Normal & Pathological Responses to Bereavement

A Volume in MSS' Series on Attitudes Toward Death

Papers by
John Ellard, Vamik Volkan, Norman
L. Paul et al.

MSS Information Corporation
655 Madison Avenue, New York, N. Y. 10021

Library of Congress Cataloging in Publication Data
Main entry under title:

Normal and pathological responses to bereavement.

(Attitudes toward death, v. 2)
A collection of articles previously published
in various journals.
1. Bereavement--Psychological aspects--Addresses,
essays, lectures. I. Ellard, John. II. Volkan,
Vamik. III. Wallace, Elspeth. IV. Series.
BF575.G7N67   155.9'37   73-10473
ISBN 0-8422-7146-5

TABLE OF CONTENTS

CREDITS AND ACKNOWLEDGEMENTS

Bergman, Abraham B.; Margaret A. Pomeroy; and J. Bruce Beckwith, "The Psychiatric Toll of the Sudden Infant Death Syndrome," *General Practice*, 1969, 40:99-105.

Chethik, Morton, "The Impact of Object Loss on a Six-Year-Old," *Journal of the American Academy of Child Psychiatry*, 1970, 9: 624-643.

"Death in Childhood," *Canadian Medical Association Journal*, 1968, 98:967-969.

Ellard, John, "Emotional Reactions Associated with Death," *The Medical Journal of Australia*, 1968, 1:979-983.

Gramlich, Edwin P., "Recognition and Management of Grief in Elderly Patients," *Geriatrics*, 1968, 23:87-92.

Hilgard, Josephine R., "Depressive and Psychotic States as Anniversaries to Sibling Death in Childhood," *International Psychiatry Clinics*, 1969, 6:197-211.

Kaij, L.; A. Malmquist; and Å. Nilsson, "Psychiatric Aspects of Spontaneous Abortion. II. The Importance of Bereavement, Attachment and Neurosis in Early Life," *Journal of Psychosomatic Research*, 1969, 13:53-59.

Kennell, John H.; Howard Slyter; and Marshall H. Klaus, "The Mourning Response of Parents to the Death of a Newborn Infant," *New England Journal of Medicine*, 1970, 283:344-349.

Maddison, David, "The Consequences of Conjugal Bereavement," *Nursing Times*, 1969, 65:50-52.

Maddison, David, "The Relevance of Conjugal Bereavement for Preventive Psychiatry," *British Journal of Medical Psychology*, 1968, 41:223-233.

Maddison, David; and Wendy L. Walker, "Factors Affecting the Outcome of Conjugal Bereavement," *British Journal of Psychiatry*, 1967, 113:1057-1067.

Pacyna, Dorothy A., "Response to a Dying Child," *Nursing Clinics of North America*, 1970, 5:421-430.

Parkes, C. Murray, "'Seeking' and 'Finding' a Lost Object: Evidence from Recent Studies of the Reaction to Bereavement," *Social Science and Medicine*, 1970, 4:187-201.

Paul, Norman L., "The Use of Empathy in the Resolution of Grief," *Perspectives in Biology and Medicine*, 1967, 11:153-169.

Silverman, Phyllis Rolfe, "The Widow-to-Widow Program: An Experiment in Preventive Intervention," *Mental Hygiene*, 1969, 53: 333-337.

Volkan, Vamik D., "The Linking Objects of Pathological Mourners," *Archives of General Psychiatry*, 1972, 27:215-221.

Volkan, Vamik, "The Recognition and Prevention of Pathological Grief," *The Virginia Medical Monthly*, 1972, 99:535-540.

Wallace, Elspeth; and Brenda D. Townes, "The Dual Role of Comforter and Bereaved," *Mental Hygiene*, 1969, 53:327-332.

PREFACE

Emotional reactions associated with death are complex and varied. It is well known, however, that feelings of grief suffered at the loss of a love object are central to the future adjustment of the individual. This volume focuses on the process of bereavement and the problems found in the management of grief.

Selected papers discuss the normal process of grief — through shock, sorrow, apathy, and assimilation of the loss, as well as the recognition and prevention of pathological grief. The importance of empathy and the role of the comforter are also considered, as are the particular problems of the aged whose confrontation with death is more frequent and closely attached to their own fears of impending death.

Conjugal bereavement is considered in a separate section. Factors affecting the outcome of conjugal bereavement and the relevance of conjugal bereavement for preventive psychiatry are stressed.

The loss of a child or infant provides an especially painful problem for the family and physician. The importance of bereavement, the mourning response and psychiatric toll of sudden infant death syndrome and the frequency of depressive and psychotic states at anniversaries to sibling death in childhood are topics receiving particular attention in this section.

Finally, this volume also explores object loss, grief, and the ways in which both adults and children seek to recapture the lost object. The pathological and normal uses of linking objects, the impact of loss on young children, and the process of "seeking" and "finding" a lost object are among the topics examined.

Management of Grief

EMOTIONAL REACTIONS ASSOCIATED WITH DEATH

JOHN ELLARD, D.P.M., F.R.A.C.P., M.A.N.Z.C.P.

FOR a while, growing older brings with it enough consolations and rewards to make the process acceptable or even welcome. We acquire new skills and more possessions, and if we are fortunate, we may learn to love others more than we love ourselves. After a while, the equation becomes sufficiently unbalanced to require our attention, and the thoughtful person cannot escape the contemplation of its final solution. We are confronted with the certainty of death, not only the death of our patients, our family, and our most loved companions, but also with our own personal death.

For some at least, this must be a melancholy prospect, and yet death seems to concern most of our acquaintances little, if at all. Indeed, so rarely is our own occasional cold anticipation reflected in the community that we might be pardoned for believing that the secret of immortality had been privately revealed to everyone but ourselves. As doctors we can acquire a temporary refuge in the contemplation of the great works of scientific medicine, provided that we have wit enough to avoid mortality tables, but our patients face the business end of it all, and are in need of comfort. Death requires looking at, if we can bear to do it, but that we cannot do so with a level gaze can be deduced not only from an examination of our own minds and the minds of those about us, but also from an inspection of the medical literature.

In 1906, Osler described the dying of 500 patients, but thereafter there was little more in the literature for the next 40 years. The last decade or two have produced a number of articles about death and dying, but there is nevertheless a most remarkable scarcity when one weighs the importance and frequency of death against the triviality of some of the matters discussed frequently and at length.

It may be asked, do people die comfortably or miserably, or at any rate as well as they might? Are we as wise in managing the universal condition of dying as we are clever in treating the rarer and more fascinating biochemical disorders? Can we reflect upon the man who died with comfort and dignity under our care with the same satisfaction that we feel when we recognize the most recently described intractable and disastrous chromosomal disorder?

It may help to consider some aspects of the problem separately. First, there is the setting, the backdrop against which the final scene is played. Here one is concerned with the cultural background of death, for it seems to change its meaning in different places and times. Secondly, there will be the stage, the immediate environment of death. For most doctors most of the time, this will be the hospital, but less commonly it will occur in some more public or catastrophic circumstance such as war or natural disaster.

Thirdly, there will be the family and the friends. Sometimes they will be deeply involved in one way or another: too often they will be unseen, either because they wait offstage, or because quite determinedly we avoid acknowledging their existence and their needs.

Fourthly, there will be the central actor who may be a child, an old man, a suicide, or what you will. It is the one starring part we shall all play in the end.

Fifthly, there will be the nurses and ourselves. Our parts are obscure, our roles difficult and changing, and no one has written our lines for us.

Sixthly, there will be the clergy, the traditional comforters. Although community attitudes towards religion are not the same as they were a generation ago, there is evidence that the clergy, by examining their function as counsellors, are thinking as much of the current necessities of the bereaved as of the posthumous vicissitudes of the deceased.

DEATH AND MAGIC

When presented with an intractable problem, man uses a characteristic solution—magic. Rational exploration of the problem of death is recent and tentative, but the various magical systems have played a prominent part in thought and literature for as far back as one can see. This is relevant to our problem, not only in so far as it shows man's almost limitless capacity for denial (in the psycholanalytic sense), but also because we must relate the patient to his particular system of belief to understand what is in his mind. If we do not do this, the probability is that we shall project our own beliefs and anxieties on to him, and then attempt to deal with them as though they were his. This may do something for us,

12

but is of problematical benefit to the dying man. If his medical attendant is afraid of fire and brimstone, he is unlikely to engender serenity in his patient.

There are so many unassimilated cultural systems represented in Sydney now that no one is capable of guiding us through their intricacies, and we must do the best we can on inadequate knowledge. A newcomer from Calabria or Mitylene is not going to face his death in the same way as will a dowager from Potts Point, and the doctor will need to modify his role accordingly. We are so much embedded in our own cultural matrix that it is not easy to comprehend the extent of the differences that exist. This is not the place to develop such a theme fully, and I am not competent to do it, but the views of others may be illuminating.

Borkenau (1955) points out that in so-called primitive societies, many things were and are done to and for the dead. They may be painted or their bodies may be preserved in ways which surely must be designed to ensure immortality. Their possessions and occasionally their servants may be entombed for their later use, indicating that the expected immortality had very much the flavour of a continued earthly existence. Sacrifices may be performed to propitiate them, and in general, the living seemed to be trying to do two things: to keep the dead alive, and to keep them away.

In early Egyptian society, only Pharaoh was certain of immortality, and all others of extinction, as Borkenau puts it. Later, the aristocracy contrived to improve their chances through mummification, and later still, the life everlasting became possible for all. Then followed a gradual loss of belief in direct immortality, there arising instead the notion that there was a different and better world to be reached after death, provided that one complied with certain ritualistic and magical rules while alive. Our own culture is approximately in this state now.

These matters are mentioned to indicate how much one's attitude might be conditioned, not only by the century of one's birth, but also by the social status one had achieved or inherited. It was much more comfortable to be a Pharaoh than a fellah. Most members of our society more or less adhere to one of several systems of belief which proclaim that death is not death at all, but something quite different, often associated with a system of rewards and punishments. In some places, it is either illegal or improper to examine these contentions scientifically, because society as a whole is involved in the denial. Many people become very angry when their religious beliefs are discussed: the possible loss of security is too dangerous to be endured.

Denial of death may be taken so far as to become preposterous. One cannot forbear from quoting Jessica Mitford's (1965) reference to medium-priced metal caskets equipped with the "beautyrama adjustable soft foam bed: quality mattress fabric is used, and height adjustment is accomplished by patented means which eliminate cranking . . . the bed is soft and buoyant, but will hold firm without slipping".

THE FEAR OF DEATH

First, let us look at the problem of whether there is indeed a general anxiety about death, which is denied,

13

or whether people are not really concerned about it. Alexander's (1957) study is helpful. In it, 31 Princeton undergraduate volunteers had their psychogalvanic response recorded, in the belief that the Sanborn recorder was being tested. There were 27 words, 18 of them basal, three relating to sexual matters, three to school and three to death—the last three being "funeral", "death", and "burial". The words were balanced for their number of syllables, their length and their frequency of usage.

The sex, school and death words produced a response differing from the basal words at a highly significant level, but there was little difference between responses in these last three areas. This would indicate that there was something like the same amount of anxiety about these topics in a group of young men, although, of course, one cannot extrapolate with any confidence.

Secondly, it is worth looking at some of the attitudes revealed by Fulton's (1963) study of the American public in this respect. Fulton made an extensive survey, using direct interviews and posted *questionnaires*. Again it cannot be assumed that the data might equally be derived from an Australian population, but it seems reasonable to quote his results in the absence of a local series. One of the groups came from memorial clubs, which perhaps approximate our funeral funds; another was a group of householders selected from telephone directories. In his sample, the members of the memorial clubs were older, better educated and of higher occupational status.

There were several significant differences between the groups. Belief in God was acknowledged by 69% of the householders, but only 22% of the memorial club members. Whereas 19% of the householders thought that death equalled the finish of life and everything else, 53% of the club members took this view. Almost exactly opposite numbers in each group believed that death meant going to heaven, or some similar transformation. Few in either group throught that the funeral is primarily a religious event; the club members in particular being inclined to the view that it is a way of comforting relatives or allowing one to pay one's last respects.

Another interesting study is that of Diggory and Rothman (1961). Five hundred and sixty-three non-random subjects were given a *questionnaire* and as'ked to rank the following seven statements in order of importance to the subject.

1. My death would cause grief to my friends and relatives.

2. All my plans and projects would come to an end.

3. The process of dying might be painful.

4. I could no longer have any experiences.

5. I would no longer be able to care for my dependants.

6. I am afraid of what might happen to me if there is a life after death.

7. I am afraid of what might happen to my body after death.

In general, most people were most perturbed about their death causing grief to relatives and friends, next about all their plans and projects coming to an end, and next about the process of dying being painful. Fear of what might happen if there was life after death ranked sixth, and the least concern was expressed about what might happen to one's body after death.

There were some minor variations when the population was examined in other ways, but in general, the significant variations were as follows: in those aged more than 40 years, worry over dependants was the greatest problem of all, superseding all others; in those of the Roman Catholic faith, worry about the hereafter rose and reached third position. In Jewish patients, and in those patients of low socio-economic status, fear of a painful death ranked first, and amongst the atheists, the principal regret was of there being no more experiences and of all one's plans and projects coming to an end.

In general, it seemed that a person feared death because it eliminated his opportunity to pursue goals important to his self-esteem. Fear for dependants depended more on one's social role. I could say much more: the conclusion argued is that concepts of death vary widely, and that the doctor cannot manage his patients satisfactorily unless he takes due notice of this and does his best to appreciate the patient's own position.

DEATH AND DOCTORS

Perhaps war and natural disaster may be disposed of very briefly. Here the fear of death can be overwhelming. Once more, the usual mechanism of defence is denial: a denial which may be present not only amongst those actively engaged, but also amongst those who are concerned with their problems. Few medical texts have death as an entity in the index: it is fascinating to note that one of of the early standard works on Air Force combat stress (Grinker and Spiegel, 1945) lists neither death nor fear of death, although it lists fear of the dark. In any case, the military doctor has a special role. It is his function to keep men facing death as long as they can, and therefore he must not analyse the repressive and reality-denying psychological forces of denial, ritual, and magic. They are his most potent allies: his task is to note when they are about to fail, and to take some sort of action.

Here the doctor is deflected from his proper role by harsh necessities over which he has no control, and which he can but deplore. How much better, then, should things be managed in an environment created by doctors themselves so that they can practise their art in their own way? Probably more than a quarter of the population die in hospital, so we cannot complain that we lack an opportunity to demonstrate our *expertise*. Yet it is difficult to deny that the modern general hospital is inhospitable to both the living and the dying. The teaching hospital is probably worst of all, for here the communication from patient to treating doctor and back again is often indirect, unsatisfactory and emotionally attenuated.

The rigid hierarchical structure of the ward ensures that those who spend most time with the patient have the smallest voice in his management. The nurses who wash his back, make his bed and give him his medicines are uniquely placed, for it is upon them that the patient must obviously depend. They attend to his bodily comfort, and it is not surprising that he should often turn to them for emotional comfort as well. Nevertheless, they are usually uninformed about his illness and what it might mean to him, and uninvited to the informal conferences

15

which determine what is to be done for him. Worse than this, they are often so busy doing the work of clerks, domestics and waitresses that there is insufficient time for them to fulfil their proper function. I have known more than one general ward in which the nurses were firmly discouraged from speaking to the patients since it "wasted time".

Another problem in teaching hospitals is the frequent orientation towards research and training in preference to the other aspects of medicine. These are most worthy objects in themselves, but there is sometimes reason to suspect that in the search for knowledge, the patient's comfort may be jeopardized rather than enhanced. Hinton's (1963) observations, to be discussed later, make it clear that at least in some hospitals there is room for improvement in this area.

THE FAMILY

It is not always easy to perceive what sort of family the dying patient is from, and it is particularly easy not to make the observation if one does not meet its members. Here the teaching hospital game can be played as one prefers—the anxious or bereaved relatives can be kept at arms' length and the consultant's own anxiety preserved for weightier matters—if this is his choice. I do not suggest that this defence is often used, but it could not be said that it is unknown.

In a rough way, one may talk of two sorts of families. In the first group, there is the large, extended family, interdependent and generally mutually supportive. Because of the multiple relationships in such a family, each member is less vulnerable to the loss of another member, not only because there is more support, but also because relationships tend to be a little diluted by their multiplicity. Further, the general pattern of life goes on: the dying man knows that his children will be brought up in a relatively stable family circle, which is certainly not the case in the more typical Australian nuclear family. The stereotype of the large, warm Italian family approximates to what I am trying to describe. There are many difficulties within such a structure, but the best features seem to come out under circumstances of the kind that interest us.

In the smaller family, two things may happen. Either the marital couple may share their friends, their entertainments, their chores and generally their lives, or perhaps more commonly in many areas in Sydney, they may have separate circles of friends, separate relaxations and interests, and quite separate relationships with their own families. This is often more marked on the wife's side, when her life revolves around her close female relatives.

These two types of families tend to work quite differently. In the first case, the individuals derive most of their support from within the family, in the other from other relatives and from non-mutual friends. Impending death or bereavement will produce different stresses in those involved, and support must come from quite separate directions. The doctor responsible for the situation must have some notion of what is going on if he is to intervene usefully.

16

There is another point. A little close scrutiny of what may be called the separate-role nuclear family will often reveal that one or both of the principals are leading quite isolated lives, with few or no relationships of any significance in them. This is particularly the case if the parents or siblings are dead or in another city. Here one finds an isolated person, a person whose isolation may become more marked as death approaches. It is a critical time for the spouse. It may be that reserves of concern, love and tenderness will be uncovered by the tragedy which has befallen the other member, or it may be that the club will be sought even more eagerly as a refuge from the anxieties at home. Many people acquire a marital partner with less exercise of their judgement than is involved in buying a new car, and the irrationality of their choice may be fully exposed when they are most in need of support.

The segregation of the dying is well established in many cultures, and, if anything, is becoming more marked in ours as a general pattern of dealing with the aged. Nothing destroys an aged person so quickly as the removal of familiar things, places and relationships, and there is no need to detail all the social trends conspiring to produce this. Nor is there need to comment on the way such matters are dealt with in large general hospitals. The point to be emphasized is that there is often a general tendency for the dying and the aged to be left alone before they are dead. Sometimes the relatives deal with their own anxiety by moving out, and sometimes the dying person is being paid back for years of rejection and domination of those who might have comforted him now. It is wise not to judge hastily, and not allow anxiety about one's own death to lead to condemnation of the absent comforters.

There are many things to be said about the effect of death on the surviving members of the family. No one really knows what normal bereavement is, but it seems clear that the general morbidity in the bereaved is significantly greater than that in a controlled population. There are some groups at special risk, and the physician has a responsibility in ensuring that this morbidity is reduced as much as possible.

BEREAVED CHILDREN

One special situation to be mentioned is that which arises when a child is disturbed by the death of a sibling. The whole topic is covered most admirably by Cain *et alii* (1964). In this study, 58 children aged two and a half to 14 years who had lost a sibling were investigated intensively. Approximately half of them showed marked guilt combined with considerable depression. The guilt appeared not only as sheer misery, but also in many other neurotic ways which were not always easy to understand. Significantly, in some cases, there was a direct reason for guilt to be present; either the child had been angry with his sibling at the time of his death and had wanted him dead or, more directly, the child had done something which had contributed to his sibling's death.

Parents typically did everything that they could to deny the whole situation to the child (and probably to themselves), and as a result the surviving child had no chance to deal with his guilt and depression. In slightly less than a quarter of the cases, guilt was imposed on the

17

child because his parents considered that he did not show a proper amount of grief. Sometimes the child had merely honestly said that he was glad that his sibling had died, but there were often more complex reasons for an absence or apparent absence of reaction. The parents were disturbed by such a state of affairs, particularly if they had their own problems in their relationship with the dead child.

Many of the surviving children developed distorted concepts of doctors, hospitals and religion. Many of them developed phobias of death and other peculiar ideas were entertained. In about 40% of the cases, the living child reproduced some of the dead child's prominent symptoms. Sometimes this occurred as an anniversary reaction, sometimes as an immediate reaction to the death. Naturally this was a threat to their own identity, which the parents had often further compounded by comparing the living child to the dead child, and then unfavourably.

Finally, one should mention the anniversary reaction described by Hilgard (1963) in the United States in one of a number of articles and by Brown (1961) in England. To put the matter simply and a little inaccurately, if a person loses a parent in his childhood, he is the more likely to have a depressive illness later in his life. He is at particular risk when a child (perhaps the oldest child, or the one most identified with) has reached the age at which he was when the parent died.

It is interesting that under the law of New South Wales, one may sue for "nervous shock". This nebulous term may be taken to include neurotic illness following the death in an accident of a loved person. In the small series that I have seen, death of a parent in the patient's childhood is a remarkably common circumstance in the history of the person who is later overthrown by his bereavement.

It is not proven, but I suspect that one of the important things to do is to ensure that so far as it is possible, the child of a dead parent mobilizes his feelings and expresses them. They will include perhaps not only grief at the loss, but anger at the abandonment. The child who takes the death of a parent calmly and apparently with fortitude is a child at risk in later life, and the adults who assist him in the repression of his feelings are probably neither helpful nor as altruistic as they would like to think.

The physician has a responsibility which extends beyond that normally understood. He must do all that he can to comfort his patient, but further, he must recognize that death is a situation involving the whole family, and that harm may be done to some of the surviving members. It is important that everything be done to deal with this risk at that time, since it may well be that no sign of harm will appear for decades to come. More than this, the sufferers or potential sufferers may not present themselves for medical inspection, since it is expected neither by the doctor nor by society that he had any role at the time other than that of dispensing platitudes and sedatives. The emphasis on diseases rather than on whole people is rarely further astray, and further from the needs of those involved than it is here.

DYING IN HOSPITAL

Most people do not die in large hospitals, and the manner of their dying is little known. A significant number die under our care, but only recently have attempts been made to observe the process in detail, and to see how inadequately or adequately we handle it. I know of no series compiled in this city, but it is a reasonable assumption that Hinton's (1963) observations may be transferred to the local scene without doing too much violence to them. He interviewed (in the end) 102 matched pairs of patients, one of the pair being about to die, and the other seriously ill. The seriously ill member was followed to ensure that he recovered; naturally his recovery was anticipated from the beginning.

Of 91 patients who might have been expected to experience physical suffering 31 (more than a third) did not obtain sufficient relief from their suffering. A little less than half experienced a distressing amount of depression; depression was more common in those with unrelieved physical distress. Dyspnœa and intractable nausea were particularly associated with anxiety. The very religious and those without faith were most free from anxiety, while the most anxious were those with some belief who rarely went to church.

Obvious grief, noticeable by the nurses, occurred in about a quarter of the patients before they died. In the last week, 43% had physical distress for all or some of the time. Since 11% were unrouseable for most of the last week of life, and 34% were unconscious for more than 24 hours before their death, it is obvious enough that there was more suffering attached to the process of dying than is perhaps normally admitted. In the last month, more than 75% acknowledged the possibility of death, and in the last week 20% were quite sure that death was at hand. Since patients often spare their doctors, there can be little doubt that the true figures are higher.

Hinton makes the important observation that only two patients were disturbed by the interviews, and that this occurred only after the first interview and before the patients knew who the interviewer was and what he was about. Most patients were comforted by his presence and welcomed the opportunity to discuss their anxieties and fears. The simple companionship of having someone to talk to was important, and he also found evidence of emotional isolation and the "bereavement of the dying" described by Weisman and Hackett (1961). He also noted the very definite beneficial effect of the traditional morphine and cocaine mixture when it was given.

Aldrich (1963) makes another important observation. One of the measures of maturity is one's capacity to form deep, warm and meaningful relationships with other humans. Accordingly, the more mature one is, the more such relationships one will have, and the more there are of them, the more there is to lose. To put it shortly, the more mature the dying person, the greater his potential psychological suffering. His maturity may help him to contain his suffering the better, but his physician should not misinterpret the situation, and in particular should not allow his own anxiety to lead him into a conspiracy of pretence with the patient.

SUMMARY

There are many more things to be said about the dying patient, and many of them have been pointed out in the recent literature. However, perhaps at this point I might try to bring together some of the things mentioned in the foregoing in a way which the practising doctor might find helpful.

First, there are certain things which the doctor must look for in himself and come to understand as well as he can. There is his own cultural position and his own attitude to death. Probably this will be partly realistic and partly neurotic, and it is necessary to look carefully before deciding that a position is as reasonable as it seems to be at first sight. The physician should also look at his own habitual modes of defence; whatever they are, they are likely to be brought powerfully into play when he is confronted with an intractable problem such as this one. Importantly, he should look at his relationship with the particular patient. There may be guilt from therapeutic failure, anger from defeated omnipotence, and indeed the whole complex range of countertransference problems may enter into the situation. It is through this filter that he will see his patient and his needs.

Secondly, he needs to understand as well as he can what sort of patient he is dealing with. He needs to know his cultural background, the sort of family he comes from and how it works. He should know the number and depth of the patient's relationships with others and in what stead they are going to stand him now. Particularly should he pay attention to what seems to be the patient's habitual mode of defence and to his proneness to denial; for a time, his neurotic defences may be his best friends, and there is no particular reason to rush forth and analyse them.

Thirdly, he should look at the immediate environment and see if anything needs to be done to it. Are communications in the ward open from the newest probationer to the most exalted physician? The more junior the nurse, the more time she will spend with the patient, and the more he will turn to her for comfort and for knowledge. If the doctor's own communication with the patient is bad, the situation is particularly difficult.

Fourthly, he should bear certain things in his mind. The patient probably knows that he is going to die, or has a good idea of it, so that the essential problem is not to decide whether or not the patient needs to be told. It is necessary to remember that the patient is as likely to be kind to the physician as the physician is to be kind to the patient, and that the temptation to take refuge in this may be almost irresistible. It must be remembered that the patient will probably be depressed, and that he will probably suffer physically, particularly if he is vomiting or has dyspnœa, and that meticulous attention to medication may make a lot of difference. The physician needs to be sure that depression and grief are being distinguished from physical suffering, and he needs to know that the patient can get medication when he needs it, and not when some harassed and inexperienced resident in another building thinks that he needs it. Above all, it is necessary to remember that the nearer the patient's death approaches, the greater his fear of loneliness and abandonment.

Fifthly, the doctor needs to avoid denial in himself. There is a particular form of it which is difficult to resist; that is, the fantasy that he has done all that he can do for the patient, and that therefore he should busy himself with more important or apparently rewarding things. What the doctor can do for the patient is not to be measured by the size of the liver, the opacities in his lungs, nor by the appearance of his marrow. It is measured by his needs, and the one thing that he needs above all is a continuing relationship with the doctor who undertook to help him in the first place. If his own doctor no longer comes to see him, from whom else may he expect comfort?

Perhaps the total management of the patient can be related to the three phases described for the cancer patient by Ruth Abrams (1966). When the patient's condition is diagnosed, he needs to be told three things, in words that he can understand. He needs to be told what is wrong with him, what it may possibly mean in the future, and what medical science has to offer him. If these three things are advanced carefully, the patient can make some reasonable arrangements and may also bring his usual defences to the situation at whatever level he finds necessary. There is then the second stage of waiting and fearing, in which all the considerations I have tried to outline above should occupy the mind of the doctor.

Finally, there is the stage of inevitability. In this stage, the fear of abandonment, physical suffering and depression are likely to be present, and this is when the doctor and the nurse need all the resources they can derive from their training and their personalities.

When it is all over and he can retreat from what has been a painful situation, the physician must then remember his responsibilities to the family and to his assistants and his nursing staff. It is the present custom to pretend that situations which increase the physician's own anxiety leave them unscathed. I suppose that one day we will be confident enough about ourselves to help them.

REFERENCES

ABRAMS, R. D. (1966), "The Patient with Cancer", *New Engl. J. Med.*, 274 : 317.

ALDRICH, C. K. (1963), "The Dying Patient's Grief", *J. Amer. med. Ass.*, 184 : 329.

ALEXANDER, I. E. (1957), "Is Death a Matter of Indifference?", *J. Psychol.*, 43 : 277.

BORKENAU, F. (1955), "The Concept of Death", *The Twentieth Century*, April.

BROWN, F. (1961), "Depression and Childhood Bereavement", *J. ment. Sci.*, 107 : 754.

CAIN, A. C., FAST, I., and ERICKSON, M. (1964), "Children's Disturbed Reactions to the Death of a Sibling", *Amer. J. Orthopsychiat.*, 34 : 741.

DIGGORY, J. C., and ROTHMAN, D. Z. (1961), "Values Destroyed by Death", *J. abnorm. soc. Psychol.*, 63 : 205.

FULTON, R. (1963), "The Sacred and the Secular: Attitudes of the American Public Towards Death"; reprinted in "Death and Identity", 1965, Wiley, New York.

GRINKER, R. R., and SPIEGEL, J. P. (1945), "Men under Stress", Blakiston, Philadelphia.

HILGARD, J. R. (1963), "Parental Loss by Death in Childhood", *J. nerv. ment. Dis.*, 137 : 14.

HINTON, J. M. (1963), "The Physical and Mental Distress of the Dying", *Quart. J. Med.*, N.S. 32 : 1.

MITFORD, J. (1965), "The American Way of Death", Penguin Books, Middlesex.

WEISMAN, A. D., and HACKETT, T. P. (1961), "Predilection to Death", *Psychosom. Med.*, 23 : 232.

21

The Recognition and Prevention of Pathological Grief

VAMIK VOLKAN, M.D.

THIS PAPER is derived from an extended study (1966-1971)[1,2,3,4,5,6] of 55 patients aged 17 to 46 whose problems dated from the death of a loved/hated intimate. The contact with these patients ranged from psychoanalysis to psychotherapy given during a relatively short period (average one month) of hospitalization on the psychiatric ward. Their disturbances had manifested themselves either at the time of the death, soon after it, or at a later time on an anniversary of its occurrence.

Many people have studied the ways in which men deal with the [death of someone close to them.] Bowlby[7] identified three phases of mourning, and Parkes[8] saw four—numbness, yearning to recover the lost one, despairing disorganization, and, finally, behavioral reor-

Presented at the Annual Meeting of The Medical Society of Virginia at Arlington, October 15, 1971.

ganization. An analogy is suggested[9] between the process of grieving and the process whereby a wound heals. The grieving process can become complicated, just as a wound can become infected. This report describes signs and symptoms by which a physician can identify pathology in the initial reaction to death, and recognize established pathology in grief reactions to death which persist more than six months after the loss has been suffered.

Initial Responses to Death

The initial response to death depends on several factors. A. The first is whether or not the death had been anticipated. A family is seldom deeply shocked when an aged chronic invalid dies; a sudden death is obviously a more crushing event. B. The second consideration is the mourner's rapport with the one who has died. The more mature this has been, the greater the likelihood that what is experienced by the mourner will be a deep sadness—sadness being a feeling without guilt, a personal and intimate feeling like love itself, and one more difficult to convey than depression.[10] When the relationship had been highly ambivalent and stormy, however, the reactions of the mourner are apt to be complicated ones with a variety of component feelings. C. The third issue is the mourner's emotional makeup. The more dependent his personality is, the more likely he is to have complicated grief reactions. Or he may have unfinished business with the one he mourns, and for this reason unconsciously try to keep him alive. An example of this is provided by a patient whose father died suddenly when the boy was courting the girl he planned to marry. Since the father had checked his genital growth during puberty, and conveyed anxiety about his potency, the boy had a psychological need to prove his manhood to the father he was trying to keep alive, and accordingly made his fiancee pregnant.[5]   D. The fourth consideration concerns whether death was caused by self-destruction or violence, or came about through illness. In the case of any kind of violent death, any resonation with the mourner's angry feelings toward the dead person tends to evoke oppressive feelings of guilt. E. The fifth factor is whether or not the death has brought about changes in the real world for those left behind, changes such as the loss of a home or reduction of financial circumstances, which are in themselves stressful.

Lindemann[11] described the manifestations of *acute* grief as including: 1. waves of somatic distress 20 minutes to an hour in duration, accompanied by sighing respiration, complaints of weakness and digestive malaise—"food tastes like sand", etc.; 2. a feeling of remoteness from others, a slight sense of unreality, and a view of others as being small and shadowy; 3. preoccupation with the image of the deceased; 4. strong guilt feelings leading to a painstaking review of the past for any lapse in dutiful devotion to the deceased; 5. feelings of debility and heightened hostility toward others; and 6. interruption of usual patterns of contact, such as a rush of speech, particularly in speaking of the dead. These symptoms appear strongly after a sudden death, but following an expected death they are usually less destructive to the mourner's daily routine. They appear also in established pathological grief, in which they may manifest themselves on a delayed basis at the time of an anniversary or when the mourner re-focuses on his

24

loss. The family physician will want to evaluate the quality of initial grief for complications which could presage the establishment of pathological grief reactions, clinical depression, etc.

A comparison of four cases may point the way. The first is an example of uncomplicated grief reaction, and concerns a young woman who had previously undergone psychotherapy during which her complex relationship with her father had been worked through, so that at the time of his death it was satisfactory. Upon learning of his death the daughter felt numb, had a dry mouth, and at first felt disbelief, despite the father's heart disease and advanced age. Through the mechanism of splitting, part of her kept him alive. She felt aimless for an hour or so after the news came but was able to talk to her husband about her feelings. She saw other people as shadowy, and felt remote from her environment, but was able to do what was expected of her, calling relatives and arranging for the funeral. She was able to travel to the city where death had occurred. She cried the first night, and again from time to time during the first week. At the funeral she felt anger at an aunt who had been unkind to her father during his lifetime, but the anger was under control. She went through the funeral and took part in the burial rites, later returning to the graveside for a visit. Her crying spells diminished and became no longer deeply disturbing, although they occurred occasionally. She continued to be preoccupied with her father's image. He had visited her two days before his death, and she had taken him for a walk in windy weather. At first she felt guilty lest this walk had hastened his death, but this misgiving left her after a short time.

Two months after the death she fantasized the decaying body that lay in the earth, and for a while she regarded these fantasies as bizarre and wanted to get rid of them. By the second month they no longer came to her, and by the time two months had gone by she felt the return of free energy and the ability to become involved in new objects and activities. Her husband gave her a puppy and she became fascinated with her new pet. Hers was an uncomplicated grief, passing from initial shock and disbelief with its splitting of the ego, guilt, and preoccupation with the image of the dead, to fantasies about the decaying body, and an ultimate release of energy and attention.

Her preoccupation with the decaying body, however macabre, was transient. In contrast, one of our patients suffering from pathological grief had daydreams and sleeping dreams a few times each week for over three years in which he saw his father's body in its coffin with no evidence of decay, but with water dripping over the face. The young woman's anger toward her aunt illustrates a characteristic component of uncomplicated grief; when the anger is directed toward others and especially toward the dead person it marks the acceptance of death. This anger may, however, take exaggerated forms when the initial grief reaction is itself exaggerated. We had one young patient who had lost the grandfather who had been both father and mother to him during his childhood, and upon whom he remained dependent even after marriage. His anger led him to the top of a mountain parkway where he planned to shoot passersby in their cars. He had been ambivalent toward the old man, depending on him but also desiring escape from his influence. He went each night to sit on the grave so that his weight would keep the old man down; but he carried a shovel in his car in the fantasized event of his grandfather's returning to life and needing help to do so.[4] This patient's initial reaction was a highly exaggerated one which was prevented from turning into established chronic pathological grief only by treatment supplied during the beginning phase of his disturbance. The antithesis of his reaction would be the absence of any display of grief. Deutsch[12] made it clear that this negative response is also pathological and anticipates the later appearance of pathological grief. One of our patients, seen a month after his brother's fatal car accident, reported that there was no reason for him to grieve since he believed that his brother had died only in his dreams. He was not at that time psychotic except for this focal break with reality. In treatment, fully realizing his brother's death, he manifested symptoms of acute grief, even gathering the family together for simulated funeral rites.

Established Pathological Grief Reaction

It is evident that loss, actual or threatened, may precipitate mental illness and account for neuroses, psychoses, and psychosomatic conditions of various kinds.[13] Here I limit discussion to the reponses to an actual loss—death, which is considered a specific stress—in a specific clinical entity[3,4,6,14] known as established pathological grief reaction. We consider this diagnosis when, six months or more after a death, we observe an attitude toward the loss indicative of intellectual acknowledgment of its occurrence accompanied by emotional denial. We find the pathological mourner

27

clinging to the dead person in the *chronic hope* of his return, while at the same time dreading this possibility. This chronic hope critically differentiates pathological grief from depression, since in depression the ego is in a state of helplessness.[15] The contradiction in this fearful but eager and absorbing search reflects the ambivalence with which the dead person had been regarded in life. Both the negative and positive aspects of this search are unconscious and become clear only through psychotherapeutic investigation. The pathological mourner typically speaks of the dead in the present tense—"My father has curly hair."—"My brother likes cars." He characteristically dreams about the dead person, who appears undisguised and engaged in a life-and-death struggle from which the mourner tries to rescue him in a painful effort thwarted each time by his awakening.[3,4] The dreams repeat, and are inconclusive each time. Preoccupation with the dead person often increases to the point where the mourner loses the thread of his daily life. One of our patients, for example, changed his wife's place of burial three times in three years, and was about to effect a fourth change when he came into treatment. He was preoccupied with the thought of her not being happy with his choice. Typically, the patient feels that the dead person is "buried" in his breast like a foreign body there (an introject). Some carry on inner conversations with their introjects. The historical knowledge of the death is there, but doubt nevertheless surfaces unexpectedly and with compelling force, particularly on an anniversary. It was four years after the death of his father that one of our patients, while walking, saw on the street a man whose appearance from the back reminded him of

his father. Although he *knew* full well that
his father was dead, he felt compelled to run
past the man and turn to look into his face
to see if this was his father. Such patients are
typically fascinated with the concept of reincarnation[3,4,5] which engenders in them dread
as well as hope. They usually manage to deny
the existence of the grave by staying away
from it, and sidestep the responsibility of providing a gravestone, which represents evidence
of death and burial in a symbolism which is
unacceptable.

I will review some related developmental
concepts to account for another characteristic
we found among all our pathological mourners—the use of what we came to call a *linking
object.*[6] Psychiatrists have long been able to
demonstrate that it takes the first 36 months
of life for the infant to individuate,[16] to break
away from the mother-child unit, and to feel
and behave on his own behalf and not simply
as an extension of the mothering figure. In
his clinical practice the psychiatrist sees many
adult patients whose problems stem from this
separation-individuation process, and some
who have never achieved a complete differentiation from the mother-child unit in spite of
advance in chronological age.

One of the familiar devices employed by
the young child to handle the problem of
separation from the mother is the "security
blanket" which readers of Peanuts comics will
connect with Linus. Typically, an object like
this blanket—something soft and recognizable
by its odor—is adopted by the child for solace,
especially at bedtime, and clung to. Psychiatrists call these "transitional objects"[17] in recognition of the fact that each represents a
bridge across the chasm that is opening be-

29

tween the child and its mother, and even a *place* for the pondering of the first blurred awareness of the world outside. The transitional object is a manifestation of a normal developmental phase, and it is laid aside spontaneously when it has served its purpose.

The anxiety of some children over psychic separation from the mother is so intense, however, that their comforting objects are used in bizarre ways, and with undue concentration. They represent the mother herself, and convey to the child in a magical fashion the actual presence of the mother. In this case we call them childhood fetishes.[16,18,19]

Our pathological mourners adopted their linking objects in a similar fashion and for the like purpose of dealing with a specific separation (death). I have dealt elsewhere with the similarities and differences between the transitional and the linking object, and the fetish and the linking object. The latter are chosen from among:

1. The belongings of the dead, sometimes something he wore, like a watch.

2. Something the dead person once used as an extension of his senses, like a camera (an extension of seeing).

3. A symbolic or realistic representation of the dead person, the simplest example of which would be a photograph.

4. Something at hand when the news of death was received, or when the mourner saw the body. These we call *last-minute objects* since they recall the last moment during which the full impact of the living personality of the other was available. For example, one patient received word of his brother's accidental

30

death just as he was sitting down to play a stack of phonograph records, and these became his linking objects.[6]

Linking objects should not be confused with the kind of keepsake which is simply treasured and put to appropriate use. Anyone might value and use his father's watch, perhaps attaching considerable sentiment to it. But the patient who clings to a linking object would put the watch away, be fastidious about knowing exactly where it was at all times, and at the same time certain of being able to avoid it when this suited him. It is as important to be able to avoid the linking object as to touch it. One of our patients had his linking object in a car that was wrecked. He took extravagant pains to rescue it, and it was the only thing he did salvage from the wreckage.

The linking object represents a *place* external to the self in which the mourner can magically accomplish reunion with the dead person. By avoiding this *place* he can also reduce the anxiety generated by the thought of such reunion. The deceased is not resting in peace, but the mourner is engaged in the dilemma of killing him or saving him. The basic formulation of a fearful search may await the triggering effect of an external event such as an anniversary.[20,21] Perhaps the most important thing to remember is that when it does appear it may be concealed behind the false mask of another condition. Two of our pathological mourners had been diagnosed as schizophrenic, and this diagnosis would have been adhered to had not their symptoms quickly given way to the brief psychotherapy we call re-grieving,[1,2,5] designed specifically for the relief of the pathological mourner. The suffering of pathological grief reaction is well worth guarding against; the possibility that a pathological mourner's disturbance may be attributed to a more severe and resistant clinical condition and require prolonged hospitalization on that account adds even more weight to the importance of (a) preventing its appearance whenever possible, and (b) suspecting its existence when symptomatic behavior can be correlated with the occurrence of a death.

The Role of the Family Physician

The family physician should be alert to the absence of appropriate response to death. He should appreciate the part anger plays in grief and understand that he need not be defensive against it when it is directed toward himself. Our experience with men who had lost their fathers in puberty indicates the wisdom of helping the grieving family to understand that they should not "spare" a young boy mourner, or weight him down unduly with busywork to distract him, but that they should encourage full expression of grief and full participation in funeral rites. Those who have gone through puberty can grieve like adults.[22,23] Children's reactions to death[23] differ according to age, but these are beyond the scope of this paper since our study dealt with adults only. However, even the young child needs to know that the dead do not return and that grief is an experience that can have a beginning and an end. It is important for the child to see adults grieve and survive their grief. It is often within the province of the family physician to allay guilt, and it is to him that the mourner will bring imitations of the dead person's illness, as when the widow of a coronary infarction victim complains of chest pains; this may indicate depression, especially when accompanied by low self-esteem. The physician presented with either guilt or somatic disturbances can encourage the expression of his patient's reactions.

The most immediate and evident characteristic of pathological grief is its excessive and disproportionate nature and its protracted course.[24] To diagnose established pathological grief the physician may, six months after the death, ask about dreams and be on guard if repeating dreams of the dead or the interruption of the patient's daily routine by his preoccupations persist beyond the sixth month. If he finds himself unable to relieve the patient and turn aside the development of pathological grief reaction, he may consider psychiatric referral.

One may expect uncomplicated grief to persist for approximately six months. During this time disbelief, anger at others, anger at the dead, and the struggle and hope of keeping the dead alive will appear. Its course will include the sad surrender of this hope, disorganization of behavior, fantasies of killing (rekilling) the dead, and eventuate in the freeing of energy toward new people or things. The physician can stand by in a therapeutic relationship although he refrain from interfering with this natural course. Familiarity with the process enables the physician to help the patient to thaw any freezing that may threaten this normal course, and to point the way to psychiatric help should that become necessary.

Summary

I have sought to acquaint the physician with what to expect from the bereaved, and the identification of grief reactions that can presage pathology. When the process of grieving over a death does not take its usual course,

33

the mourner may have complicated initial responses or develop later pathological reactions. Established pathological grief reactions are sufficiently specific to be described as constituting a unique clinical entity in spite of the fact that death may also trigger other neurotic, psychotic, or psychosomatic conditions. This paper deals with both the natural and pathological course of grief, and offers suggestions for the family physician in preventing the development of the latter and dealing with it should it occur.

References

1. Volkan, V. D.: Normal and Pathological Grief Reactions—A Guide for the Family Physician. Virginia M. Monthly 93:651-656, 1966.
2. Volkan, V. D. and Showalter, C. R.: Known Object Loss, Disturbance in Reality Testing, and 'Re-Grief' Work as a Method of Brief Psychotherapy. Psychiat. Quart. 42: 358-374, 1968.
3. Volkan, V. D.: The University of Virginia Study in Pathological Mourning. Tip Dunyasi (Istanbul) 42:544-551, 1969.
4. Volkan, V. D.: Typical Findings in Pathological Grief. Psychiat. Quart. 44:231-250, 1970.
5. Volkan, V. D.: A Study of a Patient's 'Re-Grief' Work Through Dreams, Psychological Tests and Psychoanalysis. Psychiat. Quart. 45:255-273, 1971.
6. Volkan, V. D.: The Linking Objects of Pathological Mourners. Arch. Gen. Psychiat. (in press) 1972.
7. Bowlby, J.: Process of Mourning. Int. J. Psycho-Anal. 42:317-340, 1961.
8. Parkes, C. M.: Seeking and Finding a Lost Object: Evidence from Recent Studies of the Reaction to Bereavement. Soc. Sci. & Med. 4:187-201, 1970.
9. Engel, G. L.: Is Grief a Disease? A Challenge for Medical Research. Psychosom. Med. 23:18-22, 1961.

10. Smith, J. H.: Identificatory Styles in Depression and Grief. Int. J. Psycho-Anal. 52:259-266, 1971.

11. Lindemann, E.: Symptomatology and Management of Acute Grief. Am. J. Psychiat. 101:141-148, 1944.

12. Deutsch, H.: Absence of Grief. Psychoanal. Quart. 6:12-22, 1967.

13. Schmale, A. H.: Relationship of Separation and Depression to Disease: I—A Report on a Hospitalized Medical Population. Psychosom. Med. 20:259-277, 1958.

14. Parkes, C. M.: Bereavement and Mental Illness: Part 2—A Classification of Bereavement Reactions. British J. M. Psychol. 38: 13-26, 1965.

15. Bibring, E.: The Mechanism of Depression. Affective Disorders ed. P. Greenacre. New York: International Universities Press, 1953.

16. Mahler, M. S.: On Human Symbiosis and the Vicissitudes of Individuation. Vol. I. New York: International Universities Press, 1968.

17. Winnicott, D. W.: Transitional Object and Transitional Phenomena. Int. J. Psycho-Anal. 34:89-97, 1953.

18. Sperling, M.: Fetishism in Children. Psychoanal. Quart. 32:374-392, 1963.

19. Speers, R. W. and Lansing, C.: Group Therapy in Childhood Psychosis. Chapel Hill: University of North Carolina Press, 1965.

20. Pollack, G. H.: Anniversary Reactions, Trauma, and Mourning. Psychoanal. Quart. 39: 347-371, 1970.

21. Pollack, G. H.: Temporal Anniversary Manifestations: Hour, Day, Holiday. Psychoanal. Quart. 40:123-131, 1971.

22. Wolfenstein, M.: How Is Mourning Possible? Psychoanal. Stud. Child 21:93-123, 1966.

23. Nagera, H.: Children's Reactions to the Death of Important Objects—A Developmental Approach. Psychoanal. Stud. Child 25:360-400, 1970.

24. Wahl, C. W.: The Differential Diagnosis of Normal and Neurotic Grief Following Bereavement. Psychosomatics 11:104-106, 1970.

THE USE OF EMPATHY IN THE RESOLUTION
OF GRIEF*

NORMAN L. PAUL, M.D.

Rage, terror, profound sadness, helplessness, acute loneliness, and despondency are among those feelings that both children and adults find most difficult to bear; all are associated with the state of grief. Through the expression of grief and empathic responses among family members, each member can be freed from these painful feelings for the pursuit of more constructive and satisfying activities. This paper explains the crucial role of empathy in the resolution of grief.

One difficulty in describing empathy, its sources, and induction lies in the limitations of language. George Engel, in his attempts to develop an adequate classification of the phenomenology of affects, or raw feelings, readily acknowledged the inadequacy of language: "We still recognize not only that in nature affects do not exist in pure, unalloyed form but also that to deal with affects in written, verbal, or conceptual terms is fundamentally inconsistent with their nature and can succeed only at the expense of their oversimplification and impoverishment" [1]. Despite the constrictions with which language hems us in, we must persist in the exploration and assessment of empathy because of its importance in human experience.

Empathy

Empathy is an interpersonal phenomenon that occurs when the empathizer, or subject, recognizes that he shares kindred feelings with another person, the object. When empathy is reciprocated, it may be regarded as love. Olden defines empathy as "the capacity of the subject instinctively and intuitively to feel as the object does. It is a process of the ego, more

* Presented as part of the Edward A. Strecker Award in Philadelphia, October 21, 1966.

specifically, an emotional ego expression . . . the subject temporarily gives up his own ego for that of the object" [2].

It is imperative to make a clear distinction between empathy and sympathy. Although these terms are often used interchangeably, they describe different and mutually exclusive kinds of interpersonal experience. The two words share a common measure of meaning; both express a preoccupation with the assumed affinity between a subject's own feelings and the feelings of the other person. ("Object" and "other" are both used in this paper to designate the recipient of sympathy or empathy.) In sympathy, however, the subject is principally absorbed in his own feelings as projected into the object and has little concern for the reality and validity of the object's special experience. Sympathy, then, bypasses real understanding of the other person; he becomes the subject's mirror image and is thus denied his own sense of being.

Empathy, on the other hand, presupposes the existence of the other as a separate individual, entitled to his own feelings, ideas, and emotional history. The empathizer makes no judgments about what the other should feel but solicits the expression of whatever feelings may exist and, for brief periods, feels them as his own. The empathizer oscillates between such subjective involvement and a detached recognition of the shared feelings. The periods of his objective detachment do not seem to the other to be spells of indifference, as they would in sympathy; instead, they are evidence that the subject respects himself and the object as separate people. The empathizer, secure in his sense of self and his own emotional boundaries, attempts to nourish a similar security in the other. The empathic relationship is generous; the empathizer does not use the object as a means for gratifying his own sense of importance but is himself principally concerned with encouraging the other to sustain and express his feelings and fantasies as being appropriate to himself. The empathizer thus makes clear the other's individuality and his right to this individuality without apology, thereby avoiding the induction of guilt in the object, a common ingredient of sympathetic interactions. Such guilt induction is associated with the development of a hostile-dependent relationship that binds the object to the sympathizer and vice versa.

There are two kinds of empathy, intellectual and affective, both of which may exist simultaneously in the same person. Intellectual empathy describes a reciprocal process where each of two (or more) persons identifies with the other in terms of the other's verbalized thoughts, incorporating them as his own for the moment. This process seeks to understand the other's thoughts, as spoken, and the sources of those thoughts, in short, to meet the intellectual needs of the other. Two types of intellectual empathy, cognitive and associative, have been delineated. Cognitive empathy describes a structured situation in which a teacher, parent, clergyman, or other authority attempts to impart a clear body of knowledge to the other. The imparter understands both the motivations and resistances to learning that exist in the other and selects those techniques that minimize resistance. Associative empathy, by contrast, has no structured or specified goal beyond the sharing of verbalized thoughts in an effort to broaden an area of knowledge. There is a peer relationship between participants, each of whom can oscillate between the roles of empathizer and object. "Brainstorming" is one use of associative empathy. Another is that psychological treatment of neurotic patients where patient and therapist alternately respond to each other in terms of the verbalized thoughts of the moment.

This paper is concerned with affective empathy, the principal focus of my interest and work. Affective empathy seeks to meet emotional rather than intellectual needs and involves all feelings, not only those that are verbalized. Affective empathy presupposes the existence of honest, direct communication without value judgments and includes the empathizer's accepting, for a brief period, the other's total emotional individuality. In other words, the empathizer accepts the existence within himself of not only the simple emotions of the other but the other's whole state of being —the history of the other's desires, feelings, and thoughts as well as other forces and experiences that are expressed in his behavior and have produced his current adaptation to his own situation and to those around him. The empathizer is not only aware of the other's various experiences but finds himself sharing the reliving of those experiences. The object senses the empathizer's response and realizes that, for a brief point in time, they two have fused. If he then takes the initiative by communicating more of his experience, he provides a basic stimulus for what can become an affective empathic process.

Often it is difficult for an outside observer to identify the existence of empathy. It is difficult even for the participants to recognize when empathy is being induced, when it exists, when it has existed. The difficulty of recognizing the state within a therapeutic situation is further compounded by the need for the therapist's empathy to be effectively communicated and then substantiated by a response in the patient. The situation is analogous to that between a mother and infant. The mother's love, or affective empathy, may be real, but it must be communicated in some way, usually through physical contact and tone of voice, to reach the infant before its effect can be observed. The larger process of which observed communication may be merely a surface signal is expressed by Pinter when he says: "So often, below the words spoken, is a thing known and unspoken" [3]. Difficult as it is to define and describe, affective empathy, because of its importance for the growth and development of the human being, warrants more attention and research. Eventually, experiments using such psychophysiological techniques as polygraph measurements may succeed in identifying those physiological reactions associated with the beginning of empathy between two persons—that point at which their feelings become synchronized—and those reactions that mark the duration of empathy.

The material of this paper may be used to illustrate the three kinds of empathy just described: intellectual (including cognitive and associative) and affective empathy. The reader should, if the paper fulfils my intentions, experience cognitive empathy in following its development. I have organized the material so as to facilitate the transfer of information, shifting back and forth between the roles of writer and reader in order to make the presentation effective. Only through feedback from the reader can I learn whether this effort has been successful. If the reader were to follow not this paper but the tapescript of excerpted materials from a series of family therapy sessions I have conducted, he would be experiencing associative empathy induced by the dialogues as written down. To take the material back one step farther toward its origins, if the reader were to become, instead, a listener and follow the actual recordings of those sessions, he would have the opportunity to share in reliving of experiences by family members, to experience affective empathy. Each reader, while listening to those emotionally charged recordings, would observe points at which he could easily empathize and other points where he would have an aversion to doing so. There seems to be a direct relationship between a listener's ability to tune in empathically on such experiences and his own acceptance of comparable feelings in himself.

Affective empathy, referred to hereafter as empathy, is important to every person because it allows him to feel that he is not alone in his passage through life. Children often admit the existence of empathy more freely than adults; sometimes they speak of their feeling that one or the other parent is "with them inside." A large part of our cultural heritage, however, as presented both at home and at school, acts to inhibit rather than to nurture the empathic potential. Adults frequently resist empathy. Pinter expresses his insight into this resistance in saying: "To enter into someone else's life is too frightening. To disclose to others the poverty within us is too fearsome a possibility" [4]. He emphasizes a double aversion—to empathizing with someone else and to becoming the object of empathy. Apparently, the aversion is especially strong against empathizing with such uncomfortable feelings as guilt, terror, and helplessness. Before a person can empathize with an object who has these feelings, he must have been able to accept their existence within himself. But one may be unable to do this because of a natural human tendency to avoid pain and distress. Consider, for example, the reactions among the audience to certain empathic experiences on a theater stage or screen; expressions like "schmaltzy," "corny," or "childish" suggest that the dramatic portrayal of feeling has been recognized by the viewer as one of his own feelings, but that he wishes to cancel out this recognition with verbal reactions that minimize and negate his feeling.

The dearth of studies of empathy, or even of allusions to it, in scientific literature, can, perhaps, be explained both by the difficulties of coping with an essentially non-intellectual experience and by the general aversion to empathy which the scientist shares with the rest of society. Sullivan reflects on this aversion:

I have had a good deal of trouble at times with people of a certain type of educational history; since they cannot refer empathy to vision, hearing, or some other special sense receptor, and since they do not know whether it is transmitted by the ether waves or air waves or what not, they find it hard to accept the idea of empathy. . . . So although empathy may sound mysterious, remember that there is much that sounds mysterious in the universe, only you have got used to it; and perhaps you will get used to empathy [5].

The artist, poet, or playwright is perhaps better suited than the scientist to discourse upon experiences of empathy and their relationship to frustration, loss, love, and tenderness. One can feel some of the discomforts associated with empathy in viewing the three-dimensional art forms of Edward Kienholz. Kienholz wants to jolt the viewer out of his apathy by enveloping him in some of life's most unpleasant realities. In "The Wait," for

40

example, a very old woman, made of cow bones and wearing a necklace of Mason jars containing figurines that represent her memories of different periods in her life, sits wasting away and waiting to die among her moldering living-room furniture. On the wall and on an adjacent table are photographs of people who once filled her life. Her cow's-skull head is fronted with an oval picture of her face as she must have appeared fifty years earlier, the image of herself that she still maintains.

One is immediately aware of the pull to empathize with this sad creature whose deluded self-image is of one still young and vibrant. Yet it is repulsive to empathize with her because the scene is so thoroughly unpleasant. Kienholz seems to be demonstrating that each of us is living with a deliberately ignored anticipation of his own death and the deaths of those he loves. "The Wait" is repulsive because it reminds us of this mortality and thereby forces us to deny the truth of death even more vigorously. It may be that Kienholz is asking the viewer to face resolutely the ugly realities of existence and to use those energies customarily spent in avoidance in the pursuit of a fuller life.

Grief

Why do we feel such strong aversion to this confrontation with death? Although we are not always aware of it, each of us presumably has the deep conviction of his own God-like uniqueness. Each believes that he is immortal, omnipotent and, in fact, that he is the only real acting force in the world. These fantasies thrive because the content of our own consciousness is the only thing with which we have direct experience; they are reinforced by the continuity of our daily experiences, in which people and situations appear predictably and recurrently. Such narcissistic fantasies are threatened not only by death but by all kinds of changes that affect us.

Searles [6] believes that one of the critical sources of anxiety against which the schizophrenic patient unconsciously defends himself is the idea of mortality. This anxiety is so intense that the schizophrenic frequently imagines himself as not alive and thus beyond the reach of death. Furthermore, his behavior often suggests that he cannot discriminate between a minor change or loss and the major loss incurred in the death of a near person.

The total configuration of responses to a major loss, or death, is called "mourning." Mourning includes physical behavior, both formal and spontaneous, and psychological processes, both observable and covert, which are set in motion by loss. "Grief" is a more restricted term applied to the subjective state of mourning and excluding all the ritualistic and behavioral elements of mourning. Grief usually consists of such feelings as helplessness, anger, despair, and bewilderment, which overlap and vary in intensity from person to person as well as within any one person during the mourning process. I am primarily concerned with grief rather than with all of mourning because grief is entirely subjective and personal and so directly accessible to empathic intervention in grief work.

In their broadest uses, "grief" and "mourning" can be applied to the loss of anything valuable—the fantasy of being loved, a job, a part of the body, status, even symptoms. Here, however, the terms are restricted to situations involving the loss of a loved person through death. Grief and mourning may precede the actual loss in cases where the latent fear of death is activated by circumstances which might involve fatality. The news that a loved person has been in an automobile accident or is suffering from a serious illness may bring about the onset of grief and mourning. The wish for someone's death may be so strong as to make the death seem real for a moment and touch off a momentary reaction of grief to replace the anger that caused the wish. Anxiety about separation or the dread of being abandoned are feelings that may induce anticipatory grief and mourning.

The psychological treatment of grief has, up to now, generally been undertaken in the individual therapy setting. Such treatment has included the patient's cathartic reliving of his relationship with the lost object and his more cerebral and reflective view of this relationship. The form of treatment derives from the clinical insights of Freud [7], Abraham [8], Klein [9], and Deutsch [10], among others. Each of these has emphasized the importance of the patient's anger toward the lost object. The bereaved is angry because he feels helpless in finding that his fantasy of object constancy has been shattered; the environment that he supposed was inviolable has been suddenly and terribly changed by the disappearance of a loved person. His helplessness and anger become intensified whenever he becomes aware of the loss; one of the ways in which he tries to diminish these feelings is to imbue others with characteristics of the deceased.

In their studies of large numbers of persons suffering from grief, Parkes

[11] and Lindemann [12] collected data that reveal the close relationship between unresolved grief and various degrees of disability. Parkes concluded: "Grief may prove to be as important to psychopathology as inflammation is to pathology" [13]. The clinical mandate for treatment of the condition was provided by Deutsch: "The process of mourning as reaction to the real loss of a loved person must be carried to completion" [14].

Anthropologists have been active in studying the role of ceremony and ritual in promoting the resolution of grief in other cultures. Psychiatric literature, however, generally neglects this area; those discussions of grief that it does include concern individuals whose grief has taken such a form that treatment seems advisable. In most other societies, children and adults are prepared for death through elaborate rounds of ceremony and ritual accompanied by mythical explanations of the meaning of life and death. Whereas our approach to grief is individualistic, these cultures have traditional forms of mourning that require the active participation of all bereaved family members together with the whole community. Such ceremonies have been lost to us through secularization, urbanization, and a smug reliance on rationality, and we have discovered no viable substitute. Our abbreviated and restrained mourning observances are often carefully hidden from children, who grow up without experiencing empathic understanding or catharsis. All of this tends to foster a dehumanization of the individual, who finds himself increasingly alienated not only from others in his life but from himself. Mourning is a way of emphasizing the difference between life and death, the separation of the dead from the living. When this difference is minimized and glossed over, it is not surprising that the young seem void of feeling for others or flirt casually with the idea of suicide. We have obviously neglected the broad implications of Freud's thesis, "If you want to endure life, prepare yourself for death" [15].

Implications for Treatment

What can therapy do to meet this painful human need? Foreshadowing later uses of empathy for resolving grief in the context of the family, Melanie Klein wrote, "If the mourner has people whom he loves and who share his grief, and if he can accept their sympathy, the restoration of the harmony in his inner world is promoted, and his fears and stress are more quickly reduced" [16]. The provision of these conditions, aimed at empathy rather than sympathy, is one major purpose of family therapy.

43

My work with a family is conducted on an out-patient basis. I use a variety of settings—interviews with individual family members; conjoint interviews with husband and wife; meetings which involve the couple, their children, and other members of the household; and larger gatherings where several nuclear families come together. The choice and sequence of settings is dictated by attempts to provide opportunities for the expression of feelings which have been suppressed in the family's own pattern of interpersonal relations.

My underlying hypothesis is that there is a direct relationship between the maladaptive response to the death of a loved person and the fixity of symbiotic relationships within the family. A husband (or wife) may have suffered the loss of a parent or sibling many years ago, before his current family came into existence. The response to that loss may have been incomplete or unsatisfying. If there was little empathy within the bereaved family, his grief may never have been resolved. In such a situation, his feelings toward the deceased may remain unchanged through the years, lingering with him to influence his adaptation to his new family. A family's inability to cope with an original loss may produce a family style that is variably unresponsive to a wide range of changes, including new losses and disappointments. Such unresponsiveness is expressed in attempts to deny the passage of time; these often bring about the family's unwittingly keeping one of its members in an inappropriately dependent position. That member, struggling in vain to free himself from the role imposed upon him, acts in ways which annoy or alarm the others. Sometimes they decide that he must be mentally ill. Such family systems, it seems, often need a scapegoat in their midst to preserve the family's equilibrium.

My studies, some in conjunction with George Grosser [17-20], have disclosed that families containing either neurotic or psychotic patients manifest a set of family relationships variably resistant to change; this resistance is especially obvious in attitudes toward the patient. These attitudes and the resulting behavior, including the patient's reactions to his family, have been regarded as expressions of a "pathologically stable equilibrium," a relatively fixed state to which the family tends to return when it is disturbed; this state often relies upon the scapegoat or patient as a point of familiar stability. The fixation is symbiotic insofar as the family needs to keep the patient and, perhaps, its other members in a kind of dependency that prevents their emancipation, which is viewed as a threat to the family unit. The patient is a symbol of the family's defense against their recognition of grief. The difference between families with neurotic patients and those with psychotic patients is that the state is maintained with greater rigidity in the latter.

Family systems, like all other social systems, tend to maintain equilibrium. In the normal family, however, this equilibrium gradually evolves and alters in response to aging and the changes in roles that life demands of its members. It appears that the way to dislodge the pathologically fixed family is to expose and set in motion toward their appropriate objects those feelings that have been distorted for the maintenance of equilibrium. Once such feelings are released, they can be neutralized and resolved in the therapeutic setting through empathic intervention. Those affects or feelings most tenaciously withheld from sharing, even from exposure, are the ones associated with grief.

Bowlby's analysis of the mourning process helps to explain the reactions of the bereaved. He has indicated that mourning, in both its observable and hidden reactions, occurs in three overlapping phases: (1) the urge to recover the lost object, (2) disorganization, and (3) reorganization, the last two being adaptive processes. The first phase is triggered by the shock of numbness when one learns of the death, and it expresses the survivor's attempt to deny that the loss has really occurred. The second phase is the disorganization of the personality associated with the reluctant acceptance of the death as fact. The third phase, the reorganization of the personality, includes a revised perspective of the loss associated with both a detachment from the loss and the integration of the mourning experience. Bowlby has suggested that an individual can become fixated anywhere in this process [21, 22]. I think it is also possible for a survivor to be fixated in a pseudo-reorganization phase that masks the fact that the first two stages have, to a degree, been avoided. Controlled hypomanic states suggest this pseudo-reorganization. Furthermore, it seems that the smaller the amount of empathy the bereaved receives from those about him for coping with his grief the greater the possibility that he will become fixated in the mourning process.

Since such fixation within the mourning process seems to be at the root of both individual psychopathology and a family's pathologically stable equilibrium, a corrective grief experience, even though belated, seems to be the means for overcoming the fixation. A specific therapeutic technique has been developed that deliberately introduces a belated grief experience and emphasizes the elements of the mourning process. This technique focuses on the reactions induced by direct inquiry about responses to actual past losses sustained by specific family members. The therapist, in assuming an empathic stance toward both the resistance to review and, ultimately, the poignant review of the loss, presents himself as an empathic model. In accepting the reality of the belated mourner's resistance and grief, the therapist encourages him and the other family members to experience empathy. The therapist's role also includes empathizing with the others in their resistance to sharing the grief experience.

The therapist does this by imagining himself to be alternately the belated mourner and the other family members. He can thus feel within himself everyone's disinclination to review a painful experience. As the therapist acknowledges the depth of this resistance, the mourner begins to expose his distress.

At this point, other family members often deny the importance of the loss and attempt to prevent further exposure of grief with such sympathetic responses as, "You can pull yourself together," "I don't know why you're worried about it now," or "Don't listen to Dr. X. He doesn't know what he's talking about." It is obvious that family members, including the mourner himself, unwittingly conspire to deprive the mourner of his right to grieve. The therapist must empathize with these expressions and explain them as difficulties family members have in sharing the pain of grief. At this stage, the therapist should emphasize the long-range influence of the loss by pointing to the mourner's present behavior. The bereaved is, by this time, downcast, possibly beginning to weep.

The therapist also feels saddened as he shares the distress of the bereaved; empathy is furthered when the therapist feels that he is living through the mourner's experience at the time of the loss. He encourages and supports the mourner in his expression of intense emotions, while remaining alert to the emergence of sympathetic resistance to the progress of the cathartic review. Frequently, this process or parts of it need repeating in later interviews because of recurring resistance within the family unit. Families with a schizophrenic member show the strongest aversion to admitting the existence of grief and require the most skilful application of empathy in repeated attempts to induce a belated experience of grief.

The therapist, after a detailed review of the loss experience as it was lived, encourages expression of the belated mourner's inner feelings. Other family members are then invited to reveal both empathic responses and other feelings generated by observing the reactions of grief. Reciprocating expressions of empathy lead to a lessening of family tensions, a sense of relief, and expressions of goodwill and love toward one another. The procedure permits children, often for the first time, to observe their parents expressing intense feelings and provides a forceful lesson in empathy. Children and parents can acquire a sense of emotional continuity between generations.

It is essential that the therapist assure every family member that these exposed feelings are natural. Because of social taboos, there is one emotion that family members may have particular trouble in regarding as normal—hostility toward the deceased. The bereaved often feels angry toward a loved person who has died, who has taken away his presence, shattered the environment, and abandoned the survivor to shift for himself. But in our culture it seems ungenerous to speak or think ill of the dead, so such hostility is often deflected from the deceased toward some other, living member(s) of the family. Once the hostility and its real object are identified, the family can understand the situation more clearly. At this stage, the person who bears the brunt of the displaced hostility may exhibit separation anxiety or threaten to remove himself from the family or both. Such responses tend to diminish and disappear as the experience of grief is worked through.

The ability of the therapist to empathize with grief and other painful states seems related to his capacity for reflective review of feelings generated by comparable situations in his own life. Loewald described tendencies on the part of analysts to resist this affective regression required for empathy because of an underlying fear "lest we may not find the way back to higher organization" [23]. To empathize with the other's grief, however, the therapist must be able to empathize with himself as he once was.

The foregoing observations support Bowlby's thesis that "three types of response—separation anxiety, grief and mourning, and defense—are phases of a single process and that when treated as such each illumines the other two" [24]. The family coming to treatment presents a problem which, I submit, masks either separation anxiety or a defensive reaction to this or both. The family sees the problem as residing either in one of its members or in a disturbed relationship. The presenting complaint, after being initially acknowledged, is set aside while historical background is explored. Such exploration, which includes scanning the lives of senior family members, usually converges on unresolved grief. It is curious to observe that, while this grief is being resolved through empathy, the symptoms that brought the family to treatment seem to fade away.

At the same time, the family equilibrium shifts from its dependency on the original scapegoat, that is, the labeled patient or disturbed relationship, to a fluid situation; as the therapist underscores the responsibility of each family member in perpetuating the original equilibrium, that member takes a turn as scapegoat. In this stage, individual disorganization and heightened intra-family frictions appear. This disorganization is equivalent to Bowlby's second phase of the mourning process. Family members need empathic help in coping with the beginnings of dissolution of their symbiotic patterns. The original scapegoat finds himself newly free, but he and other family members are ambivalent about the changing intra-family relationships that this freedom activates.

The therapist must be alert to a variety of psychological and psychosomatic disturbances that usually emerge at this stage—anxiety states, temporary paranoid reactions, depression, mood swings, and gastrointestinal disorders that simulate organic disease. To escape the intensity of feelings related to the grief work, family members may often start to search frantically for the counsel of other physicians, lawyers, and clergymen; they may become immersed in a variety of "busy-work" activities. These actions are attempts to block the recognition and expression of regrets that the family has wasted so many years in senseless discord. Empathy toward the resistance to sharing such regret leads to genuine declarations of remorse. This phase is most difficult to achieve in both parents and grandparents of schizophrenics. Such senior family members often threaten to withdraw from treatment and sometimes actually terminate their visits. Once regret is fully expressed and reviewed, the family settles into a more harmonious equilibrium where each member is able to assume his proper responsibility for the presenting complaint and the related family dissonance.

The family unit is unwittingly prepared for the experience of losing the therapist through the corrective grief experience. It seems that the belated completion of mourning for the original loss enables them to cope adequately with new losses. Another technique that encourages successful termination (the main goal of treatment whether for individuals, couples, or families) is a self-confrontation procedure where, at home, they listen to and discuss audio-tapes of their own therapy sessions. Each member is confronted with real evidence of how he functions with the others in mutual and spiraling provocations. By assessing a disturbance and his own part in it, he can begin to avoid being provoked on future occasions. The therapist must empathize with the resistance family members feel toward hearing how they actually sound. Often an individual has the greatest difficulty in empathizing with the self revealed on tape, a feeling comparable to the disgust or embarrassment some people feel when reading letters they wrote long ago. Once resistance is overcome, however, and family members achieve increasing self-control, they are freed to explore the relevance of the past to the present under circumstances where the effect can be most enduring, that is, at home in the absence of the therapist.

My work with a family unit includes the induction of the belated grief experience as part of the general focus on the critical life experiences of each family member. My approach is distilled from psychoanalytic theory as adapted for both individual and group psychotherapy, and includes dream interpretation and free association. It relies on more direct inquiry and topical focus than is usual in individual psychotherapy. After family diagnostic studies, groups are assembled for therapy, and this group work is integrated with individual psychotherapy for selected family members; I usually conduct the individual as well as the group sessions. Each family requires its own pattern of meetings. The therapist acts as a group leader whose catalytic role is gradually incorporated into intra-family patterns of action. He remains, however, sufficiently an outsider to represent both social reality and an object on whom unresolved conflicts can be projected and displaced. In contrast to individual psychotherapy, he is not the sole focus of transference, since other family members are also objects of fluctuating transference phenomena. Because the transference is scattered rather than concentrated, the therapist is in a favorable position to clarify not only the ambivalence expressed toward him but also similar expressions between family members.

My work is directed toward certain goals for each family member: an increased empathic understanding of himself and others; a greater tendency to validate against reality his impressions about the attitudes of those around him; and an ability to tolerate and accept differences, frustrations, and failure. Above all, this form of treatment aims at developing firmer individual identities through the establishment of each member's sense of self, while simultaneously reinforcing the viability of the family.

Broader Implications

There is probably a need to consider empathy as important in general as well as in therapeutic situations. Each of us appears to have a basic hunger for empathy, a wish for the intimacy that can erase, if only for a moment, the individual's sense of emptiness and aloneness. Paradoxically, we want to satisfy this hunger, but, at the same time, we erect façades and barriers to prevent our being touched by real people. This conflict can be imperfectly resolved for brief periods through the vicarious satisfactions provided by novels and the theater. In *A Long Day's Journey into Night*, for example, we can empathize with the characters without risk because we know that our engagement will be confined within the limits of the play. We know too that our empathy as spectators will involve little pain, for we are not asked to expose our own distress. And we know that the actors will not be hurt by their revelations of emotion because they are merely assuming their roles. Empathy is so vital a nutrient that human beings deliberately seek it in fiction. Would it not be desirable that they be encouraged to satisfy their hunger for empathy in real life?

In our society, the nuclear family is that social unit most responsible for the development and maintenance of personality. Each member's level of self-esteem depends upon the emotional climate of the whole family. If parents can share with each other and their children their innermost joys and sorrows, each member can observe and accept the existence of helplessness, sadness, and aloneness underneath the façades we all erect to conceal them. Parents are the most enduring models for their children's behavior and attitudes; so it is appropriate that from them each child learn the value and reality of empathic understanding. Sympathy, by precluding this sharing, promotes only frustration and isolation among those who should be closest and most real to each other. Whereas sympathy triggers mutual regression, empathy fosters mutual growth.

These considerations have generated a recent series of radio broadcasts called *A Chance to Grow*. The eleven programs in the series demonstrate the value of empathic review among "normal" people living through significant changes in the life cycle, such as graduation from school, marriage,

50

and retirement. The listener can hear family members as they talk among themselves and with me and can share their feelings about events and their interactions with each other. The series is designed to encourage listeners to consider the important part empathy might play in their own lives.

Of all the changes in the life cycle, one of the most difficult seems to be the death of a loved person. Throughout this paper, I have tried to show the persistent and damaging consequences of unresolved grief. Such unresolved grief is probably widespread among us. Geoffrey Gorer, following his survey of reactions to bereavement in his own country, concluded: "I think that the material presented has adequately demonstrated that the majority of British people are today without adequate guidance as to how to treat death and bereavement and without social help in living through and coming to terms with the grief and mourning which are the inevitable responses in human beings to the death of someone whom they have loved" [25].

What social patterns can we devise to meet this widespread need? I am unable to go far in answering this question, but I believe that it may finally be found that, just as grief is at the root of psychopathological blight, so empathy may be the principal element of the healing process. Modern man needs a situation that provides the climate for empathy to resolve grief, a situation analogous to the primitive mourning rituals of his ancestors.

If a man does away with his traditional way of living and throws away his good customs, he had better first make certain that he has something of value to replace them.— BASUTO PROVERB.

REFERENCES

1. G. L. ENGEL. *In:* P. H. KNAPP (ed.). Expressions of the emotions in man, p. 267. New York: International Universities Press, 1963.
2. C. OLDEN. Psychoanal. Study Child, 8:111, 1953.
3. H. PINTER. Evergreen Rev., p. 81, Winter 1964.
4. ———. *Ibid.*, p. 82.
5. H. S. SULLIVAN. The interpersonal theory of psychiatry, pp. 41–42. New York: W. W. Norton, 1953.
6. H. F. SEARLES. Psychiat. Quart., 35:631, 1961.
7. S. FREUD. *In:* J. STRACHEY (ed.). The standard edition of the complete works of Sigmund Freud, vol. 14, p. 137. London: Hogarth Press, 1957.
8. K. ABRAHAM. Selected papers in psychoanalysis, p. 137. London: Hogarth Press, 1949.
9. M. KLEIN. Int. J. Psychoanal., 21:125, 1940.
10. H. DEUTSCH. Psychoanal. Quart., 6:12, 1937.
11. M. C. PARKES. Brit. J. Med. Psychol., 38:1, 1965.

12. E. LINDEMANN. Amer. J. Psychiat., 101:141, 1944.

13. M. C. PARKES. Brit. J. Med. Psychol., 38:25-26, 1965.

14. H. DEUTSCH. Psychoanal. Quart., 6:22, 1937.

15. S. FREUD. *In:* J. STRACHEY (ed.). The standard edition of the complete works of Sigmund Freud, vol. 14, p. 300. London: Hogarth Press, 1957.

16. M. KLEIN. Int. J. Psychoanal., 21:145, 1940.

17. N. L. PAUL and G. H. GROSSER. Family Processes, 3:377, 1964.

18. ———. Amer. J. Orthopsychiat., 24:875, 1964.

19. ———. Community Ment. Health J., 1:339, 1965.

20. N. L. PAUL. Psychiatric Research Report No. 20, p. 175. American Psychiatric Association, 1966.

21. J. BOWLBY. Int. J. Psychoanal., 42:317, 1961.

22. ———. *Ibid.*, 41:89, 1960.

23. H. W. LOEWALD. Int. J. Psychoanal., 41:26, 1960.

24. J. BOWLBY. Int. J. Psychoanal., 41:91, 1960.

25. G. GORER. Death, grief, and mourning, p. 126. Garden City, N.Y.: Doubleday, 1965.

The dual role of comforter and bereaved

ELSPETH WALLACE, R.N.
BRENDA D. TOWNES, M.A.

Normal processes of mourning in adults
and the assumptions concerning personality
development affecting the mourning process
have been reviewed and discussed by
Bowlby.[1] A controversy exists over theoretical assumptions concerning early personality development and its relationship to
processes of mourning.   Mourning is
represented as a manifestation of early
depressive feeling by Lindemann,[2] Bowlby,[1]
Chodoff and co-workers,[3] and Pollack,[4]
whereas Klein,[5] Grinberg.[6] and others view
the mourning process as a manifestation
of persecutory anxiety. (All authors agree,
however, that the work of mourning involves detachment from the lost person
through the demands of reality and the

The work here reported is supported, in part, by
research grants MH 12548–01 and CA 04937–07 from
the U. S. Public Health Service and by Bureau of
State Services grant NIH 5 107A66.

establishment of new relationships.) The normal process of mourning in adults has been defined by these authors primarily through observation of adults in psychoanalysis relating in retrospect their feelings toward loss of a parent during childhood.

Richmond and Waisman,[7] Natterson,[8] Knudson,[9] Friedman,[10] and their colleagues have conducted longitudinal observations of mothers and, to a lesser extent, of fathers of children with neoplastic diseases on an inpatient ward. Their conclusions, based on interviews and observations of ward behavior, are in agreement: in the presence of prolonged illness and death of a child, the anticipatory mourning process in parents follows a triphasic pattern.

The first phase of anticipatory mourning is characterized by denial of reality and attempts either to screen it out or to reverse it. Parental behavior is characterized by shock, disbelief, hostility toward doctors and other medical staff, outbursts of grief, guilt, and anger, and refusal to accept the diagnosis. In the second phase of anticipatory mourning there is acceptance of the reality of the diagnosis, but not the prognosis. This is seen in the parents' demands for information relative to the disease, concern over the treatment of the child, overprotection of the child, fear of separation from the child, and expressions of personal guilt. In the final phase of anticipatory mourning, the parent accepts the reality of the diagnosis and the prognosis.

Characteristic parental responses include a redistribution of time, with more time devoted to the rest of the family, the development of close friendships with parents of other afflicted children, a wish for the suffering of the child to end, and a shift from hope for a miracle cure for their own child to hope for a future cure for similarly afflicted children. Natterson and Knudson[8] found that a minimum of four months between diagnosis and death is needed for successful development of the entire triphasic anticipatory mourning process.

The purpose of this paper is to consider the reactions of medical personnel to the dying child and his parents. The medical staff, whose role is that of healing and whose experience is one of repeated loss, is subjected to sustained psychologic stress. Observed stress reactions of staff in the form of anticipatory mourning and its parallel to the triphasic mourning process in parents will be illustrated through case material.

There are approximately fifty children concurrently under treatment for leukemia at the Oncology Clinic of the Children's Orthopedic Hospital and Medical Center, an affiliated teaching hospital of the University of Washington School of Medicine, Seattle. Within the group of fifty children there is an almost predictable rate of two deaths and two newly diagnosed children with leukemia per month. Furthermore, in the past two decades the life span in childhood leukemia has been increased from a median of three months to a current median of 21 months.[11] Thus, instead of the past expectation of imminent death, the medical staff and the parents of the child with leukemia are now exposed to the prolonged anxiety of a critically ill child for whom painful medical procedures, hospitalizations, remissions, and ultimate death are predicted.

When the diagnosis of childhood leukemia is established, the clinic physician meets with the parents, who are then told about the diagnosis and the prognosis. The present limitations of chemotherapy are discussed with the parents, and they are requested to allow their child's participation in the national research program that seeks optimal induction and maintenance of remission of leukemia by chemotherapy. The typical course of alternating relapses and remissions is explained, and the hope is sustained that through their child's participation in ongoing drug studies they may assist in finding a future cure for similarly affected children.

The child with leukemia is seen at the clinic at regular intervals of approximately two to three weeks for about three hours per visit. During these visits blood tests, physical examinations, and often bone marrow aspirations may be completed. The last is a painful procedure that provokes anxiety in parents, child, and clinic staff. Thus, the clinic nurse, aide, laboratory technician, and social worker, as well as the physicians, experience in the course of the day and the week the anguish surrounding the dying child and his parents. The child may be in the initial phase, in remission, or in the terminal phase of the disease. Reactions to the psychologic stress of sustained pain, mourning, and death may vary within the clinic staff members, as it does within the parents, according to their own previous experiences and personality.

The authors, involved in an investigation of the healthy siblings' adaptation to chronic illness and death of a child with leukemia, observed within themselves and the clinic staff mourning processes that closely parallel the previously described anticipatory mourning in parents of a dying child. These reactions are described in the following composite case illustrations of the parents and of staff.

Case illustration 1: Tommie, age 5, was diagnosed as having acute lymphocytic leukemia. He was an inpatient for five days and responded well to therapy, so that he reached a remission within four

56

weeks. On admission Tommie was very ill, with a high fever and unsightly bruises on his body. His mother, who accompanied him to the hospital, was in a state of shock and complete despair. His father wept when told of Tommie's diagnosis and returned to talk with the physician the following day. The father was very angry and demanded that the bone marrow examination be repeated, as he was sure that an error had been made. Tommie actively fought having to stay in the hospital and resisted any attempt to make him more comfortable.

During the first days following the diagnosis of Tommie's leukemia, the social worker, nurse, and aide, as well as the doctors who would care for him at the clinic after his hospital discharge, visited the ward. The staff tended to place high social value on Tommie and commented on what "good" parents he had. Everyone from the physician to the ward aide joined in praise of Tommie, his behavior, attractiveness, and intelligence. They assured each other that he didn't look ill and "wasn't too bad," and that a remission would soon be achieved. Although the father was overtly hostile to the physicians and the mother was almost incapable of responding to any overtures of friendship offered, the clinic staff was sure that the family would soon fall into the routine demanded by the treatment of leukemia.

Tommie's father continued to demand further proof of his son's illness and became very disturbed about his bruises. He was as adamant in requesting a repeat of the bone marrow examination as he was in requesting that someone make the bruises vanish. He demanded that Tommie have repeated warm baths because he felt this would cure the petechiae and then his son would be well again. He was unable to admit that Tommie was too upset to tolerate even limited nursing care, much less repeated baths and the painful re-examination of the bone marrow.

In response to the father's anger and grief, the staff's complete attention was turned to helping the father to accept the diagnosis. It was decided to repeat the bone marrow examination a few days earlier than usual. The physician who would repeat aspiration of the marrow was given strong support and praise for his decision to do so from the staff.

A growing irritation with the father was experienced by the group, as he seemed unable to respond to the situation in the accepted father role it had assigned to him. Under the impact of the father's hostility, staff members became warm and supportive of each other. They praised the skill of the physicians and responded eagerly to assurances from the director that this was not abnormal behavior on the part of the father. Care was taken that not one member of the staff received the full force of the father's anger. Tommie's room, where the parents stayed with him, was visited by the staff in two's and three's rather than singly. A laboratory technician who refused to give information to the father that she felt was not appropriate was able to come to the clinic nurse to report that the father was angry with her. She was warmly reassured by the nurse, "I thought he might try that [to get information from other than the usual source]; you certainly handled it well. I am sure it will make no difference to his adjustment later. I am pleased you came and discussed this with me, as we must all work together to help this family."

Anticipatory mourning for the dying child occurs in staff as well as in parents. The response to the stress of working with the terminally ill child and his parents is varied.[12] Behavior characteristic of the first phase of anticipatory mourning is experienced when there are a number of deaths or new admissions within a brief period of time. Those involved seem to ignore the reality of the diagnosis and to dwell on the attractiveness of the child or to dismiss the painful course of the disease for the hope of a quick adjustment to clinic routine. There may be little mention of the child's ultimate death, of his place in the research program, or of a remission.

Under the impetus of parental inability to accept the diagnosis, anxiety is generated around the staff's and the parents' ability to accept the treatment program and the finality of death. The usual method of coping with this anxiety is a typical third-phase response of internal support and efforts to help the parents adjust. As illustrated by the case of Tommie, however, the technician's uneasiness in denying information to the father and the staff's anger at the father's unreasonable demands are typical first-stage reactions—that is, pervasive feelings of anger or rage are present that may be free-floating or directed toward a specific person.

Case illustration 2: When Henry died suddenly before a remission was produced, a general feeling of guilt and sorrow affected the entire group. Individual expressions of this feeling were manifested among staff members. One physician who was not on duty when Henry died attempted to contact the parents to express his sympathy and suggest they return to discuss the nature of the child's disease. He was attempting to extend his care of the family beyond the death of the child, a common occurrence. His efforts were praised by the rest of the group. Because this doctor was involved in the attempt to contact the parents and seemed particularly touched by the death of this child, the other doctor, unasked, took on a larger share of the routine work for that day.

Henry's mother had only one friend among the other mothers, and the ward aide wondered if the clinic should not inform this friend of Henry's death. The social worker helped the aide to work through her feeling of responsibility for the unexpectedness of the child's death.

Stress is also handled in ways consistent with the philosophical resignation of the third phase of mourning. Staff members display a willingness to attempt to help one more child and to risk the painful loss again, to recognize the needs of each staff member and to attempt to support one another.

Case illustration 3: Willie was admitted to the hospital, no longer responding to therapy, with severe nose bleeds and evidence of gastrointestinal bleeding. He was irritable and was in evident pain. Willie was apprehensive and expressed his fear by great anger toward his parents. He attempted to hit his father with his intravenous arm-restraint board, cried when his mother left his side even briefly, and demanded her immediate and constant attention.

Willie responded in a friendly fashion to the staff, who, he felt, could make him well and whose withdrawal he could not risk. One nurse responded to his needs by becoming very protective of Willie.

59

She doubted the ability of others to give him adequate care, returned during her time off to sit with him, and actively resisted any attempt made by her supervisors to separate her from him.

The physician suggested that Willie's mother might be able to help the families of newly diagnosed children. The mother was eager to talk to the parents, but the ward nurse felt this would exhaust her and would only reluctantly agree to the plan. As Willie's parents lived from day to day with the threat of Willie's imminent death, they sought more and more detailed information about his condition and therapy and wanted more of the physicians' and nurses' time. These demands were met by a feeling on the part of the staff of "What's there to explain now?" More newly diagnosed children or those with more time to live demanded their energy. The ward nurse interpreted this attitude on the part of the physicians as cold and unsympathetic. She felt that everyone but her had forsaken the dying boy.

The clinic nurse, who had been a warm friend to the mother and child during visits a few months previously, found it difficult to find time to visit on the ward. The mother complained, "They were so good at first when I had to be told he would die. Why do they seem afraid to stop and talk with me now?"

When Willie died, a nurse who was not on duty responded by saying, "Oh, God, I should have been there." She stated the common hope that she could have prevented his death or made the experience easier for the mother and child.

The casual conversation in the clinic touches upon the myth that each child who dies will be replaced within a few days by a new patient. When a death occurs, tensions mount within the clinic. Reports are misplaced, patients appear who are not scheduled, and some infighting goes on in the form of "hospital humor." One member of the team may be singled out to receive undue criticism for management of patients. In casual conversation, this "damned" disease is discussed, and the hopelessness of ever finding a cure is mentioned.

When faced with the death of a child,

60

some other strategies are employed to deal with the failure to cure the child. The staff has to admit its own limitations and face a lack of professional gratification. The ward nurse who had been very involved with Willie just before his death and had had less time to prepare herself for the event displayed reactions and feelings resembling in many ways those of an early phase of anticipatory mourning. She was angry at her co-workers and felt only she could care for the child. She resented separation from this patient to the extent of returning after hours to care for him and finally felt guilty at his death, as if she could have prevented the event by her presence.

A shift of time and interest to children who might still respond to therapy and provide new information relative to the research goal clearly is a third-phase mourning response. The difficulty in remaining comfortable through reliance upon intellectual pursuits is manifested by occasional disruption in the clinic functioning and in the interpersonal relationships of the workers. Communications seem to deteriorate first, as evidenced by unscheduled patients, hospital humor, misplaced memos and reports, and mild misunderstandings. "Will we ever find a cure?" is a common plea. The human despair and doubt are shared with the parents.

Discussion

The dual role of comforter and bereaved is a heart-breaking one. For the staff, motivated to enter the healing professions by a desire to help people and relieve suffering, the expectation of a cure for the disease is frustrated from the time of diagnosis. Secondary goals that fulfill the needs of the comforter must be developed or the rage, anger, and depression may become overwhelming. The painful and exacting nature of many of the procedures performed at the clinic allows each person to use his skills to the full extent. Seeing a child well enough to enjoy Christmas or his birthday gives great satisfaction!

There is an essential and inherent conflict between the roles of comforter and bereaved. We support, treat, and offer hope even as we mourn for the child. We are burdened with the image of being able to "take it," to accept death casually. The antagonism between the two roles results in a persistently high level of psychologic stress.

The death of a child is a difficult and inexplicable fact of human life. Our culture values life and equates death with punishment and failure. We are activity oriented, seeking mastery over nature; and "death may be conceived of as a thwarting of man's struggle for ultimate supremacy; it hence constitutes a serious threat to his sense of mastery over nature. As such, it is a source of anxiety and fear." [13] In our culture "the idea of death is so threatening there exists a strong defensive attempt to deny its significance." [13] The children's cartoon characters and comic heroes who are dismembered and flattened by various lethal devices and instantly become whole again exemplify our primitive reluctance to accept mortality.

While we are asking, "Why must the child die?" we are seeking the meaning of our own death. Success in our internal struggle to find meaning in death is determined by our previous experiences. Are we not finding partial solutions to our own dilemma through our involvement in the death of others? Perhaps we can achieve within ourselves, and assist others to arrive at, a personal equilibrium that does not deny the reality of death.

Most preconceived ideas of how it will feel to work with the dying child do not take into account the amount of personal involvement that occurs. Neophyte staff members, especially, are assailed by feelings of despair and frustration. They question the value of the research, the attempts to prolong the lives of the children, and their own effectiveness.

We all wish to see an end to the suffering of the child and within ourselves. We feel guilty at our own failure to live up to a self-image of comforter. As we become more familiar with the scope of the medical research, we learn that these children's deaths do have a meaning. Each time we risk our identity to care for a child with leukemia, we grow in maturity and self-knowledge, or else we must seek other avenues of effectiveness. As we cast aside the magic beliefs, the denial, and the anger, we find satisfaction in making meaningful what remains of the child's life. When we see our discomfort in the framework of a process that has a reasonable expectation of a hopeful outcome, we can function more effectively in the total medical effort. We learn that shock, anger, fear of separation from the child, and personal guilt are normal preparations for the establishment of new relationships.

REFERENCES

1. Bowlby, J.: Psychoanalytic Study of the Child, 15:9, 1960.

2. Lindemann, E.: American Journal of Psychiatry, 101:141, 1944.

3. Chodoff, P., Friedman, S. B., and Hamburg, D. A.: American Journal of Psychiatry, 120:743, 1964.

4. Pollack, G. H.: International Journal of Psychoanalysis, 42:341, 1961.

5. Klein, M.: Contributions to Psychoanalysis, 1921–1945. London, The Hogarth Press and the Institute of Psychoanalysis, 1948, pp. 311–338.

6. Grinberg, L.: International Journal of Psychoanalysis, 45:366, 1964.

7. Richmond, J. B., and Waisman, H. A.: American Journal of Diseases of Children, 89:42, 1955.

8. Natterson, J. M., and Knudson, A. G., Jr.: Psychosomatic Medicine, 22:456, 1960.

9. Knudson, A. G., Jr., and Natterson, J. M.: Pediatrics. 26:482, 1960.

10. Friedman, S. B., Chodoff, P., Mason, J. W., and Hamburg, D. A.: Pediatrics, 32:610, 1963.

11. Krivit, W., et al.: Cancer, 21:352, 1968.

12. Glaser, B. G., and Strauss, A. L.: Trans-action, 2:27 (May–June), 1965.

13. Howard, A., and Scott, R. A.: Journal of Existentialism, 6:161 (Winter), 1965–66.

Recognition and management of grief in elderly patients

EDWIN P. GRAMLICH, M.D.

Grief is a ubiquitous bodily reaction to emotional injury and loss, not unlike bodily reactions to physical injury. Known throughout the ages as an important cause of illness, it is diffuse in the aged and obscured, if not completely overlooked, in this age of scientific medicine.[1] If it is not truly a disease, as suggested by Engel,[2] it is certainly a state of dis-ease, with organic and physiologic changes. In its uncomplicated form grief follows a typical and predictable course.[3-7] As with many reactive processes, however, it may follow deviant and atypical courses which are easily confused with other disease processes.[6,8] The more devious patterns of grief are found in the young and the old.[6] It is stated by Nemiah that melancholia is at the bottom of everything, since nothing lasts and all that is loved or shall be loved must die or be lost.[9] Aging, therefore, subjects individuals to more and more loss. Loved ones are lost, health is lost, cherished goals are unrecognized and lost, cherished occupations and sources of pride and value are lost in the progress of time.[4,10,11]

Grief in elderly people has been studied scientifically only on a few occasions[12-15] with contradictory results. Several complete studies of elderly people suggest that grief, as such, may not be a significant event.[15-17] According to the theory of aging proposed by Cummings and Henry, aging people progressively disengage from their environmental attachments and live in an increasingly detached state.[18] It may be, however, that this state is one of a chronic depressive withdrawal and is associated with the continued accumulation of losses and overwhelming grief.[1] The recent work of Kastenbaum and Birren supports the general theory that aging is associated with a progressive disengagement from the environment.[15,16] Their theory proposes that grief in itself is not an essentially important factor, but only one of many

65

stresses applied to the aging individual. Other studies, however, have shown that grief is the precipitating factor in many states of illness and tends to aggravate preexisting organic and psychosomatic disorders.[3, 10, 13, 19-21] The death rate of widows and widowers exceeds that of the population by a significant degree, and it is legendary that many have died of, or at least during, grief.[21]

Definition   To understand grief in the elderly patient, one must have a firm understanding of the general syndrome of grief. The grief process is initiated by awareness of a significant loss. The first reaction to the loss is that of shock and disbelief. This state may be intense and associated with hallucinations and delusions in an effort to deny the loss in fantasy. If the loss is denied by the individual a state of numbness prevails.

Usually the loss can be denied only for a short time. It then becomes painfully obvious to the bereaved person that an extremely important other person has died. This initiates a stage of intense physical distress accompanied by feelings of deep loss and emptiness, associated with intense sadness and sorrow. Physical pain is common, especially headache, muscle and joint pain, and pain and pressure in the neck, chest, and abdomen. It is an all encompassing and disorganizing emotional reaction. It tends to come in waves of pain and distress accompanied by weeping.

This stage usually passes to a more chronic stage of mourning associated with a prolonged feeling of depression and sadness and with periodic memories of the lost person. It is debatable whether typical grief carries with it intense feelings of guilt and hostility. Some authors state that it does, others that it does not.[9, 24] However, it is common to feel intensely hurt and injured. The intensity of the hurt and injury calls for some explanation and meaning on the part of the grieving person. Intense guilt and self-blame often occur and may be of an entirely irrational nature, depending upon the ambivalence of the relationship with the lost person.

Following the guilt, hostility is common. Friends and family members may be confronted with anger and rejection. Efforts to offer comfort may meet with intense hostility. The person views the world as a hostile place, and projects blame to anyone who comes near. As the grieving person continues to do the work of mourning and to cope with the many memories associated with the lost individual, the process slowly subsides over weeks and months until energy is once again available to invest in new people to replace the lost one. This enables the grieving individual to go on and live a life free from the entanglements of the irretrievable past.

Atypical grief   Atypical grief follows one of three general forms: [1] In delayed grief, the loss may be denied for months or years and grief occurs later, inappropriately associated with a reminder of the loss. This frequently occurs on an anniversary of the loss, the individual having experienced no grief prior to that time. [2] Inhibited grief occurs in individuals in whom mourning seems to be subdued; however, it is longer lasting and associated with disturbed behavior or physical symptoms. It is common in young people. [3] Chronic grief is a prolongation and intensification of the normal grief process. It may be associated with states of overactivity without much sense of loss. It may occur in conditions where the grieving individual has identified with the lost person's illness and has developed symptoms similar to those of that illness. These symptoms may persist. It is as though the lost one has become a part of the grieving individual, who attempts to maintain contact with the deceased through illness, or sympathy pain.

Other patterns of chronic grief have to do with chronic isolation and apathy with depression, chronic hostility with paranoid thinking, and lengthy disorganization of preexisting life patterns. Physical symptomatology is a common part of grief, and chronic grief may be manifested by chronic physical symptoms either due to diagnosable psychosomatic conditions or ill-defined symptoms of pain and dysfunction. Parkes[10] lists osteoarthritis, colitis, migraine, asthma, bronchitis, ulcerative colitis, spastic colon, urticaria, and rheumatoid arthritis as disease entities which may be precipitated or aggravated by a loss.

Inhibited grief in the elderly Typical grief is thought to be uncommon in aged individuals. More often it follows a pattern of inhibited or chronic grief. The most common manifestation of grief in the aged, therefore, is overt somatic pain and distress. Many aspects of grief do not manifest themselves as clearly and are not as well defined as in younger people. It has been shown that elderly patients, who are grieving, frequently present themselves to physicians with physical complaints. They commonly have gastrointestinal symptoms, or joint and muscular pains, or both.

The most important aspect of the diagnostic process is the preceding history of an important loss, perhaps on its anniversary. One should suspect a grief reaction, regardless of the symptomatology, when one sees an individual who has sustained a major loss within the two years prior to the presenting complaints. Most commonly the physician is consulted within six months of the loss and studies have shown that the incidence of office visits is two to three times as great during the six months following a loss than it was during the six months prior to the loss. Since the grieving process is not experienced as intensely on a conscious level in elderly people, it appears that more of the emotional reaction is suppressed and finds an outlet through somatic expression. Most elderly patients actually hurt rather than complain of emotional pain. In my experience, many grieving elderly people also show symptoms of overt emotional and mental disorder, contrary to some of the literature on the subject. This is particularly evident if one takes the time to inquire about the patient's life after the somatic complaints have been investigated. It is my contention that one cannot rule out the grief process in a symptomatic widow unless there is a definite organic disease to explain the symptomatology. Even then, grief may be a strong contributing factor.

Case report An 81-year-old Caucasian widow was seen in psychiatric consultation four months after the death of a favorite but very disappointing son. She complained of abdominal discomfort and lack of appetite. She had been constipated and unable to sleep. She was nervous and frequently tearful. As an occupant of a nursing home, she had been overtly and covertly admonished and accused of being a baby because of her tendency to cry copiously. She had, in effect, been told to "shut up and stop grieving," which increased her grief and denied her an outlet. She expressed much guilt over her son's poor history of accomplishment in life. With encouragement to allow her tears to flow freely, she wept for most of one hour and part of another. The nursing staff was encouraged to assist her in her process of grief and to allow her to weep freely. As soon as this was accomplished, the patient's attitude changed markedly and her symptoms subsided. She developed a more optimistic attitude and began to socialize anew with the members of the nursing home. She resumed her cultural role there as a gossip and on follow-up visits showed only little evidence of residual grief. As the anniversary of her husband's death arrived and of her son's approached, she again experienced her symptoms, but with less intensity.

Treatment The management of grief in elderly people must be preceded by recognition and understanding of the underlying process. Once the physician is relatively certain that his patient's symptoms are those of grief the course of action is clear, with few exceptions. In the very old patient who is able to deny the loss and live in a state of unreality free from grief, it might be prudent to avoid challenging the denial. However, in the patient with existing symptoms, denial has been unsuccessful. Here, "grief work" must be at least partly done before the patient can be symptom-free to work toward new human relations and some form of partial engagement with the environment. The term "good grief" conveys the concept that grieving is good, necessary, and therapeutic. "Grief work" consists of remembering the lost individual and of working through the pain, guilt, and anger that go with the memories.[9, 23] I encourage grieving patients to cry frequently and to freely share their tears with close members of the family, physicians, nurses, and ministers. Paradoxical intention probably operates here, as many people unconsciously do the opposite of what they are told.

I think it important to share guilt, so that it can be forgiven and its irrational aspects rejected. Those who deal with a grieving patient should accept hostility, not react to it with counterhostility. Sharing of guilt feelings often functions to relieve intolerable guilt and may prevent suicide. Also, if it is understood that the patient is simply venting his anger at being hurt by what seems to be an irrational and unjust world, the anger can be accepted as a natural emotional reaction similar to the inflammatory reaction that naturally follows a burn. An angry reaction from a hurt patient should not be taken personally. A tolerant attitude toward it will help the grieving person accept anger and will keep him from directing it inwardly or suppressing it entirely. As this is accomplished, it is important to encourage the process of resocialization and finding new friends to begin, at least, to substitute for the important lost one. Sometimes the grieving process can interfere with current relationships and it is helpful to explain to friends and relatives that the person's hostility or symptom is a part of grief and will subside if they are patient. New living arrangements may have to be made by family members. Tranquilizing and antidepressant drugs can be used, depending on the target symptoms. They help in subduing emotional reactions and allow the individual to take the grief in smaller doses.

Grieving patients should be told that they are in the process of grief and mourning, for many of them do not connect their pain and misery with their loss. They have worked to deny or avoid memory of the loss, with the idea that not thinking about the loss would make the pain go away. Some say it is silly to cry and it does no good to mourn, not realizing that they only fool the mind. The body and emotional self react anyway as the loss is jerked from the very heart of the being and many wounds are opened that must heal. Many interpret their symptoms as a sign of physical disease or mental illness and need to be repeatedly reassured that the symptoms do not represent those dreaded conditions. A few extra minutes of a physician's time and understanding at this point can be exceedingly helpful to a bereaved patient.

Summary   The process of grief in general, and in the aging patient in particular, is outlined. Grief is viewed as a psychosomatic reaction to an extreme environmental stress that every physician should be cognizant of and alert for, especially in the elderly patient in whom it may be hidden behind a facade of somatic complaints. A program of management and treatment is outlined whereby grief can be shortened and prevented from becoming a more chronic and disabling, if not fatal, disease.

REFERENCES

1. MILT, H.: Grief. Trends in Psychiatry. Vol. 3, No. II. West Point, Pa.: Merck Sharp & Dohme, 1966.
2. ENGEL, G. L.: Is grief a disease? Psychosom. Med. 23:18, 1961.
3. KOLLAR, E. J.: Psychological stress. J. nerv. ment. Dis. 132:382, 1961.
4. VOLKAN, V.: Normal and pathological grief reactions: A guide of the family physician. Virginia med. Mth. 93:651, 1966.
5. PARKES, C. M.: Bereavement and mental illness. Part I. A clinical study of the grief of bereaved psychiatric patients. Brit. J. med. Psychol. 38:1, 1965.
6. PARKES, C. M.: Bereavement and mental illness. Brit. J. med. Psychol. 38:13, 1965.
7. LINDEMANN, E.: Symptomatology and management of acute grief. Amer. J. Psychiat. 101: 141, 1944.
8. ENGEL, G. L.: Grief and grieving. Amer. J. Nursing 64:93, 1964.
9. NEMIAH, J. C.: Foundations of Psychopathology. New York: Oxford: University Press, 1961.

10. PARKES, C. M.: Effects of bereavement on physical and mental health: A study of the medical records of widows. Brit. med. J. 2:274, 1964.
11. SCHMALE, A. H., JR.: Relationship of separation and depression to disease. Psychosom. Med. 20:259, 1958.
12. KAY, D. W., ROTH, M., and HOPKINS, B.: Aetiological factors in the causation of affective disorders in old age. J. ment. Sci. 101:302, 1955.
13. STERN, K., WILLIAMS, G. M., and PRADOS, M.: Grief reactions in later life. Amer. J. Psychiat. 108:289, 1951.
14. PERLIN, S., and BUTLER, R. N.: Human Aging. U.S. Department of Health, Education and Welfare, National Institute of Mental Health, Bethesda, Md., 1963, p. 159.
15. BIRREN, J. E., BUTLER, R. N., GREENHOUSE, S. W., SOKOLOFF, L., and YARROW, M. R.: Human Aging. U.S. Department of Health, Education and Welfare, National Institute of Mental Health, Bethesda, Md., 1963, p. 314.
16. KASTENBAUM, R.: New Thoughts on Old Age. New York: Springer Publishing Co., 1964.
17. SIMON, A., and ENGLE, B.: Geriatrics. Amer. J. Psychiat. 120:671, 1964.
18. CUMMINGS, E., and HENRY, W. E.: Growing Old. New York: Basic Books, 1961.
19. KRUPT, G. R.: Identification as a defense against loss. Int. J. Psycho-Anal. 46:303, 1965.
20. FREUD, S.: A General Introduction of Psychoanalysis. New York: Washington Square Press, 1960.
21. YOUNG, M., BENJAMIN, B., and WALLIS, C.: The mortality of widowers. Lancet 2:454, 1963.
22. KRAUS, A. S., and LILIENFELD, A. M.: Some epidemiological aspects of the high mortality rate in the young widowed group. J. chron. Dis. 10:207, 1959.
23. PAUL, L.: Crisis intervention. J. Ment. Hygiene 50:141, 1966.

70

Conjugal Bereavement

The Consequences of Conjugal Bereavement

David Maddison, FRACP, FANZCP

In the past two decades the topic of death and its consequences has been substantially freed from its traditional taboo in western society. During this period much has been written about the normal and abnormal processes of mourning and about the physical and psychological effects of death on the bereaved survivors. Particular attention has been given to studies of conjugal bereavement, using the general framework of the so-called 'crisis model'. This postulates that, following bereavement, a state of crisis is almost invariably experienced, in which the individual's normal coping techniques are ineffective so that he experiences various physical and psychological symptoms as he attempts to master his grief. This state of crisis however, like other crises, must be resolved in some way sooner or later. In bereavement this task of resolution is often referred to as the 'grief-work'.

The Phases of Grief

Uncomplicated or normal grief runs a consistent course in which there are three phases:

(1) The initial phase in which the bereaved is shocked and cannot accept the fact that the loss has really occurred.

(2) The stage of developing awareness of the loss in which sadness, hopelessness and helplessness become

overwhelming. Often grief is accompanied by self-blame, painful self-questioning, shame, guilt and anger. Although emotional disturbances usually predominate it is quite common for alterations in physical health to accompany or even overshadow the troubled feelings. Bodily symptoms, such as insomnia, fatigue and loss of appetite, are usually reported by the bereaved. Some may complain little of their grief and are more aware of symptoms such as indigestion, muscular pains, dizziness, headaches and constipation.

(3) The phase of recovery is usually longer than the two earlier phases. Gradually the bereaved begins to accept the permanence of the loss; the grief subsides and the previous state of health and well-being is re-established.

The Prevalence of Serious Consequences

Previous studies have clearly demonstrated the frequency of important and serious consequences following bereavement in the middle-aged woman. Bodily symptoms may result in substantial physical ill-health, and emotional distress may develop into well-recognized psychiatric disorder. In one series of 72 widows, residents of London's East End, who were interviewed approximately two years after their husbands' deaths, only 14 considered themselves to have recovered completely; 31 reported a lasting deterioration in their health and 57 reported continuing difficulty with sleep. It has been shown, in a study of persons admitted to a psychiatric hospital, that the number of patients whose illness followed the death of a spouse was six times greater than expected, suggesting that the bereavement must have been one causative factor in the development of the illness. Another study has shown that widows under the age of 65 consulted their general practitioner because of psychiatric symptoms three times more frequently than they had done during a control period before the bereavement.

Dying of a 'Broken Heart'

It is known that, for some time after the death of their spouse, widows and widowers run a considerably greater risk of dying than married people of the same age. The increase in mortality occurs in the first two years after bereavement and is particularly marked in the first six months, when there is a rise of about 40% in the expected mortality rate. One North American study revealed that the death-rate is particularly increased for young widowed people under the age of 35. In this study and in separate studies in England and Wales it has been demonstrated

73

that the mortality rate for widowers is twice as high as that of widows. Dying of a broken heart may be due to a number of conditions; self-neglect and suicide make some contribution.

Our Studies in Sydney and Boston

Our studies employ the widow's self-report of her physical and mental health during the 13 months following bereavement as an index of the extent to which she has mastered the crisis situation in an effective way. There are good reasons for believing that the development of new physical and mental symptoms, or the substantial aggravation of symptoms previously existing, are reliable indicators of unsatisfactory crisis resolution. Using consecutive death records, we have gathered information about the health status of 132 widows in Boston, Massachusetts, and 243 widows in Sydney, making a total of 375 bereaved subjects.

Each of the 375 subjects completed a detailed questionnaire about her health since the bereavement, comparing this with her state before her husband's death. Inspection of the questionnaires enabled us to decide on a level of health deterioration which undoubtedly represented a 'bad outcome' and, using these criteria, we found a prevalence of health deterioration of this magnitude in 21 % of Boston subjects and 32 % of Sydney subjects.

In view of the possibility that this health deterioration might have been due to middle age itself, rather than bereavement as such, comparable data were gathered from a matched control group of married middle-aged women in Boston and Sydney. Approximately 7 % of these women reported a comparable deterioration in health in the space of a year, the difference between this and the previous figures being highly significant.

Analysis was undertaken of the relationship between health deterioration and the social and personal characteristics of the widows. In Boston a significant correlation was found between young age of the widow and subsequent health deterioration, but this finding was not repeated in the Sydney sample. In conflict with much of the mythology about bereavement, no clear correlation was found between bad outcome and social class (rich people may fare as badly as poor people), nor between bad outcome and the amount of warning the widow received of her husband's death, that is, sudden, unexpected death is *not* more likely to lead to a bad outcome. Religious affiliation and racial origin appear to play no part in the type of outcome.

Factors Contributing to an Unfavourable Outcome

Research in my department is ultimately aimed at the development of preventive techniques which might, when introduced at the height of the crisis, reduce the frequency of bad or potentially bad outcomes. Having determined the frequency of bad outcomes, the second stage of our study has involved intensive interviews with 80 subjects from our total sample of 375 widows. The life situation and social network of 40 subjects for whom bereavement had serious consequences were compared with a carefully matched group of 40 widows who had passed through the crisis without serious ill-effect. By noting the subject's response to a large number of statements concerning her personal relationships, we were able to measure the extent to which she had perceived the people in her environment as helpful, passively neglectful or actively opposed to her needs.

Our findings suggest that the widow who is dissatisfied with the help available to her during the crisis is very likely to proceed to an unfavourable outcome. Some specific forms of behaviour were also shown to be important. In general terms bad outcome subjects, when compared with good outcome subjects, felt that their expression of feelings (grief, guilt and anger) had been blocked. They tended to consider that persons around them had, actively or passively, opposed their wish to review their past lives and talk at length about their husbands. Attempts to encourage the development of new interests, new activities and new romantic relationships tended to arouse great anger, and also seemed to be associated with a bad outcome.

Despite its overwhelming importance the quantity and quality of the support available in the environment is obviously not the *only* determinant of the widow's outcome. Other factors may make their contribution: the quality of the marriage; the presence of markedly unusual personality characteristics before the bereavement; the mode of death, particularly when this involved disfigurement or grossly protracted pain and suffering; the presence of additional stresses such as another independent crisis situation (for example, death of mother) or a pathological reaction to the death by another family member, usually a child.

Illustrative Cases

The following illustrative cases, in which all the subjects had bad outcomes in terms of health deterioration, provide examples of the diverse complications which may follow bereavement.

75

Case 1

Mrs. A., aged 49, had a large number of unmet needs and unhelpful experiences during the crisis. A good deal of anger and bitterness had been aroused by the financial circumstances in which her husband's sudden death had left her. These had involved substantial debts and a near bankrupt business. Her husband's relatives had been most unco-operative, flatly refusing to lend money or to advise in business matters. Her 20-year-old son, 14-year-old daughter and elderly mother were considered to be the only helpful people in her environment; however they did not allow her to express her feelings about the death. Her son had also upset Mrs. A. with his moodiness and uncontrolled distress.

Mr. A. had been a well-liked and highly respected member of the local community and Mrs. A. had high expectations of a return of his past services. Yet offers of help, visits to her home and invitations out were conspicuously absent. It is most likely that Mrs. A's neurotic character and long-standing pessimistic outlook on life had antagonized many people and thereby contributed largely to her lack of environmental support.

Case 2

Mrs. B's network of support had been small because all Mr. B's relatives were still in Europe and her own siblings lived in a distant State, and had returned to their homes after a brief visit for the funeral. Her own daughter had been seen as helpful, as had one particular friend, but she felt very badly let down by several people and agencies from whom she had expected support. She had been angered by the staff of the hospital in which her husband had been treated during his last illness, in that they insisted that he be taken home despite an obvious steady deterioration in his condition. She considered that they were abrupt and unsympathetic towards her. Her parish priest on his only visit had irritated her by his attempts to distract her from her grief. Her local physician failed to take seriously her complaints of bitter depression and suicidal thoughts. Mrs. B. had felt neglected by her neighbours and distressed by their attempts to focus her attention on the possibility of future relationships, including the statement 'we've found a new boyfriend for you.'

Case 3

This 49-year-old subject illustrates the problems posed for the widow when the marriage has been a stormy one. Mr. C. had prolonged periods of alcoholism, though sometimes he was sober for as long as 18 months, and at these times he was said to have been an excellent father and charming companion. His death occurred following an extended drinking bout. Mrs. C. denied any resentment about his alcoholism or the manner of his death, but recognized that the post-bereavement problems of her two teenage sons were related to their previous difficulties with their father. Her older boy, aged 15, suddenly developed a good deal of absenteeism from school, became 'accident prone' and had a number of what Mrs. C. called 'imaginary illnesses.'. Her 12-year-old son became extremely insecure and developed hysterical symptoms. She considered that these reactions had made it essential for her to prevent the boys seeing any display of grief, and she felt that there was nobody else in her relatively limited social network to whom she could freely express her distress. Because of a long-standing family feud Mr. C's relatives did not attend the funeral, let alone provide Mrs. C. with any support.

Implications

Our research to date has concentrated on the identification of those widows at maximum risk of health deterioration, and it is hoped to construct a measuring scale which will give, quite soon after the death, a reasonably precise indication of those women who are likely to proceed to an unfavourable outcome. Such a device will enable community workers to concentrate their efforts on these particular widows during the crisis.

Ultimately it is hoped that people such as general practitioners, clergymen and social workers in various community agencies will be able to provide a service to the bereaved in the form of brief interviews of the type referred to as 'preventive intervention.' This function will be supported by psychiatric consultation and fortified with the more sophisticated knowledge of the various reactions to bereavement which should come from our own and other research studies. At present we are concentrating on the development of such preventive techniques, applying these to a group of high-risk widows, and comparing the outcome with that of a matched group of widows who receive no such intervention.

Much work still needs to be done, both in terms of hard research and in the translation of research findings into community action, before we have anything approaching a satisfactory programme for the care of the bereaved person and the prevention of the illness which may follow.

The relevance of conjugal bereavement for preventive psychiatry

By DAVID MADDISON

In the past decade great emphasis has been laid on the importance for preventive psychiatry of various developmental and accidental crises. If such crises not infrequently act as direct precipitants of mental disorder, or lead the individual to use more regressed defences which increase his predisposition to develop a psychiatric illness at a later time, then the study of persons in crisis becomes an essential task for psychiatric research. Not only should the crises themselves be examined descriptively and dynamically, but tests must be made of the hypothesis that preventive intervention during crisis (Caplan, 1964) will lower the incidence of serious sequelae.

This paper confines itself to an examination of the material available from a detailed study of one such crisis, conjugal bereavement in 132 young and middle-aged women. The findings of an earlier phase of this study show that approximately one in five widows in this age range will sustain a substantial health deterioration in the year following bereavement (Maddison & Walker, 1967). This physical and/or mental deterioration is our criterion of unsatisfactory crisis resolution, and can be validated in later interviews. Much other evidence points in the same direction; e.g. Marris (1958) and Parkes (1964). Those widows in our study who were rated as having a 'bad outcome', when interviewed 15 months after their bereavement, reported a high frequency of perceived unhelpful interactions with persons in their social network during the 3 months following their husband's death, and also experienced a large number of their needs as unmet during the same period. These findings, when compared with the interview data obtained from 'good outcome' widows, reached a high level of statistical significance.

The most likely explanation is that the degree and quality of the support which is available to the widow during crisis is of importance in its own right in determining the manner in which the crisis is resolved. This does not deny that long-standing personality characteristics may contribute to the eventual result, nor does it detract from the relevance of the purely intrapsychic aspects of grief and mourning. Crisis theory, however, stresses that intercurrent events, though the perception of them will be determined in part by the individual's experiential background and habitual defensive operations, are in constant and reciprocal interaction with intrapsychic processes, this interaction being in fact of maximal significance during the state of crisis.

A widow is faced with two concurrent tasks: she is required, through the processes of mourning, to detach herself sufficiently from the lost object to permit the continuance of other relationships and the development of new ones; at the same time she has to establish for herself a new role conception as an adult woman without a partner. Her poorly defined status in Western society (Gorer, 1965), and her frequent financial problems, do nothing to assist her with these tasks. Existing social agencies, including the medical profession and the clergy, seem relatively powerless to help her, not only because of their own anxieties about death, but due to substantial ignorance of her real needs. It is small wonder, then, that a sizable group of women, grief-stricken, bewildered, often (perhaps always) angry (Pollock, 1961) and frequently burdened with guilt, are profoundly affected by the quality and quantity of the support that is available to them through their pre-existing relationships, through previously unused facets of their social network, and from the helping professionals who become involved with bereaved people.

WIDOWS AT SPECIAL RISK

For the development of any preventive programme, the first challenge is to identify those women at maximal risk of an unsatisfactory outcome following bereavement.

Perception of the environment. Our own data, derived from semi-structured interviews with 40 widows, 20 in each outcome category, stress the importance of the perceived supportiveness or non-supportiveness of interactions with the environment during the crisis. By coding the subject's response to a large number of statements concerning interpersonal relationships, we were able to measure the extent to which she had perceived her environment as helpful, passively neglectful or actively opposed to her needs. Important specific categories of interaction could also be defined. The findings are complex, and reference should be made to our previous work for a full account of them (Maddison & Walker, 1967).

Two general points can, however, be made. Firstly, the results of a multivariate discriminant function analysis demonstrate the overwhelming importance of unmet needs in differentiating between bad outcome and good outcome widows. Whatever one may think about the reasonableness of such needs, and to whatever extent it may be considered that the subject's own personality dynamics have determined the feeling of need, the fact remains that such an expression of dissatisfaction with the available environmental resources strongly suggests the likelihood of an unfavourable outcome. Secondly, while there is no one interchange which is consistently helpful or consistently unhelpful for every widow, nor which in itself differentiates between good and bad outcome groups, patterning of interactions can be detected by statistical treatment of the data, some differences in patterns between the two groups also reaching acceptable levels of significance. In general terms, bad outcome subjects felt that they lacked permissive support from the environment, and considered that their expression of affect had been blocked, overtly or covertly; sometimes affect expression had seemed to them to meet an overtly hostile response. As a group, they perceived environmental opposition to their wish to review the past and talk at length about their husbands; conversely they saw many persons in their environment as trying to arouse their interest in new activities, new occupations, even new romantic relationships, and this usually aroused great anger.

There were, however, a few subjects in whom our findings at interview did not conform to the above pattern, which is that of the bad outcome group as a whole. Other factors need therefore to be considered in the individual case, but under the headings which follow (except in relation to age and parity) we did not gather information of a quantifiable nature. In many instances, however, even when the widow was not a deviant subject in relation to our major hypotheses concerning environmental support, one or more of the following additional problems was clearly relevant.

Age and parity. Our findings on 132 North American widows, whose husbands died between the ages of 45 and 60, show that there is a significant relationship between bad outcome and young age of the widow ($P < 0.05$). Regardless of statistical findings, however, we early became aware of a subgroup of younger widows for whom the bereavement had been particularly traumatic in that sexual involvement with the husband had still been intense, his person being extremely highly cathected. Kraus & Lilienfeld (1959), using an epidemiological approach, have observed that the excess mortality previously noted in widows is greatest, relative to the death-rate of married women generally, in those aged 34 or less. It seems unlikely, however, that the explanation of this phenomenon by Young, Benjamin & Wallis (1963) is correct; they attempt to relate this to the usually sudden death of younger men, whereas our own findings do not suggest any relationship between outcome and the length of time for which death has been anticipated. Perhaps the comment of Krupp & Kligfeld (1962) on the 'timeliness' or otherwise of the death is the most useful explanatory hypothesis, though one which would be difficult to test.

There is also a suggestion that widows with dependent children tend to do badly, though it is impossible to disentangle this factor from that of age. Although young children are often highly valued by the widow because they are considered by her to provide some partial distraction from her own problems and to give meaning to her continued existence, they in fact create several major problems, not the least of which is that mothers may feel that they must hide their grief in their children's presence, their own mourning being therefore impeded (Langer, 1957). Moreover, at the height of crisis, when the widow feels relatively helpless and is craving dependent gratification, it is difficult for at least some women to fulfil the dependency needs of others. The reaction of some children to the death itself may provide an additional burden, and this is further dealt with below. Conversely, the outward manifestations of the mourning of the child or adolescent may seem inadequate to the grieving mother, and may add to her resentment. Additional problems will arise as she struggles, as she inevitably must to some extent, to fill some aspects of the paternal role.

Pathological marital relationship. We considered it to be completely impracticable, 15 months following bereavement, to assess the quality of the pre-existing marital relationship and use this information statistically. Nevertheless our interviews uncovered a great deal of material in this area which justifies some comment.

There are certainly no grounds for assuming any clear-cut one-to-one relationship between a previously disturbed marriage and an unsatisfactory outcome to the bereavement crisis. Some of our subjects were functioning adequately in their new role and had maintained their usual health, yet they discussed their marriage in terms which clearly indicated an almost complete absence of intimacy between the partners and, in some instances, an open recognition that the relationship had been a failure. In some other subjects much evidence pointed in this direction even though the husband and the marriage had been idealized after his death (Stern, Williams & Prados, 1951). This small group of women appeared to have a substantial degree of character disorder which had largely insulated them against the normal effects of loss because of their generally tenuous attachment to objects. Prospective studies would be required to determine whether these women had in fact experienced a state of crisis following bereavement.

There was another group of women, however, where pathology in the marriage seemed to have a direct connexion with their unfavourable outcome. Not surprisingly, in view of the importance for mourning of ambivalent feelings towards the lost object (Freud, 1917), this was particularly marked when the marriage had shown unequivocal sado-masochistic aspects. (Dependence and identification in the marital relationship must also be assumed to have relevance for the mourning process and its outcome.) Direct expression of hostility towards the deceased is usually prevented by superego restraints and by the expectations of the culture, though displacements of this rage are very common. Conversely, there was one very striking instance of an extremely disturbed marriage, where the wife's outstanding response to the death had been guilt stemming from her almost complete lack of grief, yet where the eventual outcome was clearly favourable. The quality of the marital relationship obviously does not by itself predict the nature of the outcome which will be achieved.

Overt neurosis in the widow. In addition to those subjects with the type of character disorder described above, there were several other women who gave a lengthy, sometimes virtually lifelong, history of overt neurotic symptoms or behaviour, and where this seemed to be of importance in their subsequent deterioration. Traditionalists may argue that neurotic characteristics must have been present in all bad outcome cases and that we were simply unable to detect them in many of our subjects during our limited contact. While it is fruitless to deny this possibility without prospective and intensive studies in depth, it nevertheless appears equally reasonable (and of far more practical relevance) to assume that overtly neurotic women are, in general, more likely to need environmental support and more likely to sustain a symptomatic deterioration if this support is unavailable. Moreover, neurotic behaviour, especially if long-continued, may in itself be a factor in alienating those individuals within the social network who might under other circumstances have provided support.

It should be noted that there were occasional subjects, of considerable theoretical interest, who reported a marked alleviation of pre-existing neurotic symptoms following bereavement. Conversely, neurotic symptoms appeared for the first time following bereavement in several subjects whose lives till then seemed to have been singularly free from neurotic distortions. It does not appear therefore that overt neurosis is in itself an inevitable pointer to, nor an essential precursor of, subsequent maladaptation; nor does the converse proposition hold any greater degree of truth. The studies of Lindemann (1944) would suggest that he shares this viewpoint.

Mode of death. There were several subjects for whom the mode of the husband's death, and the stress involved on either objective or personal and symbolic grounds or both, had a particular relevance. We have previously reported that, contrary to popular belief, those women whose husbands die instantly or with minimal warning are not more prone to a bad outcome than those who have substantial foreknowledge of the death, and the evidence suggests that a protracted period of dying poses its own problems in that it may maximize pre-existing ambivalence and lead to pronounced feelings of guilt and inadequacy. When such a death has involved deformity and mutilation additional intrapsychic problems are involved

for the wife, as well as the physical strain of heavy nursing or repeated hospital visiting and the torment resulting from close contact with her husband's pain and suffering.

So much do we insulate ourselves from a detailed knowledge of the processes of dying that we tend to be unaware of the grotesque suffering which is not uncommonly involved. The most outstanding instance in this series concerned a woman whose husband had suffered from carcinoma (presumably originating in the parotid gland) for 25 years and had endured 32 operations. Several years before his death his tongue had been amputated, and for 8 years he had fed himself by nasal tube. He emitted an extremely bad odour and his face was grossly disfigured. Somewhat more typically, several subjects had been required to nurse their husbands, often in highly complex and intimate ways, through terminal phases which lasted six or nine months or more. One subject, who in fact proceeded to a satisfactory outcome (largely in our view because of an extremely supportive environment), had nursed her husband at home for 2 years prior to his death, towards the end of which period he was doubly incontinent and sometimes needed to be changed as often as 14 times in one day.

Pathological reaction in another family member. Though there were many subjects who considered that the extreme grief of one or more family members had added to their own problem, it was relatively uncommon for the bereavement to have produced a clearly pathological reaction in such a person, such sequelae being confined in our sample to the widow's children. When this did occur there was some tendency for it to be associated with an unfavourable outcome for the widow herself. The magnitude of the child's disturbance was not always easy to evaluate, and at times it appeared probable that some degree of projection on the mother's part was involved, for example in one subject who seemed to be, at least in part, expressing her own feelings of withdrawal and isolation when she described her son as being 'remote from everybody' since his father's death. As has also been found by other authors (e.g. Clarke, 1961), delinquent or quasi-delinquent behaviour was reported in some teenage children, the onset of the disturbance having a clear relationship to the bereavement. Clearly there is a need for studies, preferably prospective ones, of the impact of death on the total family network.

Multiple crises. Relatively few subjects reported that they had experienced another distinct but unrelated crisis in close temporal relationship to their conjugal bereavement, but this was important when it did occur, though it was not inevitably associated with a bad outcome. One subject discovered, seven weeks after her husband's death, that her unmarried 17-year-old daughter was pregnant; the extremely prolonged death of the girl's father may well have had dynamic relevance for this pregnancy, as the widow reported that there had existed an unusually close, perhaps pathological, father–daughter relationship. Because of acute financial stringency, a few subjects had been compelled to leave their own homes during the bereavement crisis and seek cheaper accommodation, this being experienced as an additional object loss and increasing the severity of the mourning task (Fried, 1963). Case 2 further illustrates the occurrence of multiple crises.

Disturbed relationship with mother. As the majority of our subjects were of middle age there were relatively few whose mothers were still alive and available to the widow during the crisis. Where the relationship had long been a mutually gratifying one the mother's support seemed to have been invaluable, but each subject who reported mother as unhelpful at this time, or as failing to meet her needs, proceeded eventually to an unfavourable outcome. Some of the mothers in this latter group had themselves been widowed at a relatively early age, and claimed to have all the answers to the problems of bereavement—answers, however, which were quite unacceptable to their daughters. One mother, described by her daughter as 'always headstrong and domineering', was reported to have told the subject's

friends, the day after the funeral, 'Don't worry about her—she's a *rich* widow', and on the same day she engaged in vigorous verbal battles with the subject's adult son.

Problems with the husband's family. Marris (1958) has pointed out that widows, particularly in lower socio-economic groups, are unlikely to receive much aid or support from their husband's families once the funeral is over. He cites only two widows (out of a total of 72 subjects) who reported that members of the husband's family visited her more often, on their own initiative, after his death. He suggests that this may be a strongly class-linked phenomenon, and draws attention to the fact that in the East End of London, the area of his study, a man tends to marry into his wife's family, sharing her company with her mother with as good a grace as he can, and visiting his own family largely on his own or with his children. The present study abundantly confirms the extent to which the two family groups may quickly drift apart following the death, particularly when there has been animosity beforehand. We noted instances of quarrels over the disposition of the husband's possessions, of painful disagreements about the funeral and burial arrangements, of failure to keep promises concerning attention to the children, and of the withholding of financial support when the subject considered that this could have been given without hardship. In some instances the widow considered that her husband's family believed that she had taken inadequate care of him, or had failed to appreciate his qualities, or had insisted on his having medical or surgical treatment which had seemingly hastened his death; some element of projection may again be involved here, though in nearly all instances the subject's reports suggested that there was considerable factual basis for her beliefs. The husband's mother in particular may create substantial difficulties, and scored relatively frequently on that interchange in our investigation which recorded individuals who had distressed and angered the subject by claiming or implying that the widow's loss was less real and less substantial than the loss suffered by one or more members of the husband's own family. For obvious reasons this seemed most likely to occur when the husband had been in a close, immature and dependent relationship with his mother.

One anecdote illustrates this problem in perhaps its most extreme form. The subject, whose husband had died only four days before the assassination of President Kennedy, had been much harassed by her mother-in-law's criticism and competitiveness immediately following the death. The climax came when she received a phone call from her mother-in-law, who said in great distress, 'terrible news has just come over the radio—Mrs Kennedy has just lost her *son*!'.

The over-valuation of independence. In roughly two-fifths of the 40 subjects whom we interviewed at length there was definite evidence, according to their own statements, of a character structure which habitually denied or attempted to suppress any manifestations of dependent needs. Seven of these women in fact achieved a satisfactory outcome, and not all came into the previously described category of persons whose character structure had apparently shielded them from the effects of object loss. There is not, then, any suggestion of a significant relationship between this over-valuation and idealization of independence and subsequent deterioration, but awareness of the potential pathogenic significance of defence mechanisms of this type should still lead us to regard such women with caution, especially in the presence of other unfavourable prognostic indicators.

These subjects typically denied, often in extravagant terms, that they felt any need for help with current problems: 'I wanted to do *everything* for myself. . .I go my own way. . . I wouldn't let anyone know how I was feeling.' From another subject: 'They would like to help me more, but I won't let them. . .I am stronger than they are. . .I don't want to be obligated.' It is possible that the relative frequency of statements of this kind might be partly related to the class distribution of the sample, for there is evidence to suggest that so-called 'blue collar' marriages tend to be characterized by a relative lack of intimacy and communication between the partners, compelling the wife to develop her own substantially independent style of existence. In many instances, regardless of outcome, it was observed that the wife had for some years, at least in her own eyes, been the controlling partner in several significant aspects of the relationship, handling the family finances in whole or in large part and contributing to the decision-making process to an extent which would be regarded as definitely atypical in marriages between persons of higher socioeconomic status. The long continued use of reaction formation and the role conception imposed by social pressure are here inextricably linked.

Deliberate suppression of affect. It has been noted that those widows who considered that the environment had inhibited or actively opposed their expression of grief and anger usually did badly. Only in a few instances did subjects report that they had themselves made a conscious decision that they would try to avoid, and actively distract themselves from, the expression of grief, and these few women all had a bad outcome. Historical factors were occasionally important in this connexion, as for example in one subject who said that her husband had always been strongly critical of her when she cried. Similar consequences ensued in those few women who attempted to deny the relevance and uniqueness of their own feelings; one bad outcome subject, for example, claimed that it had been helpful for her to remind herself that there were many people worse off than she was, though this particular interchange was almost uniformly rated as unhelpful by other subjects who had experienced it.

Idiosyncratic problems. In some women with a bad outcome there were additional individual problems which had complicated the crisis experience but which are not easily classifiable under any of the above headings. One subject experienced almost uncontrollable and fully conscious rage, this stemming as she saw it from her husband's refusal to seek medical care until the very day of his death, although it had been obvious to her and to others that he had been gravely ill for at least the preceding two weeks. Another subject, an attractive young woman with two dependent children, had succumbed to her husband's repeated pleadings and had promised him on his death-bed that she would never remarry, and she was determined to keep this vow. This probably had a dynamic relationship to her own father's remarriage when she was a small child, for she considered that this second marriage had produced disastrous effects on the family and had perceived her stepmother as hostile and rejecting.

ILLUSTRATIVE CASES

The following case summaries illustrate various combinations of the above problems.

Case 1. Mrs A, aged 55, was one of the many subjects in whom it appeared that inadequate and ineffectual support was an extremely important determinant of her bad outcome. She considered that six specific needs had been unmet, and she rated 12 interactions with her environment as positively unhelpful. In the year following bereavement a number of old complaints had been exacerbated and new ones had developed; she had sought medical help for depression, and for a period had feared total 'nervous breakdown'. She was tired and apathetic, slept badly, complained of headaches and swollen painful joints, and had repeated thoughts of her own death, wishing that she might die and join her husband.

Her network of support was relatively inadequate, even quantitatively, in that all Mr A's relatives were still in Europe and her own siblings lived in a distant state and had returned home after a brief visit for the funeral. Her only daughter had been seen as helpful, as had one particular friend, but she felt badly let down by several people and agencies from whom she had expected support. She had been angered by the staff of the hospital in which her husband had been treated during his last illness, in that they insisted that he be taken home despite an obvious steady deterioration in his condition, which she felt they tried to mini-

mize. She considered that they were abrupt and unsympathetic in their attitude towards her; moreover, they had eventually discharged him with an infected thoracotomy wound. Her parish priest had visited her on one occasion only, and her chief memory of this call was that he had irritated her by his attempts to distract her from her grief. When she complained to her local physician of her bitter depression and suicidal rumination, he had tried to be jocular and had said, 'What do you want—slow poison pills?' She considered that many of her associates in the neighbourhood had neglected her, or had acted in ways which had accentuated her suffering, particularly through their attempts to focus her attention on the possibility of future relationships, including the statement 'We've found a new boy-friend for you.' She had experienced considerable financial stress, which she claimed could have been substantially relieved by her siblings.

Whatever might have preceded this situation, in this instance the relative poverty of support available, and the ineptitude with which many people (including professionals) approached her during her crisis, were important factors in determining her outcome.

Case 2. Mrs B was aged 39 when her husband died, leaving four children ranging in age from 9 yr. to 18 mth., plus a 20-yr.-old son of a former marriage. She was deviant in terms of our principal hypothesis, in that she claimed that persons in her environment had been strongly supportive, yet she had suffered severe and persistent depression since the bereavement. She had also experienced severe recurrent epigastric pain which required gastro-enterological investigation, though no definite diagnosis had been reached.

Other possible reasons can be advanced for her bad outcome, notably her age and the number and youth of her dependent children. She was also one of the few subjects who had experienced a number of distinct crises within a brief period. Two months prior to her conjugal bereavement her 20-yr.-old son had left home and refused to return, and a few weeks later her favourite brother died very suddenly. She had also made strenuous efforts to deny her needs, and was strikingly reluctant to admit to the interviewer that she had received significant financial and practical help during the crisis. She commented: 'I am not going to depend on anyone. I would not expect anything from anybody...nothing bothered *me*, I just thought what I thought.' This brittle defensive posture seemed to be particularly common in these younger widows with a number of dependants.

Case 3. Mrs C, aged 54, reported a good deal of perceived environmental unhelpfulness, but other factors also seemed relevant. She had become markedly depressed and panicky, and had required investigations for indigestion and diarrhoea. Like many other bad-outcome subjects, of whatever age, she complained of constant exhaustion and an inability to carry out normal routines.

She recognized that she had always had neurotic problems; for many years she had been diffusely nervous and apprehensive and had been markedly agoraphobic, this last symptom in fact improving since her bereavement. Mr C had been continuously ill for 3 years prior to his death, during which period he had experienced multiple cerebral vascular accidents and had also undergone urological surgery. For the greater part of this time, and continuously during the last year, he was nursed at home. During the last months he required almost constant care, had oxygen cylinders by his bedside and was having frequent epileptic convulsions. At first Mrs C had also to cope with her demented mother, who lived with her; mother was later transferred to a hospital, but immediately following the husband's death she clamoured to be allowed home again, her repeated requests, which were supported by Mrs C's only brother, being a continuing source of stress.

She had struggled to hide her grief, allegedly because she wanted to avoid upsetting her 18-yr.-old son, though by the time of the interview she could say: 'Maybe I had the wrong idea.' Even at the time she had wished that someone would encourage and support her in affect expression, but when her symptoms led her to turn to her local doctor his unsatisfying response was 'it's just what you have been through'.

Case 4. This 49-yr.-old subject illustrates the additional problems posed for the widow when the marriage has been a stormy one, and when there are continuing problems in other family members following the bereavement. Mr D had prolonged periods of alcoholism, though sometimes he was sober for as long as 18 months, and at these times he was said to have been an excellent father and charming companion. During his extended drinking bouts he would seclude himself in his room, sometimes for days at a time, and he died suddenly at the end of one such episode. Mrs D laid quite excessive emphasis on the extent to which all his family and friends had realized that he was 'sick', and she spontaneously denied any resentment about his alcoholism or the manner of his death. While refusing to acknowledge any link between these problems and her own subsequent health deterioration, she could see that the post-bereavement problems of her two teenage sons were related to their previous difficulties with their father. Her older boy, aged 15, suddenly developed a good deal of absenteeism from school, became accident-prone and had a number of what Mrs D called 'imaginary illnesses'. Her 12-yr.-old son became extremely insecure and developed hysterical aphonia for a brief period. She considered that these reactions had made it essential for her to prevent the boys seeing any display of grief, and she felt that there was nobody else in her relatively limited social network to whom she could freely express her distress. There had been a big feud with her husband's family some 5 years before his death, and, with the exception of one cousin, Mr D's relatives did not even attend the funeral, let alone provide her with any support.

Case 5. Mrs E was also a deviant subject in terms of the principal hypothesis; there was good evidence that she was surrounded by an extensive and supportive network of friends and family, yet her health had seriously declined and in particular alcohol had become a major problem to her. She was 44 yr. old, with four children under the age of 16 and two others still living at home, and she considered that the effort involved in caring for them had exhausted her and given her little or no opportunity to accept much of the personal support which had been offered to her. Her marriage had clearly been a highly pathological one, though at the time of the interview there was considerable rationalization of this. Her husband suffered from post-traumatic epilepsy, this being the alleged cause of his subsequent increasingly severe alcoholism and decline into vagrancy. She had instituted court proceedings which had led to his detention for a period in a State Mental Hospital, and she still talked of her guilt about this action. Particularly in the light of such a sado-masochistic background his death had been a peculiarly appalling one. He had been missing from home several days and was finally found dead from exposure, this information reaching her in the middle of the night as a police message; she subsequently learnt that his body was discoloured and mutilated, and that a rat had bitten off his nose.

CONCLUSIONS

There is by now more than enough evidence of the importance for preventive psychiatry of the crisis of conjugal bereavement. The prevalence of this crisis, however, necessitates that the first step in the development of any preventive programme must be the relatively secure identification of those bereaved persons at maximal risk, and this present paper represents a first attempt at defining such a target population.

Many of the factors of importance, such as the widow's age and the simultaneous occurrence of multiple crises, are completely unmodifiable. Many other important elements, and in particular the widow's longstanding patterns of ego defence, could only be modified with difficulty, and if an approach along these lines were to be contemplated then relatively prolonged psychotherapy would be mandatory in nearly all instances. Even if more subjects were suitable for such treatment, possessing the necessary intelligence, motivation and potentiality for insight, it is inconceivable that any contemporary psychiatric service could meet the resulting demand. The most practicable line of approach, therefore, would seem to be to work with the widow during the crisis itself, in a brief series of interviews of the type which Caplan has called 'preventive intervention', and the hypothesis that such interventions will reduce the eventual incidence of health deterioration will be rigorously tested in further stages of the present research.

It is apparent that much of this interventive work will need to be carried out by non-psychiatric professionals or semi-professionals, acting in a sense as agents of the psychiatrist, rather than by psychiatrists themselves. Everyday experience suggests that the general practitioner and the clergyman are those persons outside the family to whom the widow most consistently turns for support, the funeral director not having the importance in this regard which he is beginning to achieve on the American scene. The findings in this study, as well as clinical observations made elsewhere, strongly suggest that the members of these two professional groups are not adequately trained, except in rare instances, to meet their responsibilities in this area. All of our 40 subjects, for example, had some degree of contact with the clergy, but 19 reported that this was of no help whatsoever, and three considered that it had been actively unhelpful. An even smaller number considered that they had received useful support from their local physician. It is reasonable to assume that the provision of psychiatric consultation to these and other agencies should greatly improve their role performance in these tasks, though the provision of such consultation is certainly not without problems of its own.

It is unnecessary to assume that the preventive techniques must perforce be directed at the widow herself, for in some instances it may be considered that she has the resources to work through her own problems to a satisfactory conclusion, provided that certain aspects of the environment can be modified so as to reduce the amount of interference with her own coping techniques. In case 3, for instance, much relief might have been experienced by the widow if work with the family had increased their realization that the constant pressure from her senile mother was adding to her burden, and had led to the development of mutually satisfactory alternative arrangements.

Much of the intervention would, however, need to be more direct than this. Concerning case 4, the conclusion is inescapable that the subject's denial of ambivalence, and the rapid idealization of her marriage, had been profoundly important in determining the bad outcome, probably as much for her children as for herself. In case 5 it would seem unlikely that the guilt mobilized by her husband's death, and accentuated by its particular unfortunate circumstances, could have been modified by less than psychodynamically in-

86

sightful interviewing over several weeks. It is clear that each subject, just as in the clinical setting, requires a fairly detailed and individualized appraisal and that a high order of psychotherapeutic understanding and skill would be required in the consultant, plus an ability to translate this into terms which would be meaningful and useful for the community agent in contact with the widow.

Several years will be required to produce an adequate test of the hypothesis that interventions of this type will significantly alter the course of pathological bereavement reactions. It has nevertheless been considered desirable to present some of the material available from one study of widows and to suggest some of its implications, in the hope that other workers may examine and contribute to this problem from their own particular viewpoints.

SUMMARY

Conjugal bereavement is seen to be one example of a crisis which may have far-reaching consequences in terms of physical and/or mental ill health. The research reported here suggests that widows at high risk of an unsatisfactory outcome may be able to be identified shortly after bereavement. One factor of outstanding importance in this regard appears to be the widow's perception that the persons in her environment are failing to meet her needs, or are actively blocking her expression of affect and the withdrawal of her intense libidinal attachment to her husband by means of a gradual but thorough review of her past relationship with him. Other suggestive features in individual cases appear to be: (i) a young widow (less than 45 yr. old) with a number of dependent children; (ii) evidence of a pre-existing pathological marital relationship; (iii) pre-existing overt neurosis; (iv) a protracted death, particularly if associated with severe suffering and/or disfigurement; (v) a pathological reaction to the death in another family member; (vi) additional crises in close temporal relationship to the bereavement; (vii) a disturbed relationship with her own mother or with the husband's family; (viii) long-continued reaction formations against dependence; (ix) deliberate avoidance of affect expression.

The implications of these findings for the development of a programme of preventive intervention in conjugal bereavement are briefly reviewed.

ACKNOWLEDGEMENTS

This study was carried out in the Laboratory of Community Psychiatry, Harvard Medical School, under the direction of Gerald Caplan, M.D., whose advice and support I gratefully acknowledge. Peggy J. Golde, Ph.D., offered many helpful suggestions and criticisms. Delene Rhea, M.A., gave invaluable help as research assistant and joint interviewer.

This study was supported by a grant from the Foundations' Fund for Research in Psychiatry, and by a further grant to the Laboratory of Community Psychiatry from the Grant Foundation, New York.

REFERENCES

CAPLAN, G. (1964). *Principles of Preventive Psychiatry*. New York: Basic Books.

CLARKE, J. (1961). The precipitation of juvenile delinquency. *J. ment. Sci.* **107**, 1033.

FRIED, M. (1963). Grieving for a lost home. In L. J. Duhl & J. Powell (eds.), *The Urban Condition*. New York: Basic Books.

FREUD, S. (1917). Mourning and melancholia. In *Collected Papers*, vol. IV. London: Hogarth Press.

GORER, G. (1965). *Death, Grief and Mourning in Contemporary Britain*. London: Cresset Press.

KRAUS, A. S. & LILIENFELD, A. M. (1959). Some epidemiological aspects of the high mortality in the young widowed group. *J. chron. Dis.* **10**, 207.

KRUPP, G. R. & KLIGFELD, B. (1962). The bereavement reaction; a cross-cultural evaluation. *J. Relig. Hlth* **1**, 223.

LANGER, M. (1957). *Learning to Live as a Widow*. New York: Messner.

LINDEMANN, E. (1944). Symptomatology and management of acute grief. *Am. J. Psychiat.* **101**, 141–149.

MADDISON, D. C. & WALKER, W. L. (1967). Factors affecting the outcome of conjugal bereavement. *Br. J. Psychiat.* **113**, 1057.

MARRIS, P. (1958). *Widows and their Families.* London: Routledge & Kegan Paul.

PARKES, C. M. (1964). The effects of bereavement on physical and mental health—a study of the medical records of widows. *Br. med. J.* **2**, 274–279.

POLLOCK, G. H. (1961). Mourning and adaptation. *Int. J. Psycho-Anal.* **42**, 341–361.

STERN, K., WILLIAMS, G. & PRADOS, M. (1951). Grief reactions in later life. *Am. J. Psychiat.* **108**, 289–294.

YOUNG, M., BENJAMIN, B. & WALLIS, C. (1963). The mortality of widowers. *Lancet* ii, 454–456.

Factors Affecting the Outcome of Conjugal Bereavement

By DAVID MADDISON and WENDY L. WALKER

Following the classic study of Lindemann (1944) on the various forms and possible outcomes of the reaction to bereavement, little systematic work was done in this field until the last decade. Marris (1958), in a thoughtful but uncontrolled study, interviewed 72 widows whose husbands had died at least 11 months earlier, the mean lapse of time between bereavement and interview being two years and two months. Only 14 of his subjects considered themselves to have recovered completely; 31 reported a lasting deterioration in their health, and 57 reported a continuing difficulty with sleep. More recently, Parkes (1964a), in a study of patients admitted to a psychiatric hospital, has demonstrated that the number of patients whose illness followed the death of a spouse was six times greater than expected, suggesting that bereavement must be one causative factor in the development of the illness. He has also shown (Parkes, 1964b) that widows under the age of 65 consulted their general practitioner because of psychiatric symptoms more than three times as frequently during the six months after the bereavement than they had done during a control period prior to the bereavement. The consultation rate for non-psychiatric symptoms increased by nearly a half in both older and younger widows.

Other important contributions have drawn attention to the increased mortality rate of conjugally bereaved persons, both widows or widowers, the excess mortality being more marked in those under the age of 35 (Kraus and Lilienfeld, 1959). Young *et al.* (1963) have refined this data, using a population of widowers only, by demonstrating that the increased mortality is most marked during the first six months following bereavement, when there is an increment of about 40 per cent. in the expected mortality rate.

Little has been done to define more precisely the factors which may be associated with an unfavourable resolution of the bereavement crisis, though extensive studies in conjugal bereavement currently being carried out in the Laboratory of Community Psychiatry at Harvard Medical School (Baler and Golde, 1964) may clarify a great deal that is still uncertain in this area. The present study was developed as a segment of this wider project, and was particularly concerned to examine whether a widow's perception of environmental support during the bereavement crisis could be correlated with her eventual outcome. Such a study becomes most meaningful within the framework of the so-called crisis model, in which crisis is conceived as occurring in any situation where there is "an imbalance between the difficulty and importance of the problem and the resources immediately available to deal with it" (Caplan, 1964). It is assumed that the problem-solving methods employed by the individual in attempting to resolve the painfulness of crisis can be significantly affected by certain aspects of the environment.

In considering an individual's relationship to her environment, however, it is necessary to avoid each of two extremes. On the one hand, it is clear that a study confined to those factors which are completely external to the widow—the number of accessible relatives and friends, her financial situation, the physical availability of community supports and so on—would reveal "objective", but scarcely meaningful, data. At the other extreme, knowledge of an individual's intrapsychic life, her fantasies, conflicts and defences, does not in itself provide an adequate understanding of her dynamic situation if it ignores any evaluation of the attitudes and behaviour of others which are directed towards her, and her own response to these persons.

Avoiding these two equally unsatisfactory extremes, this study was designed to examine retrospectively the widow's interaction with the environment *as seen by the widow herself*, during the bereavement crisis, here operationally defined as lasting for three months after the husband's death. More specifically, it was hypothesized that widows who ultimately resolved the bereavement crisis in a healthy manner would differ from those with a bad outcome in their perception of the supportiveness of interpersonal relationships during the crisis. We set out to ascertain, therefore, how the widow had experienced and perceived the interpersonal transactions which had taken place during the three months immediately following the bereavement. The conscious intentions of those with whom she came in contact were not sought, nor did we speculate on the intrapersonal dynamic factors which might have contributed to her evaluation of the words and actions of others.

PROCEDURE

It was decided to use the widow's subjective report of her health as the criterion of outcome of the bereavement crisis. There seems little doubt that a widow who reports a substantial decline in her level of physical and/or mental health in the year following bereavement can be assumed, *ipso facto*, to have resolved the crisis in an unsatisfactory manner, and that, conversely, maintenance of the pre-existing level of health is good evidence that the social and psychological problems created by the bereavement have been dealt with satisfactorily. Information was therefore gathered concerning the survivors of all male deaths registered in the city of Boston over a period of six months, where the male had died between the ages of 45 and 60 years inclusive, had been a resident of the city, and was believed to have been living in a marital relationship at the time of his death. Comprehensive questionnaires, with an explanatory letter, were sent to 276 widows thirteen months after their bereavement, and further letters were sent and/or personal interviews requested if no definitive result had been achieved. Adequate data was finally gathered on 132 women, 48 per cent. of the total sample. A definite rejection of our approach came from 28 per cent., while 18 per cent. could not be traced or had moved out of the research area. Seven potential subjects were definitely known to have died during the year (but this figure is possibly incomplete), and 10 were found to have been separated from their husbands for a substantial period immediately prior to his death. The loss of 52 per cent. of the subjects originally selected may have introduced some bias, but insufficient information is available concerning the non-acceptors to enable us to calculate the magnitude and direction of this.

The questionnaire, which was completed anonymously and identified by a code number only, elicited basic social and demographic information about each subject, together with her responses to 57 items which reviewed her health during the preceding year, the questionnaire being structured so that the only scoring items were those which recorded complaints which were either new or substantially more troublesome during this period. A further weighting was given to the subject's illness score if she had sought medical or hospital attention for any of these complaints for the first time during this period. Scores allotted on this basis ranged from zero to 53, and inspection of the data led to the judgment that a score of 16 or more certainly represented a substantial deterioration in health, provided that a check with the subject by telephone or personal interview confirmed the accuracy of her questionnaire responses. Scores of 4 or less seemed to represent no significant health deterioration. It was therefore decided to regard the 28 women (21·2 per cent.) with scores of 16 or more as "bad outcome" widows, and the 57 subjects (43·2 per cent.) with scores of 4 or less as "good outcome" widows. A group of 47 subjects (35·6 per cent.) had scores ranging from 5 to 15 inclusive; these were defined as the "intermediate" group and were not further considered in this study.

Statistical analysis was undertaken of the relationship between outcome, as reflected in illness score, and the social and personal characteristics of the widows. Fifty-six chi squares were calculated to assess the significance of the relationships between the social variables themselves and between these variables and outcome, but only two meaningful pairings were significant at the 5 per cent. level or better. A significant inverse relationship was found between illness score and the age of the widow, younger women tending to gain a higher illness score ($P < ·05$; biserial correlation coefficient $-·33$). A significant inverse relationship was also found between illness score and the husband's age at the time of his death ($P < ·01$; biserial correlation coefficient $-·29$). There was, of course, a positive relationship between age of widow and age of husband ($P < ·001$; product moment correlation coefficient $+·58$). It was of interest that no significant relationship could be established between illness score and low socio-economic status, for such an association is suggested by much of the literature on the relationship between illness and social class (e.g., Langner and Michael, 1963). There was also no relationship between illness score and the subject's report that she had little or no warning of her husband's death; this finding, too, is in conflict with some of the literature and a good deal of the folk-lore about the effects of bereavement.

We then proceeded to interview 20 "bad outcome" and 20 "good outcome" widows, selecting the subjects so that the resulting groups would be matched as closely as possible on all the social and personal variables on which data was available. Although a satisfactory match was obtained on such variables as religion, socio-economic status and the duration of warning of death, the heavy concentration of younger widows with a "bad outcome" forced the matching for age to be less than perfect, though the difference between the mean age of the two groups was not statistically significant. It was necessary to approach 49 widows to obtain 40 interviews, 9 subjects (3 "bad outcome" and 6 "good outcome") who had originally completed the health questionnaire declining to participate in this second phase of the study.

The interview itself was conducted, usually in the woman's own home, by the senior author and his (female) research assistant. Though it was realized that it would have been theoretically desirable to conduct each interview "blind", this was obviously quite impracticable, as the widow almost invariably referred to her state of health during the first few minutes of our contact. The interview itself lasted for approximately two hours, beginning in a non-directive manner by promoting spontaneous discussion of the bereavement and the events of the ensuing three months, but as it proceeded more specific areas were opened up by the interviewers in order to gather the data required by a previously designed schedule.

Essentially the interview had two aims. Firstly, we wished to elicit information concerning *the specific persons available to the widow* during her bereavement crisis, and to ascertain whether such persons were seen by her as helpful, unhelpful or neither. Persons concerning whom such information was sought included the medical and nursing attendants (if any) at the time of her husband's death, her parents, siblings and children, her husband's relatives, the funeral director, the clergyman or priest, her friends, strangers and casual acquaintances, and any doctor or social agency who had been consulted during the period of crisis as a direct or indirect consequence of the bereavement. For each person or group of persons in the environment, we noted on a predesigned score-sheet whether they had been perceived by the subject as "helpful", "unhelpful" or "indifferent". It was also noted whether the subject expressed the feeling that some particular individual or individuals had failed her by their inability to recognize and respond to her needs. In some instances individuals within the one category of relationship produced sharply differing effects, and this was particularly true of siblings, in-laws and children; often a favourite sister or an eldest daughter had been seen as extremely helpful, whereas other siblings or children had had little or no effect, or had even been seen as antagonistic or markedly neglectful. In a few instances there was clearly an ambivalent perception of the one person, who had been seen as making both helpful and unhelpful interventions, and here the subject was asked to make a forced choice as to whether, on balance, the predominant effect had been one of helpfulness or unhelpfulness, though the subsidiary impression was also recorded.

The second aim of the interview was to obtain detailed information about *the specific forms of interaction* which had taken place between the widow and the persons in her environment. Much of this material came out during the non-directive discussion, but in order to obtain a complete record we concluded the interview by reading to the subject a previously prepared list of 59 statements, planned to elicit evidence concerning the most important types of interpersonal transaction which seemed likely to occur following bereavement. These statements were selected with a view to focusing attention on the following categories of interpersonal behaviour:

(1) *Expression of affect:* interchanges which permitted or promoted this, or which showed sensitivity to the subject's unique feelings or which, conversely, blocked or discouraged affect expression or minimized its significance.

(2) *Review of the past* and an attempt to find some meaning and purpose in the bereavement: interchanges which encouraged or permitted the widow to engage in this activity or which, conversely, were felt to be unsympathetic or actively opposed to such behaviour.

(3) *Orientation towards the present and the future:* interchanges which attempted to direct the subject towards an active, detailed consideration of future interests and activities.

(4) *Provision of concomitant needs:* interchanges which were perceived by the widow as relating either to (*a*) her practical needs at the time, or (*b*) her needs for non-specific support and the maintenance of her self-esteem.

A list of the 59 items employed is contained in the Appendix.

Whenever the subject's verbal or non-verbal behaviour suggested that the statement had a degree of relevance for her, she was specifically asked whether the interaction had been perceived by her as helpful or unhelpful, or whether it had made no impact of any kind. She was further asked to name the person or persons who had been involved in this interchange. On the other hand, if there were no indication that she had experienced an interaction of this nature, we were interested to know whether she had felt a *need* to obtain such a response from her environment; where this was true the feeling of need was usually volunteered by the subject as soon as the statement had been verbalized by the interviewer, and particular care was taken to avoid suggesting that she might have had "needs" which she had not in fact

94

previously contemplated.

The interviewer and his research assistant independently completed a score-sheet while the interview was in progress, and subsequently reviewed their coded observations. Only rarely was there any disagreement about the categorization of a particular response, and in these few instances a mutually satisfactory decision could be quickly reached by consensus.

For each subject, then, we were able to complete a data sheet showing her perception, in a global sense, of the significant people in her environment and their effect on her, together with a statement for each of the 59 items indicating whether it had been "helpful", "unhelpful", "indifferent", "needed" or "absent". It proved impossible to rate the precise number of times a particular interchange occurred, or the number of persons with whom this interpersonal transaction had taken place, and it was decided that it was practical and legitimate to carry out the rating on an all-or-none basis. Finally an account of the interview was written up, adding detail which could not be contained in the predefined system of coded responses, and giving an overall impression of the subject, her current level of functioning and her perception of her experience during the bereavement crisis.

The material obtained during the interviews clearly supported our initial assumption that substantial health deterioration was a valid index of bad outcome, for it was clear for every subject in this group that the resolution of the bereavement crisis must have been considered to be unsatisfactory, whatever method of appraisal had been used. The converse was equally true for the individuals in the good outcome group, even though a small number of these women showed evidence of florid psychopathology during the interview; it appeared quite obvious that in these cases we were seeing long-standing personality characteristics, including neurotic symptoms and pronounced characterological deformities, which in our estimation were in no way a consequence of the bereavement or exacerbated by it, so that these individuals could be truly rated as having a "good outcome" in the rather special way in which we have defined this term. The most outstanding examples of this syndrome occurred in women of whom we inferred that gross narcissistic fixation, leading to a schizoid or "psychopathic" detachment from objects, had left them relatively unaffected emotionally by the death of their husbands, and concerning whom it might be argued that they had not experienced a "crisis" in the sense in which this term has come to be understood. They formed only a very small sub-group of the subjects rated as healthy.

RESULTS

Much valuable information was gathered from each widow about her perception of *the specific persons in her environment*, but, not surprisingly, the total number of subjects was too small to permit us to draw any definite conclusions in this area. It could be noted, for instance, that 19 of the 40 widows rated their clergyman or priest as "indifferent" and only 18 found him to be "helpful", but these judgments bore no relationship to outcome. In contrast (and perhaps a peculiarly American phenomenon), 33 women considered the funeral director to have been "helpful". Only 12 subjects had a mother who was alive and physically available to them during the crisis, and it is of some interest to note that the four women who rated mother as "unhelpful" were all in the bad outcome group. For the individuals already mentioned, as well as siblings, members of the husband's family, friends and so on, a great deal of rich data became available, much of it having important clinical and preventive implications, but of a nature which made it quite unsuitable for statistical analysis. Its inherent interest is such, and the pointers for further research so numerous, that it will be presented in more detail in a future paper.

The specific forms of interaction were, however, suitable for quantitative analysis, though the possibilities were limited by the small numbers in each group. Two kinds of analysis were made:

1. *Multivariate discriminant function analysis.* For each individual subject a profile was constructed showing the number of responses, out of the total of 59 available items, which fell in each of the five categories: Helpful (H), Unhelpful (U), Indifferent (I), Absent (A), and Needed (N). A multivariate discriminant function analysis was then carried out on the sets of profiles for the good and bad outcome groups. This procedure yields a weighting of scores to maximize the difference between two or more groups on a set or subset of items. The resulting formula was:

$$38N - 6I - U$$

This formula indicated that, over the total set of items, the responses falling into the Needed category were of overwhelming importance in discriminating between the two groups. For each individual subject a weighted score was then computed according to the above formula. The mean of weighted scores for the good outcome group was $-3\cdot45$ and the mean of weighted scores for the bad outcome group was $89\cdot6$ (a difference significant by t test at $P<\cdot001$). If 10 were taken as the cutting point of the composite distribution of weighted scores for the two groups, then five of 20 bad outcome subjects and four of 20 good outcome subjects were misclassified.

2. *Analysis of subsets of items.* As the 59 items originally had been thought to involve four somewhat different areas of interpersonal exchange, it seemed unlikely that they would function as a homogeneous group, but there were too few subjects for factor analysis or cluster analysis. The first comparison of subjects was undertaken in line with the *a priori* groupings previously discussed. Group profiles were set out for good outcome subjects and for bad outcome subjects on each of the four sets of items. Then within each set one could compare the distribution of responses (H, U, I, A and N) for the good and bad outcome groups.

Significant differences between the groups, as shown by t tests, were as follows:

(*a*) *Expression of affect.* On the items in this set bad outcome subjects gave more U responses than did good outcome subjects ($P<\cdot001$), and also more N responses ($\cdot01<P<\cdot02$). The good outcome subjects gave more A responses ($P<\cdot001$).

(*b*) *Review of the past.* Bad outcome subjects gave more U responses than good outcome subjects ($\cdot01<P<\cdot02$) and more N responses ($\cdot001<P<0\cdot01$).

(*c*) *Orientation towards present and future.* Bad outcome subjects gave more U responses than good outcome subjects ($P<\cdot001$), and good outcome subjects gave more A responses ($\cdot01<P<\cdot02$).

(*d*) *Provision of concomitant needs.* Bad outcome subjects gave more N responses to these items ($P<\cdot001$).

That is to say, significant differences between the groups were found on U responses (in three of the four sets of items) and on A responses (in

97

two of the sets of items), as well as the differences on N responses, the last being consistent with the multivariate discriminant function analysis where the N category had been found to be of overwhelming importance. These additional findings strongly suggested that the total set of items was in fact of heterogeneous composition, so that systematic differences in response patterns between the groups were probably being lost by simple addition of the responses to all of the 59 items.

A different type of empirical grouping of items into subsets was then carried out after inspection of the response profiles for each of the 59 items. For each item two profiles were drawn showing the total number of responses in each category, H, U, I, A and N, for good and bad outcome groups respectively. On nine of the items (12, 20, 26, 28, 42, 47, 48, 56 and 57) the profiles for the two groups were identical or almost identical, and these items were discarded for this phase of the analysis. On a further 15 items (3, 8, 15, 19, 30, 31, 32, 33, 34, 43, 45, 46, 52, 54 and 58) no clear pattern emerged, and these items were also ignored at this stage. From the remaining items four distinct subsets could be found where there were characteristic differences in the profiles for subjects in the good and the bad outcome groups.

SUBSET I comprised items 10, 14, 21 and 24. On each of these items almost all responses were either H or A, the good outcome group having more H than A, the bad outcome group more A than H. This subset seemed to reflect permissive support from the environment, perceived as helpful by subjects with a good outcome, but relatively absent in bad outcome subjects. The items themselves were not confined to any one of the previous *a priori* groupings.

SUBSET II comprised items 1, 2, 5, 17 and 37. Here again almost all responses were either H or A but, in contrast to the items in the previous set, the good outcome group had more A than H responses, and the bad outcome group more H than A. Apart from item 17, involving the provision of financial help (an interaction which obviously can involve far more than the mere relief of financial need), these interchanges seemed to reflect more active encouragement from the environment, especially encouragement in the expression of affects.

SUBSET III comprised items 4, 6, 9, 11, 23, 35, 36, 39, 40, 41, 44, 51, 53 and 55. On these items almost all responses were either U or A, bad outcome subjects having more U than A responses, and good outcome subjects more A than U. These items without exception seemed to describe transactions in which the subject had felt that affect expression was being blocked by the environment, either directly or as a consequence of a lack of sensitivity and empathy, sometimes coupled with covert or even overt hostility from certain individuals. Of the 14 items in this set, nine were in the original "expression of affect" category, though in a negative or converse sense.

SUBSET IV comprised items 1, 2, 7, 14, 16, 17, 18, 21, 22, 25, 27, 29, 49 and 50. On each of these items good and bad outcome profiles differed by at least two points in the N category, and if items had not been scored as N they were A, H or I; they were *never* perceived as unhelpful. They covered a range of content, including several items from each of the *a priori* categories 1, 2 and 4, but only one item from category 3, i.e., it was extremely rare for any subject, whatever the outcome, to have felt any need to be orientated towards the present and future.

On the basis of this grouping of items into subsets, each subject was given a score in the following way: she scored one point every time she gave (*a*) an A response to an item in subset I, (*b*) an H response to an item in subset II, (*c*) a U response to an item in subset III and (*d*) an N response to an item in subset IV. These scores were then added to give a total score for each subject. The mean of these scores for good outcome subjects was 3·95 and for bad outcome subjects 11·60, a *t test* showing this difference to be highly significant ($P < ·001$). If 6 were taken as the cutting point of the composite distribution, with good outcome scores 6 or below, then 3 of 20 good outcome subjects and 3 of 20 bad outcome subjects were misclassified; 4 of these 6 subjects had also been misclassified when scores were weighted according to the formula derived from the discriminant function analysis. As this latter analysis had led to the misclassification of 9 subjects, it is apparent that discrimination between the groups was improved by this division of the items into subsets.

DISCUSSION

From the discriminant function analysis one can infer with some confidence that in our population of widows those who had been rated as having a bad outcome on the basis of their health during the post-bereavement year perceived themselves as having many more unsatisfied needs in interpersonal exchanges during the bereavement crisis than did those with a good outcome. The results of the two subsidiary analyses showed that these needs were diverse, containing items in all the *a priori* categories, and it was not possible to isolate any particular need or group of needs of predominant importance. The widow may have felt that she needed more encouragement, support and understanding to permit her to indulge in a freer expression of affects, particularly grief and anger; she may have felt a need to talk more actively and in greater detail about her husband and their past life together, but had experienced the environment as failing to provide an opportunity for this; she may have felt a need for more practical help, or more general support, than she had received. In all three instances, such a widow was very likely, a year after her husband's death, to have resolved the bereavement crisis in an unsatisfactory manner.

When H responses were examined, on the other hand, it was found that there were no gross differences between the groups, i.e., widows with good outcome did *not* report that they had perceived the environment as more helpful than bad outcome widows. Perusal of the items in subsets I and II shows that there was, however, a difference in the type of interchange found helpful by members of the two groups, those with good outcome tending to perceive permissive support as helpful, those with bad outcome appreciating more active encouragement from the environment.

It is also clear from the subsidiary analyses that a widow who subsequently proceeded to a bad outcome had also tended to find the environment actively unhelpful during crisis, in addition to the perceived failure of her social network to meet certain of her needs. There were two outstanding aspects to this perception of unhelpfulness, clearly revealed by the items contained in subset III, but also shown by the significant differences in perceived unhelpfulness in the items in the *a priori* groupings 1 and 3. Concerning the expression of affect, not only was there an expressed need for more assistance from the environment in this area, but there was also the feeling that a person or persons in the environment had overtly or covertly opposed this. There was recurrent mention in this group of the belief that other people seemed to be shocked by her feelings, telling her to control herself and pull herself together, or on the other hand that attempts seemed to have been made to minimize her grief by a process of generalization, pointing out to her the sufferings of other widows, or telling her just how much grief was appropriate for a widow to feel. Other distressing and unhelpful experiences under this heading were those where the subject reported that important people in her environment were themselves upset to an extent which she believed was inappropriate or even competitive, or they were incongruously cheerful, or—yet another and seemingly important variant—they claimed to share the widow's grief and insisted that they understood how she was feeling, when this to the subject was patently untrue.

The second striking area of unhelpfulness, contained within subset III and referring to the third of the *a priori* categories, related to the widow's perception that persons in her environment were actively attempting to focus her attention on the present and the future. Remembering that the reported interchanges were those which took place during the first three months following the death, it is perhaps not altogether unexpected that many widows had a hostile response to the type of conversation which tried to arouse their interest in new activities, the development of new friendships, or the resumption of old hobbies and occupations. It was something of a surprise, however, to note the frequency with which, included in a general discussion of future possibilities, there had been an active initiation of the subject of remarriage, even at this early time. It was not uncommon for this topic to have been introduced within a few days or weeks of the husband's death, particularly with the younger widows, but the response was almost always strongly unfavourable, even though the subject often conceded that she had appreciated that her friend or relative was acting with consciously good intentions. We were left with the distinct impression that, whatever else one might say to a widow during the height of crisis, a discussion, or even a hint, of some future romantic liaison must always be a hazardous operation; only a small handful of widows found any sort of detailed discussion about their future to be of value to them, and it will be recalled from the previous section that only one item of this type was ever reported as needed.

Two of the results from the comparisons of subsets of items are not so easily interpreted. Firstly, it was found that assistance in reviewing the past was more frequently needed by bad outcome subjects, but that, in addition, different members of this same group had found some other interchanges in this category to be unhelpful. Two important items here were those with a religious orientation, where the subject had been encouraged to believe that she would see her husband again during some future existence or, even more importantly, she had been told, and often repeatedly told, that it must have been God's will that her husband should die. No distinct pattern could be observed in the responses to these two items, so that they did not help to differentiate between the two groups; it was, however, observed that such discussions were only occasionally perceived as helpful, subjects who had beliefs of this type tending to regard such interventions as gratuitous and unnecessary, while other subjects without any profound religious conviction found such attempts at comfort meaningless and often extremely irritating. A strong impression is gained that the height of the bereavement crisis is an exceedingly poor time at which to introduce religion in any evangelical fashion. It is of course also possible that those bad outcome subjects who found interchanges promoting a review of their past life to be unhelpful might have been those women who had had a distinctly ambivalent relationship with their husbands, but there was no positive evidence of this.

The other problematic interpretation relates to those items in subset II, comprising certain interchanges concerned with the active encouragement of affect expression, where it was found that those subjects who went on to a good outcome tended to rate these interactions as absent, whereas bad outcome subjects tended to find them helpful. This is the only finding in the present study which seems unequivocally to require a focus on the intrapsychic processes and longstanding personality characteristics of the widow in order to provide some meangingful explanation; there is more than a hint here that at least some of these bad outcome subjects, by virtue of their own rigid defensive structure, had felt inhibited in the expression of emotion, and had found helpful those interchanges which had attempted actively to overcome these barriers, such attempts being found to be unnecessary, and therefore presumably not encouraged, by most of the good outcome widows.

In the light of these findings and their statistical analysis, there is no doubt that our original hypothesis is confirmed, and that there are marked differences in the perception of environmental support between good outcome and bad outcome widows. We are not assuming that the quality of the environment as such, in so far as it could be measured in any objective way, is the all-important variable, for we have already made it abundantly clear that it has been the widow's perception of her environment which has been the object of this study. Certainly we have not overlooked the very real possibility that the widow's own longstanding modes of interpersonal relationship may in some instances have contributed, perhaps very markedly, to the non-supportiveness which she then perceives around her; in two cases in particular the detailed interview made it seem very likely that the widow's own behaviour, and expecially her sado-masochistic pattern of relationships, had succeeded in driving away from her, or had induced hostility in, those people who might potentially have been available as supportive figures. More frequently, however, we formed the strong impression that the widow's narrative of events had a considerable degree of objectivity; it seemed that many people in her environment (including some members of the so-called "helping professions"), had actively, and with little or no provocation, behaved in ways which, however much these individuals may have believed themselves to be helping, had been in active opposition to those psychological processes which are believed necessary for the satisfactory resolution of object loss. The early work of Freud (1917), and the more recent observations of children by Bowlby (1960), have given a reasonably clear understanding of the psychological operations which need to be completed if the processes of mourning are to be worked through to a satisfactory conclusion. The data provided by our subjects suggests that many aspects of their environment added to, rather than aided, the tasks of what has been called the "grief work" (Caplan, 1964). This inference, of course, is derived solely from an analysis of the widow's own *perceptions*. However, it is supported by a study of the abundant descriptive material available from the interviews, detailing the actions and remarks of those with whom she came in contact, but which cannot be reproduced here.

One must also consider the alternative hypothesis that much, and perhaps all, of the unhelpfulness and hostility perceived in the environment is caused by projection of the widow's own hostile feelings which, as Bowlby

104

in particular has shown, are a frequent and perhaps inevitable accompaniment of object loss. A personal study in depth of all the major participants in the social network, which would almost certainly in any event be quite impracticable, would be necessary if one wished to prove or disprove this notion, but at the present time we believe that the evidence from this study strongly suggests that, while massive projection may have been important in one or two individual instances, "objective" insensitivity, overt or covert hostility, a failure of empathy and a relative or complete ignorance of the emotional needs of the widow played a much more significant part. Here again, as in the previous paragraph, it is quite unnecessary to view this controversy on an "all or none" basis; interpersonal relationships involve the constant interplay of two personalities, the communications of each party, often at a multiplicity of levels, helping to determine the response of the other individual, a response which is itself likely to have a variable impact depending upon the first party's needs and personality dynamics. To claim an absolute relevance for either one of the two aspects of this transaction would be to ignore what we know about the subtleties of the dyadic relationship.

It is worth pointing out that the findings of this study have a variety of practical applications. If these results can be substantially confirmed using a larger group of subjects (and a replication study is currently under way), then we will have a clearer picture of the possible forms of preventive intervention (Caplan, 1964) which might be utilized during the bereavement crisis, and the complex implications of studies such as these for preventive psychiatry will be taken up elsewhere. It may well be argued, though our interview data suggest the opposite, that there is no *causal* relationship between the perception of the environment during crisis and the ultimate outcome of the bereavement; it is of course possible that both these variables are manifestations of a common underlying factor, a complex personality pattern with its roots in the historical past of the individual. But even if one does take this extreme viewpoint (which to us is untenable in that it implies that intercurrent events have no significance in the determination of adult behaviour), the data can still be put to an alternative use. For it is apparent that there is a group of women who, in the first three months following bereavement, feel that the persons in their environment are failing, relatively or absolutely, to meet their needs, or that such persons are overtly or covertly antagonistic or unsympathetic; these are the widows of whom it can be predicted, with a relatively high degree of probability, that they will eventually show signs of an unsatisfactory outcome. Further research may confirm, therefore, that these are the widows at particular risk, and it is towards this group, once techniques have been devised for their identification at the time, that a preventive programme should be most specifically directed.

SUMMARY

In this study of the sequelae of conjugal bereavement it was hypothesized that widows who resolved the bereavement crisis in a healthy manner would differ from those with a bad outcome in their perception of the supportiveness of interpersonal relationships during the crisis. In order to obtain matched groups of good outcome and bad outcome subjects, information was obtained by questionnaire from an unselected sample of 132 widows concerning their physical and mental health during the 13 months following bereavement. On the basis of this information 28 subjects (21·2 per cent.) were rated "bad outcome", 57 (43·2 per cent.) were rated "good outcome" and 47 (35·6 per cent.) "intermediate", and from the two extreme groups 20 good outcome subjects were matched with 20 bad outcome subjects for later interview. Of the various social and personal characteristics of the 132 widows recorded on the health questionnaires, only age of widow and age of husband were found to have a statistically significant relationship to illness score, with younger widows and/or widows of younger husbands reporting greater deterioration in health following bereavement.

In the main study each of the 20 good outcome subjects and 20 bad outcome subjects was interviewed. Information was elicited firstly about specific persons available to the widow during her bereavement crisis and about her perception of them as helpful, unhelpful or neither; because of small numbers only qualitative discussion of this set of data was possible. Secondly, the widows were asked about specific forms of interpersonal exchange and whether these had been perceived as helpful, unhelpful, indifferent, absent or needed, and in statistical analysis significant and meaningful differences were found between good and bad outcome groups. Over the total 59 items employed in this second part of the interview there was a gross difference between the groups in the frequency of "needed" responses, bad outcome subjects tending to perceive the environment as failing to meet their needs during the bereavement crisis. While there were no overall differences in "helpful" responses, there were significant differences between the groups on subsets of items, good outcome subjects tending to perceive permissive support as helpful and bad outcome subjects appreciating more active encouragement from the environment. Bad outcome subjects also tended to perceive the environment as actively unhelpful, the relevant interchanges usually involving either the blocking of a widow's expression of affect, or overt or covert hostility directed towards her. Attempts to focus her attention on the future, and to discourage her thinking of the past, tended also to be found unhelpful by bad outcome subjects. The results were considered to be of theoretical and practical interest.

APPENDIX

Each of the following items was read to the subject, unless the interchange had been discussed during the preceding unstructured portion of the interview. The use of the words "this person", while obviously somewhat ungainly, had the advantage of avoiding any suggestion as to the sex of the individual involved. As indicated in the text, the identity of the person, and the subject's reaction to the interchange, were th sought if she indicated that the item was relevant. (The numbers in parentheses refer to the categories of interpersonal transaction described in the text).

1. "With this person it seemed all right to cry when I felt like it." (1)
2. "I was feeling pretty angry, and with this person I was able to let it out and talk about it." (1)
3. "I was feeling pretty guilty and blaming myself a lot, and I was able to talk to this person about it." (1)
4. "I seemed to shock and upset this person if I showed my feelings." (1)
5. "This person told me it was bad to keep my feelings bottled up all the time." (1)
6. "I was told that I must control myself and pull myself together." (1)
7. "I could tell that this person really *knew* how bad I was feeling." (1)
8. "I could tell that this person was feeling very bad about it too." (1)
9. "A person I felt *should* have been very upset didn't seem to be distressed at all." (1)
10. "This person understood that sometimes I wanted to be quiet, and sometimes I wanted to be by myself." (1)
11. "This person kept trying to be cheerful when I didn't feel a bit like it." (1)
12. "Contact with this person made me see that a person could feel very upset without going to pieces." (1)
13. "This person was so upset and showed it *so* much it made me feel even worse." (1)
14. "Someone took over some of my problems without making me feel bad about needing help." (4a)
15. "I was encouraged to keep busy and do things for myself." (3)
16. "I was given good advice about my immediate problems (social security, etc.)." (4a)
17. "This person helped out with money without making me feel bad about taking it." (4a)
18. "I was given practical help (child minding, help with transport, house repairs, etc.)." (4a)
19. "I was offered help in a general sort of way, but *I* would have had to do the asking." (4a)
20. "Though I was helped with money or in other ways, somehow I felt stupid or helpless or weak about needing help." (4a)
21. "This person helped just by being around so that I wasn't alone." (4b)
22. "This person encouraged me to talk about my husband." (2)

108

23. "This person tried to stop me brooding about
my husband." (3)
24. "I was reminded how much my husband was
valued by his parents and his family." (2)
25. "I was told how much my husband was liked by
people who knew him well (e.g., work-mates)." (2)
26. "I was told how highly my husband was regarded
by people in general." (2)
27. "This person talked about my husband's good
qualities." (2)
28. "This person reminded me of the things about
my husband which were hard to take." (2)
29. "This person talked about the good marriage
we had." (2)
30. "I had to listen to a discussion of the problems
we had in our marriage." (2)
31. "It was pointed out to me how much my husband
had gotten done during his lifetime." (2)
32. "This person talked about the after-life and said
I would be sure to see my husband again." (2)
33. "I was told that it must have been God's will
that my husband should die." (2)
34. "There was a lot of talk about death in general,
but very little about *the* death that concerned
me." (1)
35. "This person encouraged me to believe that
things would be all right in the future." (3)
36. "This person talked about ways in which I
might find happiness later on." (3)
37. "I was encouraged to laugh at funny things." (3)
38. "This person acted as if they were at some social
function, without much regard for my feelings." (1)
39. "This person tried to stop me feeling sorry for
myself." (1)
40. "It was pointed out to me that there were other
people in big trouble, like other widows." (1)
41. "This person talked about the need to get out
among people again and make new friends." (3)
42. "I received cards and/or letters and/or flowers." (2)
43. "Certain things which were said to be helpful
were given to me to read." (4b)
44. "This person *claimed* to understand how I was
feeling, but obviously didn't *really* know." (1)
45. "I was encouraged to get new interests, or go
back to old ones (clubs, hobbies, job, etc.)." (3)
46. "This person backed up *my* wishes about the
funeral arrangements when other people were
trying to tell me what I should do." (4b)
47. "Somehow I got the message that this person
felt that I wasn't as upset as I should be." (1)
48. "This person claimed to be more upset than *I*
was." (1)
49. "I was invited out to visit." (4b)
50. "After a while I was helped to realize that I had
been grieving long enough." (3)
51. "This person didn't really listen to what I was

saying, but instead told me what I *should* be
feeling." (1)

52. "This person talked quite a bit about my own
good points." (4b)
53. "I was given free advice I didn't want." (4a)
54. "I was reminded that I'd managed to handle my
problems in the past." (4b)
55. "I was told stories about other widows and what
they did which seemed to carry a message about
how *I* should behave as a widow." (1)
56. "He treated the children like a father." (4b)
57. "I was frequently reminded that I had less
money than before." (3)
58. "This person was constantly showing pity
towards me." (1)
59. "I was repeatedly reminded that my husband's
death was a final thing." (3)

Acknowledgments

This study was carried out in the Laboratory of Community Psychiatry, Harvard Medical School, under the
direction of Gerald Caplan, M.D., whose advice and
support are gratefully acknowledged. Peggy J. Golde,
Ph.D., at that time the Director of the Bereavement
Project within the Laboratory, exercised an invaluable
influence on the planning and techniques of the study, and
many of her ideas and criticisms are incorporated within
it. The bulk of the data was gathered with great enthusiasm
and competence by Delene Rhea, M.A., employed as
research assistant to the project.

Agnes Viola, B.A. and Carole Abadee, B.A. assisted in
the preparation and analysis of the data, and Pearl
Harrison prepared the manuscript for publication. Paul
Ward, B.A., gave invaluable advice on the statistical
analysis.

This study was supported by a grant to the principal
investigator from the Foundation's Fund for Research in
Psychiatry, and by a further grant to the Laboratory of
Community Psychiatry from the Grant Foundation, New
York.

Bibliography

BALER, L. A., and GOLDE, P. J. (1964). "Conjugal bereave-
ment: a strategic area of research in preventive
psychiatry." in: *Working Papers in Community Mental
Health*. Boston: Harvard Medical School.
BOWLBY, J. (1960). "Grief and mourning in infancy and
early childhood." in: *Psychoanalytical Study of the
Child*, vol. 15, New York: International Universities
Press.
CAPLAN, G. (1964). *Principles of Preventive Psychiatry*. New
York: Basic.
FREUD, S. (1917). "Mourning and melancholia." In:
Collected Papers, vol. 4, London: Hogarth Press.
KRAUS, A. S., and LILIENFELD, A. M. (1959). "Some
epidemiological aspects of the high mortality in the
young widowed group." *J. chron. Dis.*, **10**, 207.

LANGNER, T. S., and MICHAEL, S. E. (1963). *Life Stress and Mental Health*. New York: Free Press of Glencoe.

LINDEMANN, E. (1944). "Symptomatology and management of acute grief." *Amer. J. Psychiat.*, **101**, 141.

MARRIS, P. (1958). *Widows and their Families*. London: Routledge & Kegan Paul.

PARKES, C. M. (1964a). "Recent bereavement as a cause of mental illness." *Brit. J. Psychiat.*, **110**, 198.

PARKES, C. M. (1964b). "The effects of bereavement on physical and mental health—a study of the medical records of widows." *Brit. med. J.*, *ii*, 274

YOUNG, M., BENJAMIN, B., and WALLIS, C. (1963). "The mortality of widowers." *Lancet*, *ii*, 454.

The widow-to-widow program
An experiment in preventive intervention

PHYLLIS ROLFE SILVERMAN, Ph.D.

Open discussion of death is usually avoided.[1] In part this is possible because the lowered death rate has made death a less frequent visitor and because most people die in hospitals or other institutions, away from the family. Only hospital personnel and funeral directors daily confront death. The former have the reputation of withdrawing from the dying person,[2] and the funeral director's job is to make the deceased look as "natural" as possible and thereby to disguise the fact

The widow-to-widow program is sponsored jointly by a local synagogue, a community-based YMCA, a Catholic women's organization, and the Laboratory of Community Psychiatry. It is financed in part by the National and Massachusetts Funeral Directors Association and in part by the National Institute of Mental Health (Grant No. MH–09214).

This paper is adapted from an address before the women's groups of the National Funeral Directors Association at their annual meeting on October 24, 1967, in Atlantic City, N. J.

of his death. We are all aware of our own mortality, but we don't like to be reminded of it.

Many caregivers who work with the dying person and his family have recently been exploring ways of being more responsive to their needs and of helping the family through its period of grief. This is happening in the medical profession, and also among funeral directors. The mental health professional has long been aware of the emotional problems that loss of a loved one and the resulting grief can cause.[3] We are, however, no more comfortable in confronting death and its consequences than are other people.

The work here reported is an attempt to find more effective ways of responding to the problems caused by death—an inescapable fact of life. The Laboratory of Community Psychiatry at Harvard Medical School is studying the normal process of grief, what human and institutional resources are utilized by bereaved people, and what might be an appropriate way to provide additional assistance.

Bereavement and grief represent a crisis and a critical transition for the family of the deceased. The crisis aspects were first studied by Lindemann,[4] when he treated victims of the Coconut Grove fire in 1942. Those he worked with were seriously depressed as a result of the major personal losses they sustained in addition to their physical injury. Lindemann observed several stages in their grieving and discovered that, unless people went through these stages, they did not recover from their physical injury or their depression. He identified the irrational aspects of grief that he saw as transient; the process of recovery was enhanced as the person was allowed to experience these transient irrational emotions.

113

Grief can be understood as a process that has a beginning, a middle, and an end, at which point the bereaved should be recovering. Some deaths are expected, such as those occurring in old age. These are normal, and most of us make some adjustment to the anticipated end. However, there are accidental crises that occur out of time in the life cycle, such as those that arose from the fire referred to above.

Our work at Harvard is concerned with the untimely death of a spouse in young families. Statistics show that young widows and widowers have a proportionately greater risk of needing treatment for an emotional disorder than would be expected from their numbers in the population. To minimize this risk, we are experimenting with ways of intervening that might ease the distress of the bereaved, carry them through the process of their grief, and lessen the possibility of their developing an emotional disorder.

Most caregivers shy away from the bereaved.[5] Widows I have talked with felt that neither friends, family, physicians, nor clergymen, for that matter, were very helpful. All wanted them to recover as quickly as possible. On the other hand, they found that other widows could be extremely helpful: they were least likely to tell them to "keep a stiff upper lip" at a time when the widows felt their lives were ended and any hope for the future gone. Other widows realized that grief was temporary and had to run its course before it was possible to feel better again.

Most mental health agencies serve people who suffer from a defined psychiatric disorder rather than those going through a life crisis. Further, most people suffering from the "hazard of living" that occurs with the death of a spouse do not typically think of turning to such agencies for aid unless they

114

have had previous contact with them.

If the most helpful person is likely to be another widow, then this is the caregiver who should be available to a woman during her time of grief. However, the distances between people in our society do not make widow-to-widow contact easy to accomplish. People tend to live in homogeneous communities; for example, married couples with children in a certain age range tend to live near each other. In this kind of a society, it is very hard to find other people like oneself if one falls into a special category, such as that of widow.

The widow-to-widow program has grown out of this realization.[6] A target community has been chosen in which all new widows under the age of 60 are offered assistance. Information about the deceased and his widow is gotten from death certificates obtained through the bureau of vital statistics; information on race and religion is provided by funeral directors.

Five widows have been recruited to offer aid and have now been working for more than a year. They represent the dominant religious and racial groups in the community. We have assumed that someone from the widow's own background and faith might be more acceptable to her. (A time when a family is in extreme grief does not seem appropriate for the initiation of integration or ecumenicalism.) In addition, the aides live in or near the community in which they work, which facilitates the easy interchange between themselves and the new widows that can come only if they are neighbors.

The aides are women without any special educational background: two of them did not go past the eighth grade; the others are high school graduates. They were chosen not because of their educational background, but because of their personal skills with people—that is, their ability to empathize and understand what the people they visit are going through. They are all women who have been active in their community in social clubs or in other kinds of volunteer activities before or since they were widowed. Four of them are in their mid-forties; the fifth is in her early sixties.

The aides have been visiting new widows since June 1, 1967. A letter is sent to each widow, on personal note paper, offering condolences, explaining that the aide is also a widow, and proposing a time when she might visit. It is suggested that the widow call if she does not want the aide to visit.

In the first seven months, 110 widows came into the sample. Of these, 19 could not be located: the letters to them were returned, or the aides learned from neighbors that the widow had moved out of town, or they could not locate the address or the apartment. Of the remaining 91, 11 told the aides not to visit; they were abrupt and disinterested. Twelve other widows thought that the program was an excellent idea, but they did not see themselves as requiring any such assistance. (Our concern is that the people who refuse aid may be those who need us the most. However, we must exercise caution; in our zeal to help, we must always respect people's right to refuse to see us.)

The aides have been in touch with 64 widows; half of these they have seen in person, and the other half they have talked with regularly, at great length, on the telephone. A question to be answered in the future is why some women are unwilling to meet the aides in person but are willing to develop, in some instances, very intimate relationships on the telephone.

At this point it is possible to talk about the contacts the aides have had with the widows within one month after the death of their husbands. It seems that the new widow primarily wants to talk. She talks about the circumstances of her husband's death, about her fear of loneliness, about financial problems and how she will manage her future, raising the children alone and perhaps needing to work. When her children are already grown, she talks about the emptiness of the house—the fact that there is no one to take care of, and no one with whom she can share her evenings and weekends. Initially, most of the widows report that they are managing since there is so much to do. They are glad for chores such as straightening out insurance and Veterans and Social Security benefits, since these give them something to keep them busy. Most people are quite able to care for themselves and really need only the special help that comes from having a friendly ear to listen and a shoulder on which they can, in a sense, cry without feeling that they are imposing or being told to "keep a stiff upper lip" and to control themselves.

The aides' responses to the widows' needs vary. They sometimes provide concrete services, such as help in finding a job; they may help the widow sort out her finances and understand how it is possible to live on her new income; they may give needed advice. Most important, they offer friendship. The following vignettes illustrate the kind of work the aides do:

1. Mrs. I. provided the J. family with *moral support* and *showed family members how to be more considerate in their expectations of a new widow;* further, she helped Mrs. J. get a job. When Mrs. I. first visited Mrs. J., the latter was not at home. Mrs. I. then talked to Mrs. J.'s sister, who complained about the new widow's not being able to make up her mind: one minute she wanted to move, the next she was very morose, and spent all her time listening to church music she and her husband had enjoyed together. Mrs. I. explained to the

sister something about the bereavement process and suggested that she be patient with her sister, encouraging her little by little to move out.

When the aide saw Mrs. J. in person the next day, she found her painting her apartment, with her teenage children's help. They were listening to church music as they worked. Mrs. J. had decided not to move, and to make her apartment more attractive. She also wanted to go back to work, doing housework so that she could be home when the children returned from school. Mrs. I. made two phone calls that evening and found Mrs. J. work for two days a week.

2. Mrs. N. offered Mrs. Q. *direct advice* about how to cope with her emotional problems. Mrs. Q. called Mrs. N. as soon as she received her letter and wanted her to come immediately. She was in a panic: she couldn't sleep and couldn't stop crying. Mrs. N. went right over.

Mrs. Q. had been accustomed to riding to work every day with her husband on the streetcar. She had gone back to work immediately after the seven days of mourning (*Shiva*) were over, but had become increasingly uncomfortable with each passing day. By the time she arrived at work she was depressed and crying. The trip constantly reminded her of her husband's death. She thought of changing jobs, of working in a different place; but she didn't want to offend her employer, who had been very good to her; in addition, she was frightened of looking elsewhere for a job at her age (50). Mrs. N. told her that changing jobs might be a good idea, but that she should first take a week's vacation, then try going back to her usual job. If she still couldn't face the situation, she should talk to her boss and look for another job.

Mrs. Q. followed this advice. She phoned Mrs. N. frequently, even when she couldn't sleep at night. In the end, she had no trouble finding a new job.

Friendship, to the aide, means visiting back and forth in each other's homes, exploring each other's experience with widowhood, and finding out about each other as people. The aides often invite the new widows to dinner, go out socially with them, and introduce them to other widows.

As we reviewed the services we were providing, it became clear that some people were able to deal with the trauma of the initial impact of the bereavement themselves, or with little assistance from either the aide or their family and friends. This did not ensure recovery, however. To meet the changing needs of the new widow, we organized group meetings to which all the widows were invited. These meetings dealt with questions that widows had raised: what to do with their leisure, what was involved in getting back to work, and how to help children understand their father's death. (We found that widows were most troubled by their children's reactions to their father's death: they had not anticipated that this event would have such an impact on their youngsters.) The meetings brought together the widows who had not seen an aide in person as well as those the aides had come to know quite well.

Our aides have reported that they got through the first few months of their bereavement in one manner or another, but that the loneliness and depression really became most difficult six months or a year after their husbands had died. By then they had in some way settled their lives so that they were carrying on, and only then did a great feeling of loss overwhelm them. Their experience in working with other widows has corroborated this.

Our program, therefore, is designed not to have just one or two interviews with people initially, but rather to develop some kind of ongoing relationship to help widows at the different stages of their grief. Our goal is to explore all of the various needs that people have during bereavement and to find ways of helping them expand their resources so they can be more effective in coping with their problems. The end result, hopefully, will be that the mourners will recover and find some future for themselves. The means to this end may be a resource they develop themselves, such as a club for widows and widowers that would, in fact, be a self-help group. If what we do proves to be effective, we hope that it may serve as a pilot program and that, eventually, churches and other agencies and groups in the community will pick up the work and carry it forward.

I believe that the base for preventive work is *not* the mental health clinic, which should reserve its highly skilled services for those who are seriously disturbed and require special care: prevention should be the work of people and agencies that deal with people as they move through the normal phases of a life cycle. I think, for example, of physicians, school teachers, clergymen, neighbors, and funeral directors—all of whom can be forces for positive mental health. Perhaps the most effective preventive program can come from self-help groups, which is basically what our widow-to-widow program is. Here we have a very specialized group of "experts": they have lived through the crisis, they have recovered, and they teach others that it can be done and how to do it. Are we perhaps simply formalizing and making applicable to urban life a procedure that would naturally be followed in rural and more closely knit communities?

REFERENCES

1. Gorer, G.: Encounter, 5:49, 1955.

2. Glaser, B. G., and Strauss, A. L.: Awareness of Dying. Chicago, Aldine, 1965.

3. Freud, S.: Mourning and Melancholia. In: Jones, E. (ed.): Collected Papers of Sigmund Freud, The International Psycho-Analytical Library, vol. 4, no. 10. London, Hogarth Press, 1953, pp. 152–170.
4. Lindemann, E.: American Journal of Psychiatry, 101:141, 1944.
5. Silverman, P. R.: Services for the Widowed. In: Social Work Practice, 1966. New York, Columbia University Press, 1966, pp. 170–189.

6. Silverman, P. R.: Community Mental Health Journal, 5:37 (Spring), 1967.

Death in Childhood

DEATH IN CHILDHOOD

THE death of a child is always attended with particular poignancy. That this has always been so is attested by its inclusion in story-telling from the earliest times. One can think of Chaucer's "litel clergeon" of the Prioress's tale and all the way up to Paul Dombey and Little Nell and later. This applies even though what appears to us, in our generation, as an appalling mortality in infancy and childhood, and confirmed by a saunter through the older parts of our cemeteries, was throughout history accepted as a fact of life. The child's evening prayer of a generation or two ago was

> If I should die before I wake,
> I pray the Lord my soul to take.

Many a school classroom choir sang the words of Eugene Field:

> But as he was sleeping, an angel song
> Awakened our Little Boy Blue.

Today, when the diseases which snatched away countless children have been vanquished one by one, the death of a child seems an even greater tragedy than it ever was.

Many deaths in youngsters are the result of violent accidents, on the road and elsewhere. These are sharp and sudden tragedies, to be suffered by the parents, not the victim. The other situation, that concerns us here, is when the diagnosis of an inevitably fatal disease has been made. Then the parents must be told of the unalterable prospect and the child has to be supervised and cared for during the course of an illness whose fatal outcome is always in mind.

There is a dearth of guidance for the physician confronted by this emotionally charged situation. There are many problems involved and certainly far more questions than there are answers. Nevertheless several thoughtful articles by pediatricians have appeared on this subject and these are decidedly helpful. Some parents have described in detail their reactions to the announcement that they would be bereft of their child and have told how they behaved and managed in the remaining time they had with him. John Gunther gave such an account in the book which took its title from one of John Donne's Holy Sonnets, "Death Be Not Proud". This attained a wide circulation and made an impact on many people.

The task of informing the parents falls to the doctor in charge of the case and cannot devolve upon a junior or a resident, even when it is not a private patient that is concerned. Granted, there are residents whose personality and resources of sympathy do qualify them for this difficult role, but parents are entitled to consideration from a senior practitioner so that his reputation for wisdom and understanding can give assurance that the problem is receiving all the thoughtful attention that is available.

Although possibly there are instances when it is better that the mother should learn the news from her husband, it is surely better that both parents should be interviewed together. It need hardly be mentioned that this interview should not take place in a hospital corridor or in the clinical atmosphere of a ward, liable to interruption by telephone or nurses. The doctor and the apprehensive parents should be able to talk together in circumstances of quiet and comfort.

In the case of a child with leukemia or a malignant tumour one may seek to spare the

123

parents the full weight of the blow at a first interview by emphasizing the seriousness of the illness with only a mention that the child may not recover. The actual diagnosis can be withheld until a later occasion. But if a direct question as to diagnosis is asked, it is best not to equivocate. The doctor must be absolutely sure of the accuracy and finality of the diagnosis in these circumstances. Any remarks about technical details to impress the parents, any assumption of credit for the elucidation of the case, must be eschewed. Verbosity and repetition do not convey the kindness that is intended and that is best communicated by a few words spoken with gentleness and gravity.

There are certain questions that are bound to be asked. How long can life be expected to last? Will the child have to remain in hospital throughout the course of the illness? Will he suffer much pain? What should the other children be told? Not only should time be taken to give considered answers to these questions, but it must appear to be given willingly and ungrudgingly. And assurance should always be given that further questions, which are bound to present themselves later, will be welcomed and answered as best one can, that further interviews can be arranged to discuss aspects of the case as they arise.

If the opinion of a consultant is mentioned, there should be no hesitation in complying, for the impression above all that one wishes to give is that nothing will be withheld that might offer even a shred of help.

Often the parents' minds will dart restlessly about in search of some failure or error on their part that may have influenced the situation. It may take repeated reassurance to disabuse them of what may seem almost an eagerness for self-reproach. It is only later, after friends and relatives have been told, that the suggestion may come that some unorthodox treatment at the hands of an unqualified practitioner to whom publicity has accrued, may be able to accomplish what regular means cannot. This is no time for indignation or taking affront. Quiet dissuasion is likely to be effective in preventing the raising of false hopes and the wasting of savings.

In those diseases where remissions can be expected, there is every reason to encourage the discharge of the child from hospital when supervision can be continued on an outpatient basis. This is so only when the home circumstances are favourable, but one must remember that what does not appear so to the doctor can be entirely acceptable to the patient. The other children in the household can be told that their brother or sister is not yet completely well and may have to return to hospital later. There will be a temptation to over-indulge the child and this is understandable, but it is better for all concerned if the order of the home is maintained on as natural a level as possible. Trips to Disneyland for such children are described in the press and receive enthusiastic support, but the contribution to the child's happiness is open to doubt. It is the parents who derive benefit from this sort of undertaking, for they are afforded the satisfaction of knowing that they spared nothing which would bring enjoyment. Since it is a means of demonstrating their love, it is not to be derided or brushed aside.

The role of the clergy in this situation cannot be easily defined. Naturally if there are close ties between the family and the church or synagogue, the spiritual adviser can be of tremendous help in supporting the parents and enabling them to face and accept permanent separation from their child. It will be realized that not all members of the clergy have the personality or temperament which fits them for these circumstances, just as it is true that many doctors, likewise, can be awkward or fail in this special role. While the personal priest or minister or rabbi will have a distinct advantage, if the family has no definite religious affiliation a call to the chaplain attached to the hospital can be suggested; in our day he is likely to be experienced in bringing help to the situation.

What of one's attitude towards the child patient? These days the older children, at least, know something about cancer and leukemia. Obviously the confused and conflicting views about what or how much to tell the adult patient about his mortal illness do not apply here. Only a simple explanation should be given for the failure to recover quickly or for the return to hospital. A child does not press for a complete account of his disease, and gentle reassurance about getting better soon, should suffice. As the course draws to a close there is the natural and merciful narrowing of awareness and lapse into listlessness that Nature provides most of us, at whatever age our exitus. Instances of mental alertness to the end, so often portrayed by novelists of the older schools, are rarely seen. The doctor's attitude throughout must be one of controlled optimism. He will never fail to draw attention to ways in which his patient is feeling better and to express hope for even more progress in the days ahead.

Visiting privileges will be granted when the terminal phase of the illness is entered. Often the mother will have satisfaction from helping in the nursing of her child and as far as is practicable this should be permitted.

A child brought up in our society has an acquaintance of a sort with death. He is familiar with scenes of violence from his exposure to the cinema and television and in his games he will enact death. But few children probably think of death as applied to themselves, even though they have had schoolmates who have been killed in a road accident. He often recognizes that it is a forbidden subject and when he is ill he may avoid mention of his fears to his parents. Those fears may be increased by the attitude of intense concern that his father and mother cannot conceal. He may therefore allude to them only to the nurse or to someone less intimately involved in his care. In the main he is more likely to be anxious about his discomforts than about dying. Other children in the household may display an acceptance of death of a brother or sister that can surprise us somewhat. When we see them out playing on the day of the funeral we may be disturbed a little, for we tend to sentimentalize the occasion.

The doctor should understand that possibly by his very attitude he may be of more service than by any words he can find. He can enable the parents to sense that he identifies himself with their anguish, as another human being as well as a doctor. At the same time he must preserve his objectivity; by failing to do so he will not only increase his own burden but he will render himself less fitted for the task of dealing with the medical problems of his patient. Often there can be a temptation, in the course of a lingering fatal illness, to omit daily visits, or at least to welcome trivial reasons for failing to see the patient regularly. It is a heavy task always to generate hope and assurance, and there will be occasions when he will indeed feel that virtue has gone out of him.

The final phase of the illness should be conducted with dignity and decorum. This is not a time for heroic measures, designed possibly to impress the parents but more likely to provide an outlet for the concern of all who are in attendance. Therapy known to be of no use in affecting the outcome has no place; the only treatment is that which will relieve symptoms and prolong life in comfort. The patient should not be allowed to suffer pain or be distressed by investigative procedures.

The doctor can help to bring some restraint into a situation which invites indulgence in sentimentality and uncontrolled grief. He can try to persuade the family to accept mortality as part of our humanity and to be grateful for the time the child was given them. As the quiet lovely notes of the little organ prelude of J. S. Bach remind us, "Alle Menschen müssen sterben."

BIBLIOGRAPHY

1. GUNTHER, J.: Death be not proud, The Modern Library, New York, 1953.
2. HOWELL, D.: J. Pediat., 1: 2, 1966.
3. KOOP, C.: Bull. Amer. Coll. Surg., 52: 173, 1967.
4. YUDKIN, S.: Lancet, 1: 37, 1967.
5. EVANS, A. E.: New Eng. J. Med., 278: 138, 1968.
6. GREEN, M.: Pediatrics, 39: 441, 1967.
7. SOLNIT, A. J. AND GREEN, M.: Pediatric management of the dying child: Part II. The child's reaction to the fear of dying. In: Modern perspectives in child development, edited by A. J. Solnit and S. Provence, International Universities Press Inc., New York, 1963, p. 217.
8. Idem: Pediatrics, 24: 106, 1959.
9. VERNICK, J. AND KARON, M.: Amer. J. Dis. Child., 109: 393, 1965.
10. DE VRIES, P.: The blood of the lamb, Little, Brown & Co. Inc., Boston, 1961.

THE MOURNING RESPONSE OF PARENTS
TO THE DEATH OF A NEWBORN INFANT*

John H. Kennell, M.D., Howard Slyter
and Marshall H. Klaus, M.D.

> Oh you, core of your father's being,
> Light of joy, extinguished too soon![1]

THERE are more deaths in the first few days of
life than at any subsequent time in childhood,
and almost all occur in a hospital. During the period when a newborn infant's condition is critical, at
the time of his death and afterward, the staff of a
hospital takes a series of actions that are presumably for the benefit of the mother. These actions are
based primarily on the staff's own personal reactions
as well as on a number of common assumptions and
customs that arise from a mixture of traditions, state
health laws, medical advances and the convenience
of the institution and its staff. There is so little information in the medical literature about the response of a mother to a life-threatening illness or
the death of her newborn infant that a physician has
no guide to either radical changes or continuation of
his present practices.

For decades mothers have been separated from
their normal newborn infants in almost all American
hospitals. When the infant is ill or premature, sepa-

*Supported in part by the Grant Foundation and the Educational
Foundation of America.

128

ration is usually complete; care is provided in another division, or even another building. In the vast majority of nurseries, although the mother may come to see her premature baby, she is denied the opportunity to touch or care for him until he is large enough to go home.

In the past many physicians have believed that a mother should not have physical contact with her ill or premature infant because of the risk of infection and for fear of an excessively severe emotional reaction in case of his death. As with many hospital practices, there has been no careful study to determine the advantages and disadvantages of such a no-contact policy. Today, with improved aseptic technics and the risk of infection no longer such a great deterrent to a mother's entry into a nursery, a few medical centers, including Case Western Reserve University and Stanford,[2] are allowing mothers early contact with their premature infants, to study whether a period of early physical contact alters later maternal behavior. These mothers scrub and gown before entering the nursery. They then see the baby at much closer range than before, reach into the incubator, touch the baby and, if medical circumstances permit, hold, feed and diaper him.

This innovation, which may prove to be desirable for the mother when the baby lives, raises a question of vital importance: Is it emotionally wise to allow the mother early contact if the baby may die?

The objectives of this study were as follows: to determine whether early tactile contact between mother and infant leads to unduly upsetting reactions after a baby's death; to investigate the importance of various factors, particularly tactile contact, in the establishment of an affectional bond between mother and infant; to observe systematically the reactions of a group of parents to the loss of a newborn infant. To achieve these objectives, we studied a **group of** mothers who had recently lost newborn infants.

The design of this study was based in part on the work of a number of investigators[3] who have postulated that the length and intensity of mourning after a loss is proportionate to the closeness of the relationship prior to death. Following this reasoning, we anticipated that the strength of the attachment that a mother had formed to her baby could be measured indirectly by determination of the length and intensity of her mourning after his death.

Grieving and mourning have been used interchangeably in this paper even though some investigators[4] have made a theoretical distinction between biologic and cultural responses to a death.

METHODOLOGY

The study population consisted of a group of mothers whose infants had died in the University. Hospitals premature nursery between January, 1968, and January, 1969. As part of a long-term study of maternal separation there were alternating three-month periods in which mothers were either permitted to enter our premature nursery to have physical contact with their infants in isolettes starting shortly after birth or restricted to visual contact through the glass walls of the nursery for the first 20 days. Whether the mothers had physical contact with their infants in those first 20 days depended upon the period in which the baby was born. The babies were all live-born, with no physical anomalies, and were, for the most part, small premature infants (range of 580 to 3000 g in weight) who lived from one hour to 12 days. Three of the infants who died had surviving twin siblings. (Although these mothers cannot necessarily be compared with mothers who have lost a singleton they were included because the deaths occurred during the period of this study.) Twenty of the 21 mothers approached agreed to participate in the study. These mothers came from a wide socioeconomic background (Table 1) and each had at least one living child.

Table 1. Study Population.

SERVICE	RACE		
	WHITE	BLACK	TOTALS
Private	9	3	12
Staff	2	6	8
Totals	11	9	20

Tape-recorded interviews were conducted at the hospital three to 22 weeks after the loss of the baby (mean of 11 weeks) and lasted for approximately one hour. They were semistructured and designed to cover three periods: the prenatal experiences — the extent of planning for the baby, the mother's feelings about the pregnancy and their changes with time; the postnatal experience, with the mother's expectations of the infant's survival, and the mother's contacts with him; and, finally, the mother's experience after the baby's death. The mothers were asked about what had happened to them and how they had felt in the days since the loss. After this, the autopsy findings were discussed, and at the end of the interview, a questionnaire covering the same topics was given to 13 of the mothers. The choice of variables for the interview and the questionnaire was determined mainly by the studies of Parkes and Lindemann,[3,5-7] who found the cardinal features of mourning to be somatic distress, an intense subjective distress, preoccupation with the image of the deceased, feelings of guilt and preoccupation with one's negligence or minor omissions, feelings of hostility toward others and a breakdown of normal patterns of conduct.

On the basis of the interview, each mother was evaluated on six key signs, which, when taken *together*, we have considered some measure of mourning: sadness, loss of appetite, inability to sleep, increased irritability, preoccupation with the lost infant and inability to return to normal activities. Every mother was rated on each of these six variables on a scale from 0 to 4 (Table 2). A 0 score was given if it seemed that one variable — sleeping, for instance — had never been disturbed. On the other hand, if there was a disturbance and it still presented an important problem one month after the loss, a score of 4 would be given.

Table 2. Numerical Components of the "Mourning Score."

SCORE	DEFINITION
0	Never a problem
1	Mild problem
2	Major problem for <2 wk
3	Major problem for 2-4 wk
4	Major problem for >4 wk

We determined an overall "mourning score" for each mother by adding the numerical score she received on each of the six variables and then averaging the total scores of two raters. If three or more of these signs were reported, mourning was consid-

131

ered to be present. Each interview was independently scored by two raters. The reliability of these two independent raters on each of the six items was tested. They agreed on 89 per cent of the items and were within one point on the other 11 per cent. The mothers' self-ratings were the same or within one point of the interview evaluations 85 per cent of the time.

The scores could not be completed for two of the 20 mothers. In one case the interview was conducted before the four-week interval; in the other the mother was unable to finish the interview because she said it would be too unpleasant to "dredge up" her feelings. The mourning scores that the remaining 18 mothers received are shown in Table 3. Theoretically, the scores could range from 0 to 24. For purposes of comparison, the mothers were divided arbitrarily into a high and a low mourning group, depending on the side of the median score on which they fell. Henceforth, the group with high mourning scores will be referred to as Group H, and that with low mourning scores as Group L.

On the basis of this study we cannot say whether the degree of reaction is more or less favorable for a mother, but other authors have indicated that a painful period of grieving is a normal and necessary response to the loss of a loved one, and that the absence of a period of grieving is not a healthy sign but rather a cause for alarm. High mourning does not refer to pathologic grieving or morbid grief reactions as described by Lindemann,[5] who believes that pathologic mourning reactions represent distortions of normal grief. On the basis of his observations he lists nine such reactions: overacting without a sense of loss; acquisition of symptoms belonging to the last illness of the deceased; psychosomatic reactions such as ulcerative colitis, asthma, or rheumatoid arthritis; alteration in relation to friends and relatives; furious hostility against specific persons; repression of hostility, leading to a wooden and formal manner resembling schizophrenic pictures; lasting loss of patterns of social interaction; activities detrimental to one's own social and economic existence; and agitated depressions. These were looked for in each interview.

RESULTS

All the mothers reported definite sadness and

Table 3. Mourning Scores of 18 Mothers.

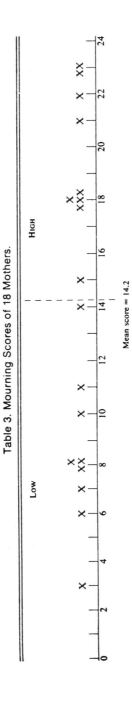

preoccupation with thoughts of the dead baby; all but two experienced insomnia and a disturbance of their usual patterns of daily life. Increased irritability was a prominent symptom for 15 of the 18 mothers, and 12 had a loss of appetite. Every mother had experienced problems in at least three of the six items noted above, and 15 of the 18 had problems in five or all six.

In comparing the group of nine mothers with high mourning scores with the nine with low scores, we found the following associations*:

High mourning was associated with the previous loss of a baby (p less than 0.05), either through miscarriage or through death of a live-born infant. Within Group H there had been nine previous miscarriages and four deaths of living children. Within Group L there was one miscarriage. The mother with the highest mourning score specifically related her intense sadness to her inability to produce a live normal child (she had one living but handicapped child). She said: "I do feel . . . a frustration about the fact that I can't have a baby. That makes me sick . . . if a woman had lost a baby and the doctor says, 'Well, in six months you can go ahead and have another baby,' — maybe she would get over it. But I think that the thing of accepting that probably this is the last child, I began to feel, am I so good? I feel less like a woman."

High mourning was associated with positive feelings about the pregnancy (p less than 0.05). All Group H mothers said that they either were initially pleased with the pregnancy or had become happy with the pregnancy by the time of the delivery. Within Group L, four mothers were initially pleased to be pregnant, and one other came to accept it favorably as the pregnancy progressed. Four of the mothers were not happy to be pregnant at the time of delivery.

High mourning was suggestively associated with touching the infant before his death (p less than 0.1). Five of the Group H mothers, and only one of the nine Group L mothers had touched their infants. It is interesting that this mother was the only one in the study who wore gloves while touching her infant. She said that because of the

*With the use of the Fisher Exact Probability Test.

134

gloves, she did not feel she had actually touched her baby. Also, her baby was one of a set of twins — the other twin lived.

High mourning was suggestively associated with a failure of communication between the mother and her husband (p less than 0.1), or in the absence of a husband, her own mother. Seven of nine Group L mothers said that they had talked with their husbands about their feelings and reactions to the loss. Only three of nine Group H mothers reported that they had been able to do so. Several of the Group H mothers said that they had tried to initiate discussion with their husbands, and had been ignored or cut off.

On the other hand, there was no apparent relation between the mourning score and the length of the baby's life, a mother's expectations of her baby's chances to live and her mourning score, or mourning and the number of living children in the household. (It is quite possible that the results would be different with mothers who have no living child.) It should be noted that all three mothers with surviving twins had low mourning scores.

Safety of Physical Contact

There were no unduly upsetting reactions at the time of physical contact or later pathologic grieving, as defined by Parkes and Lindemann,[3,5] in mothers who did not have a history of hospitalization for psychiatric disease. Pathologic grieving was present in one of the 18 mothers interviewed; a post-partum depressive psychosis developed, requiring an 11-day stay in the hospital, after the death of her infant, whom she had touched. This woman had a long history of psychiatric hospitalizations, including the development of a post-partum psychosis after the death of a previous infant whom she had *not* touched.

Useful but Incomplete Results

Although the study was not designed to include husbands, eight of the 20 mothers interviewed were accompanied by their husbands. From the discussions with them, a number of interesting observations were made.

Two husbands denied outright that they had ever grieved. These men had never interrupted their normal work and even had begun to work extra long hours. They thought that because their wives were upset, they could not afford to be. Both men appeared tense and under considerable strain. One expressed his feeling thus: "I just go on living day to day, and I have other things and other duties to perform. If I break down now, somebody will have to pick these people up . . . Somebody's going to have to pull them together and help them if I break down. So I just keep going and try to keep busy and keep from thinking and keep from worrying about these things . . . Maybe I'm doing this under a tremendous strain . . . by closing this door upon something that has happened, as if it didn't happen; maybe it's wrong. Maybe it's wrong for me four, five, 10, 15, 20 years from now."

Several husbands appeared to have grieved as long as or longer than their wives, particularly if the baby had been born in another hospital and the husband had been involved in its transportation to University Hospitals. While the baby was in the nursery the father was physically closer to him than his wife, who was in a hospital several miles away. The husband was also more aware of the details of the baby's ongoing care.

The parents of these infants were not well prepared for their own mourning responses. Their reactions worried and perplexed them, and in some families this tended to disturb the pre-existing husband-wife relationship. In several of the interviews it became apparent that a husband and wife were discussing the loss and their reactions to it with one another for the first time.

Because the interviews were conducted less than six months after the deaths of the infants and were designed to investigate the acute stages of the mourning process, it is not possible to state with assurance that later pathologic reactions, such as grief lasting for more than six months, will not occur. In addition, there was no earlier objective assessment of the intensity of mourning in these parents. Thus, we could not distinguish, at the time of the interview, between the persistence of a high level of mourning in some mothers and a diminishing but still elevated level in others.

HOSPITAL PRACTICES

In the course of the interview there were a number of interesting comments related to the mother's stay in the hospital and the experiences of both husband and wife with hospital staff members that arose repeatedly.

Mothers found association with other mothers of live healthy babies extremely difficult. Several asked to be transferred to private rooms or to rooms with other mothers with sick premature infants. When healthy babies were brought to their mothers at feeding time the mothers' feelings of sadness were accentuated.

The mothers interviewed could deal with questions from other mothers who did not know that the baby was ill or dead, but were greatly disturbed when nurses or aides would offer to bring "your baby for his feeding." These lapses of communication and apparent lack of awareness of the mothers' situation among staff personnel angered the mothers. In addition, some lapses of communication among the nursing and medical staff were also reported, which emphasized the importance of complete interstaff communication and consistency in reports given to parents.

In a few cases parents interpreted a house officer's comments to mean that if the baby survived for a certain number of days, he would live. They believe that a part of their upset state was due to their raised expectations because the baby *had* lived for the "magical" number of days, and then died.

DISCUSSION

The medical literature contains detailed descriptions of the typical mourning responses of adults to the loss of a spouse, a parent, a friend or a child with a fatal disease, but there has been no previous report in the English language of the reactions of parents to the loss of a newborn infant. The mourning score developed in this study indicates that clearly identifiable mourning was present in the mother of each infant who died — whether the infant lived for one hour or for 12 days, whether the infant was 3000 g or a nonviable 580 g, whether or not the infant was planned and whether or not the mother had touched the baby.

The reactions of the parents in this study are remarkably similar to those described by Parkes with the death of a close family member[3]:

At first the full reaction may be delayed, or there may be a period of numbness or blunting in which the bereaved person acts as if nothing had happened for a few hours or days or up to two weeks. Thereafter attacks of yearning and distress with autonomic disturbance begins. These occur in waves and are aggravated by reminders of the deceased. Between attacks the bereaved person is depressed and apathetic with a sense of futility. Associated symptoms are insomnia, anorexia, restlessness, irritability with occasional outbursts of anger directed against others or the self, and preoccupation with thoughts of the deceased. The dead person is commonly thought to be present, and there is a tendency to think of him as if he was still alive, and to idealize his memory. The intensity of these features begins to decline after one to six weeks and is minimal by six months, although for several years occasional brief periods of yearning and depression may be precipitated by reminders of the loss . . . The typical reaction to bereavement varies with the closeness of the relationship with the deceased.

The association between longer and more intense mourning and a mother's lack of communication with a close family member suggests that the experience of discussing the bereavement and expressing the associated feelings may help bring the mourning process more rapidly to a conclusion.

Affectional Bonding

The presence of mourning in all mothers implies that a substantial degree of affectional bonding *precedes* tactile contact between mother and infant. Longer and possibly more intense mourning was seen in mothers for whom the pregnancy was a positive experience (mothers who were pleased to be pregnant and those who had had a previous loss), and in mothers who had tactile contact with their infants. This indicates that both pleasurable anticipation of a pregnancy and physical contact with the baby may be important factors in the bonding process. This in part agrees with the observations of Bibring.[8]

The first objective posed in this study was to determine whether it was psychologically safe for a mother to have tactile contact with a sick infant whose prognosis was uncertain. This is a concern that has guided physicians and nurses to establish protective hospital routines to discourage mothers from having contact with premature and sick newborn infants in the first hours and days of life. The experience of viewing and touching her newborn infant is not a specific cause of a mother's mourning, because she will have a grief reaction without this (since all the mothers in this study showed mourning reactions whether or not they had physical contact with their infants). With the evidence that physical contact does not cause unduly upsetting immediate reactions or appear to result in pathologic mourning, it will be reasonable to proceed with investigations of the effects of this contact when the baby lives. Furthermore, since it is so difficult at birth to identify with certainty the babies who will die, should we not allow every mother to have physical contact with her baby if she wishes?

Mourning Customs

Averill[4] points out that "death rites are a complex blend of customs fashioned to meet the needs of society as well as those of the individual bereaved. When these needs are in conflict, social prerequisites typically take precedence over the desires and well being of the individual." In Latin America it is customary for the members of a family to come together — often traveling great distances — to join in mourning with the mother who has just lost a newborn infant, even if he has lived for only a few minutes. Over the centuries some of the basic mourning requirements of the human species may have been incorporated in these rites and in other cultural and religious ceremonies associated with death. At present when a newborn infant dies in the hospital, all evidence of his existence is often removed with amazing rapidity, and no special arrangements are made for the parents. The requirements for efficiency and for the mental comfort of the modern hospital society may have crowded out fundamental requirements for the individual.

Practical Suggestions

As a result of this study we have instituted in our hospital the changes in room assignment and communication suggested by the parents. In addition, we have made further changes in our approach to newly bereaved parents. At the time of a baby's death we tell the parents about the usual reactions to the loss of a child and the length of time that they will last. We indicate that it will be mutually beneficial if the two parents talk freely with each other about their feelings. A day or two after the death we again meet with the parents to go over the same suggestions, many of which have been missed or misunderstood owing to the emotional shock of the baby's death. Again, they are encouraged to talk and advised not to hold back their feelings. In our culture, husbands particularly need this extra advice. The parents are interviewed once more three to four months after the death, to inquire about their activities and mood as an indication of how they are working through their grief, and to discuss the autopsy findings, and any further questions are answered. These three discussions with both parents together appear to be valuable; they are especially important when there has been a previous loss.

We are indebted to Mrs. Susan Davis, Mrs. Susan Gordon and Miss Nancy Plumb for their helpful ideas and criticism.

REFERENCES

1. Rückert F: Kindertotenlieder (poems set to music by Gustav Mahler)
2. Barnett CR, Leiderman PH, Grobstein R, et al: Neonatal separation: the maternal side of interactional deprivation. Pediatrics 45: 197-205, 1970
3. Parkes CM: Bereavement and mental illness. Part 2. A classification of bereavement reactions. Brit J Med Psychol 38:13-26, 1965
4. Averill JR: Grief: its nature and significance. Psychol Bull 70:721-748, 1968
5. Lindemann E: Symptomatology and management of acute grief. Amer. J Psychiat 101:141-148, 1944
6. Parkes CM: Bereavement and mental illness. Part 1. A clinical study of the grief of bereaved psychiatric patients. Brit J Med Psychol 38:1-12, 1965
7. *Idem:* The nature of grief. Int J Psychiat 3:435-438, 1967
8. Bibring GL, Dwyer TF, Huntington DS, et al: A study of the psychological processes in pregnancy and of the earliest mother-child relationship. I. Some propositions and comments. Psychoanal Stud Child 16:9-72, 1961

The Psychiatric Toll
of the Sudden Infant Death Syndrome

ABRAHAM B. BERGMAN, M.D., MARGARET A. POMEROY, R.N.
and J. BRUCE BECKWITH, M.D.

Each year about 10,000 infants in the United States are victims of the "sudden infant death syndrome" (SIDS). Because of confusion and ignorance about the syndrome, the parents almost invariably feel responsible for their child's death. While studying all the cases of SIDS occurring in King County, Washington, since January 1965, we have been impressed with the pervasiveness of the parental guilt reaction. Needless recrimination over these deaths has taken an enormous toll in broken families and broken spirits. The problem is often intensified by a lack of knowledge about SIDS and especially its emotional sequelae.

Physicians should be familiar with SIDS because they may be asked to assist with the immediate care of the family and the treatment of guilt reactions following the sudden death of the child. Few medical problems afford such opportunities for preventive psychiatry.

Sudden Infant Death Syndrome

SIDS is defined as the sudden, unexpected and inexplicable death of an infant. A thorough postmortem examination fails to show the cause of death. The syndrome accounts for about 10 percent of deaths which occur in American infants during the first year of life. It is the leading single cause of death in infants over 1 week of age. In King County, approximately 2.8 per 1,000 liveborn infants are destined to be SIDS victims.

A number of factors can cause sudden, unexpected death in infancy. However, the vast majority of the unexplained cases follow a repetitive pattern, which suggests that they represent a distinct clinicopathologic entity.

EPIDEMIOLOGY

Most cases of SIDS occur between the ages of 3 weeks and 5 months, with a peak incidence between the second and fourth months of life. The phenomenon is uncommon before 3 weeks of age or after 6 months; typical cases almost never occur after 1 year. Most studies have shown a clear-cut seasonal distribution, with preponderance during the late autumn, winter and spring. Occasionally there is a temporal clustering of cases, which strongly suggests an infectious (though certainly not contagious) etiology.

There is an increased risk of SIDS among babies of low birth weight, among those who are nonwhite and among those born to families of the lower socioeconomic classes. To what extent these variables are interdependent has not been established. In King County, the risk of SIDS for a negro infant weighing 1,500 Gm. at birth and living in a poor neighborhood exceeds one in 80 live births, as opposed to an overall county rate of one in 350 live births.

In many cases, the victim seems perfectly healthy prior to death, although most have a history of minor respiratory symptoms during the preceding two weeks. Death during sleep is so characteristic that if an infant is observed to die, a cause other than SIDS should be suspected.

Pathologic Findings

The importance of a carefully performed autopsy cannot be overemphasized. In about 15 percent of cases of sudden, unexpected death, a lethal lesion will be found. Furthermore, the physician must be armed with the postmortem findings if he is to counsel the family with authority. Pulmonary congestion and edema, intrathoracic petechiae and minor pharyngeal erythema are the gross findings in most cases. Microscopically, slight inflammatory changes are found in the respiratory tract—but these seem too minor to account for death. In summary, when an infant between 3 weeks and 6 months of age dies in his sleep without prior alarming symptoms and shows no lethal lesion at autopsy, he can be assumed to be a victim of SIDS.

Etiology and Pathogenesis

SIDS has been called by many names and has probably been known since antiquity. Countless theories have been advanced to explain the etiology and pathogenesis. Our own feeling is that viral infection plays a major contributory role. However, neither the cause nor the pathogenesis of SIDS has been established.

It is clear, however, that SIDS is *not* due to suffocation. This is an important point because suffocation is the cause almost uni-

versally suspected by the parents. It is true
that suffocation is sometimes suggested by
the condition of the body (face covered by a
blanket, head pressed into a corner of the
crib, etc.). This appearance may be simulated or exaggerated if, as seems to be the
case, there is a brief but silent struggle during
the agonal episode. However, this interpretation becomes untenable when the total picture is viewed. The sparing of very young infants, the seasonal occurrence and the apparent association with infection—all mili-
tate against the suffocation theory. Infants
found with their faces covered differ in no
way, clinically or pathologically, from the
many who are found with their faces free.
Therefore, epidemiologic evidence leads in-
escapably to the conclusion that the vast
majority of these deaths are not due to
suffocation.

Parents' Concepts of Death

As part of our research study, all infants
who have died suddenly and unexpectedly
in King County are brought to Children's
Orthopedic Hospital and Medical Center for
autopsy. When the autopsy is completed, the
parents are telephoned by the pathologist
(J.B.B.), who explains the results and answers the inevitable questions. After several
days, each family is visited at home by the
project nurse (M.A.P.), who obtains clinical
information and provides counseling. In
addition, assistance is offered to all families
by the Washington Association for Sudden
Infant Death Study, a group of parents who
have lost children from SIDS. Families who
present unusual problems, such as severe depression or lack of affect, are visited by the
project pediatrician (A.B.B.). All the parents
are asked to express their opinions on the
cause of the child's death. The observations
which follow are a result of visits in 225
households of crib death victims.

SUFFOCATION

As mentioned before, parents most often believe that the infant suffocated. Particularly pathetic are the parents who feel they have smothered an infant who was sleeping in their own bed. SIDS used to be called "overlaying," a term originating from the time when adults and infants commonly shared the same bed. A reference to overlaying appears in the Bible (I Kings 3:19). Bodies are often found wedged into the corner of a bed or with blankets over their heads, lending credence to the false belief.

CHOKING

The second most common concept of death is that the child has choked on mucus or regurgitated food. This idea is reinforced by the frequent presence of mucus or vomitus around the mouth. However, this is a *post-mortem* finding resulting from a relaxed esophagus. Parents dwell excessively on the last feeding, harboring doubts about what they, their spouses or their baby-sitters did or neglected to do.

UNSUSPECTED ILLNESS

The third most common concept of the cause of death is a previously unsuspected illness. Parents wish they had taken the baby to the doctor, particularly if he had a cold. If the child was seen by a physician before death, they wonder "what the doctor missed." (Interestingly, physicians themselves harbor the same doubts, often for many years. A discussion of SIDS at a medical meeting invariably turns into a confessional for physicians who feel the need to stand up and re-live their traumatic experience and be convinced of the known facts.)

OTHER CONCEPTS

Other causes of death suggested by the parents include: "The other children in the

145

family must have done something to him"; "hemorrhaging" (often the body has "bruises" over the dependent portions—a postmortem change); "virus affecting the brain"; "air pollution," and "atomic testing." Parents have also attributed the death to "freezing" (the body may be cold when discovered—a postmortem change); "accident—had blood around the mouth" (pulmonary edema often results in bloody froth around the nose and mouth), and "penicillin reaction—had a shot two weeks ago."

Some parents say that the baby "cried himself to death." Often they remember hearing moans and cries during the night or recall that they let the baby cry himself to sleep. They express tremendous guilt over "not going in to check." It is important to explain that this crying did *not* occur during the agonal period.

Finally, an increasing number of parents in our community believe that their babies died of SIDS.

Family Reactions

Because of its characteristic suddenness, SIDS catches parents absolutely unprepared to deal with the death. This problem is intensified by the equally characteristic failure of postmortem examination to provide a satisfactory explanation for the death. The grief reaction seen in families parallels the classic description of this phenomenon by Lindemann.

ACUTE PHASE

In the acute phase, disbelief is the initial reaction. This is followed by considerable testing of reality. Parents often speak of the infant in a combination of present and past tenses. This phenomenon may last for several weeks. Other common reactions are anger, helplessness and loss of meaning of life. Parents are fearful, particularly about

146

the safety of their surviving children. ("I don't want the responsibility of my other children but I can't let them out of my sight.") A fear of "going insane" often occurs in the first few days and may last for several weeks. Guilt is universal and pervasive. Whether they say so or not, most if not all the parents feel responsible for the death of their babies. If a baby-sitter is involved, the situation is even more delicate. Blaming neighbors, relatives and friends augments the even heavier burden of self-incrimination.

The physical symptoms of grief are alarming to the parents and make them think they are "losing their minds." They complain of strange visceral sensations, such as "whirling around," "pressure in the head," "heartache" and "stomach pain." These sensations are accompanied by a sad expression, sighing, insomnia and restlessness. Often the parents engage in excessive activity, such as sweeping, washing or folding clothes.

LATER REACTIONS

In the weeks following the death, there is often marked fluctuation of mood. The parents have difficulty concentrating and frequently express hostile feelings toward their closest friends and relatives. Denial of death is common; the mother may continue to draw the baby's bath or prepare his food. Dreams about the dead child are common, as is a fear of being left alone in the house. One mother sat in the yard for many days when there was no one else at home. Parents with neither business ties nor close family roots frequently move soon after the child's death.

Low-income families are a special problem, particularly since crib deaths are more likely to occur among this group. They rarely have private physicians to give them support. Illegitimacy and poor housing may compound their feelings of guilt. We cannot describe their feelings since these parents tend

147

to be nonverbal. Few of them have asked for help from the Washington Association for Sudden Infant Death Study or participated in its activities. However, they seem to be grateful for the written material on SIDS which we leave with each family. Perhaps it arms them with something authoritative that absolves them from blame.

Letters from Parents

Our research study has been reported several times in the lay press and each article has resulted in a flood of letters from parents. The following letters illustrate the pervasive morbidity of SIDS.

'I AM ABOUT TO LOSE TOUCH WITH REALITY'

"To whom it may concern:

"My baby was crying, so I laid her on a heating pad on her stomach. I thought she had a stomach ache—my mother suggested that I also lay her on a pillow. She stopped crying while I was fixing supper, so I thought she went to sleep. Half an hour later, I found her lying face down on the pillow. She was dead. An autopsy was performed and the coroner told me she definitely did not suffocate. He said she died of pulmonary edema.

"Four weeks later, I read two articles which almost drove me crazy. One was about a lady who smothered her baby and buried it in her subconscious mind. Another was a statement by a pathologist which said, 'A baby deliberately smothered will show autopsy findings not different from those who die suddenly and unexpectedly.' I called the coroner and told him of my fear that maybe I had smothered my baby and buried it in my mind. He assured me she did not smother or the autopsy would have revealed it. I told him about the article the pathologist had written and he told me he didn't understand what was meant by it. As a result, I am now seeing a psychiatrist. I am about to lose touch with reality. Can an autopsy reveal suffocation or not? Please, please answer immediately."

'I TOLD EVERYONE I HAD SMOTHERED HER'

"Dear Sir:

"Our baby was born July 18, 1966. She was so healthy and such a beautiful baby. I took her in for the six-week checkup and to get her shots started. The doctor could find nothing wrong with her.

"My husband works third shift. I woke up sometime Saturday morning, September 17, and found our baby dead. The night before, she was fussy because we had to make about a 200-mile trip to take the 5-year-old to the eye doctor. When I went to bed that night, I put her in bed with me because she was fussing. When I woke up and found her, I got out of bed and carried her around with me for I don't know how long before I finally realized that she was really gone. I went across to the neighbors and they took her and called an ambulance.

"I told everyone I had smothered her sometime during the night. The doctor, the nurses at the hospital and the ambulance driver said she had never smothered. If I could only believe that. Quite a number of people have told us that when someone does smother, they turn black. I still don't have enough nerve to ask my doctor. The county coroner put down Septicemie (sic) which is a disease of the blood. I still can't convince myself that it was the cause of her death. My husband is satisfied that it did happen that way. He said the people at the funeral home said she never smothered.

"We read your article and it helped some. It helped my husband more than it did me. Maybe my letter will help someone. I surely hope so.

"In the article, it said the police questioned some of the parents. They never questioned us. It is a good thing because I

149

don't think we could have held up during that.

"I see babies her size and I break down. It is very hard for me to write this letter, so please excuse my mistakes. We just hope that soon we can have another one. We know there could never be another baby to take her place but we feel it will help some."

'I HAVE NOW LOST TWO BABIES'

"Dear Sirs:

"I would like further information regarding crib deaths, as I have now lost two babies in the same way. I do not seek this information just for myself but also for my parents who are real upset about Jimmy's death.

"My first boy was 6 months, 19 days old when he passed away. My husband at that time accused me of killing him in some way. He kept this up until we got a divorce. I have remarried since and we had a little boy. He passed away on the 30th day of November, 1966. He was 4 months, 1 day old. In both deaths, the autopsy showed that absolutely nothing was wrong with either baby.

"I would appreciate any information that you could send me.

"P.S. I would be glad to answer any questions that you might wish to ask."

The Physician's Role in Counseling

In cases of sudden, unexpected death, the physician should strongly urge that an autopsy be performed. He should explain that the examination is done with care and that it will exclude causes other than SIDS. We have observed tremendous doubt and remorse in several families who did not permit autopsies. After SIDS is confirmed by an autopsy, we stress the points listed in *Table 1*. These may have to be repeated to the parents many times.

SIDS may serve as the focus for parental guilt feelings about the child, such as those

TABLE 1.

Information Offered to Parents of SIDS Victims

1. SIDS cannot be predicted; there is no sound or cry of distress.

2. It is not preventable; death occurs during sleep.

3. The cause is unknown.

4. The cause is *not* suffocation, aspiration or regurgitation. A study by Wooley has shown that covering the faces of babies with blankets does not result in anoxemia.

5. A minor illness, such as a common cold, may often precede death.

6. There is no suffering; death probably occurs within seconds.

7. SIDS is not contagious in the usual sense. Although a viral infection may be involved, it is not a "killer virus" that threatens other family members or neighbors. SIDS rarely occurs after 6 months of age.

8. SIDS is not hereditary; there is no greater chance for it to occur in one family than in another.

9. The baby is not the victim of a "freakish disease." About 10,000 to 15,000 babies die of SIDS every year in the United States.

10. SIDS is at least as old as the Old Testament and seems to have been at least as frequent in the 18th and 19th centuries as it is now. This demonstrates that new environmental agents, such as birth control pills, fluoride in the water supply and smoking, do not cause SIDS. Despite increased attention in the literature in recent years, the incidence of SIDS is not rising.

11. SIDS occurs in the best of families. We have seen it happen in the hospital in infants admitted for minor surgery. (This point is especially comforting to young mothers who may feel inadequate in caring for their infants.)

which occur when the baby was unwanted, punished or left to cry. The universal reaction of these parents is "What did I do wrong?" The key to effective management is to uncover the specific point around which this guilt reaction is centered. Simply documenting for the parents that this factor could not possibly have caused the child's death brings comfort.

The physician should discuss the symptoms of grief with the family, reassuring them that their reactions are normal and that they are not "going insane." Temporary medication may be needed for severe insomnia or anxiety. The physician should watch for signs of marital difficulty brought on by one parent blaming the other or by relatives blaming one of the parents.

Siblings present a special problem since they are less likely to discuss their guilt feelings (for example, wishing at one time or another that the baby had not come into the family). Parents should be encouraged to discuss the death with their children and to be on the lookout for symptoms of emotional disturbance, such as nightmares, bed-wetting and school problems.

Preventive Psychiatry

Preventive psychiatry is vital in averting problems with future babies. Such infants are ideal candidates for the "vulnerable child syndrome." Any mother who has experienced the horror of finding her baby dead in his crib is likely either to reject the idea of having another child or to attempt constant surveillance of the new baby during the first few months of life. Naturally, this anxiety cannot be completely abolished. However, when the physician is aware of the anxiety, he can offer the mother anticipatory guidance.

We stress two points in this type of counseling. First, there is no known way to prevent SIDS. There is also no evidence that even being in the infant's room at the time could alter the outcome. Second, placing a child in a "glass cage" is almost certain to harm his emotional development. Thus, excessive protection is a behavior pattern that is of no proved benefit in preventing SIDS and is potentially injurious to the baby. Furthermore, there are 349 chances out of 350 that the baby will *not* die of SIDS.

Although parents are often responsive to this approach, preventive counseling may have to be repeated many times.

The National Foundation for Sudden Infant Death, 1501 Broadway, New York, N.Y., 10036, is pleased to provide information about SIDS or to assist in the organization of local parent groups.

This study was supported by grants from the National Institute of Child Health and Human Development (H.D. 01659) and the Laura Patience Paschall Memorial Fund.

Response to a Dying Child

by DOROTHY A. PACYNA, M.S.

Ego chill. . .a shudder which comes from the sudden awareness that our non-existence is entirely possible".
                              Erik Erikson

"Nurse, would you get someone to stay with me?"
"Yes, I can stay here with you. . .Is something wrong?"
"I feel so lonely."
"What makes you feel so lonely?"
"My mommy just left. I love her so much, I want her to stay with me forever."
"Tell me about your mommy."
"I wish I could go home and stay with them. I wish my mommy didn't have to go home."
"You want to be home with them. You will. Do you want to tell me about your family?"
He went on to describe vividly each one of them—how they looked and played, pausing apparently to struggle with the thought that they were now so far away. However, he even seemed to manage that obstacle, by describing how far he lived from this particular hospital, and the "very large bridge" he had to cross to get here. Finally, he said: "My name is Mark. What is yours? Will you stay with me until I fall asleep?"

Mark at this time was a complete stranger to me, a child I just happened to meet while I was spending an observational period on the pediatric ward. As I became more familiar with his stress situation, I was offered a tremendous learning opportunity. The "I feel so lonely" was cause for further study and self-growth.

BACKGROUND

For the purpose of understanding the nurse-child-parent relationship and in writing this paper, I used the general systems theory presented by Von Bertalanffy,[1] and its application as an approach toward nursing as presented by Abbey.[2] Basic to this theory is the universal tendency toward the economy of energy in the maintenance of constancy and integrity. A distinction is made, though, between maintaining constancy in inorganic systems and in living systems that maintain themselves despite constant flux. That is, in a closed energy system there is equilibrium. Open energy systems, as in the living organism, maintain themselves through a continuous change of components, so that they are maintaining a state of disequilibrium. In true equilibrium we would be dead. However, all living organisms work toward equilibration, which involves various forces needed to keep the organism near a "norm" in spite of the constant flux.

These forces, such as temperature, pressure, volume, needs, satisfactions, and growth, are the gradient that gives direction to the flux. We are dependent on this gradient for the amount of energy that is expended by the body. The parts of man also must mutually fit and interact with each other if the system is to remain whole. If they do, then we can say that man remains in good health and energy is kept at an optimum level.

All this implies that biological man is a very complex system, involved in a still more complex process of adaptation, attempting to achieve an optimal balance between the synthesizing growth process and the disintegrating death process, while continually interacting with other physical and social systems.

Living systems, throughout their life span, struggle to affirm themselves. Their boundaries are not only open, but also dynamically fluent to the changes about them. Because of these properties, the self must have mechanisms to regulate its energies. The "ego" is the functional part of the psychic apparatus which may be said to perceive, decide, and regulate the network of systems. A complex concept, it controls the mechanisms by which we keep ourselves alive and affirm our very essence. Servodynamic mechanisms develop and serve as feedback loops, working toward equilibration. Affirmed, man is able to withstand the strains of constant change and work toward his primary goals, which lead to survival.

Interestingly, all systems of the person require some degree of optimum tension for function. Above or below this point the system functions imperfectly. The forces that return over the feedback loop may, to an individual, be perceived as stressors, inhibiting his attempts toward equilibration and turning him toward entropy. The degree to which the input is perceived as a stressor affects the level of mechanism needed to work through the actual reorganization of self-maintenance. That is, the greater the stressor, the greater the potential for imbalance within the system, the greater the expenditure of energy needed to maintain the self's identity, and, therefore, the higher the mechanism required for control.

Man, as an open system, is in constant contact with the phenomenon of death. Through our very birth and in infancy we develop an unconscious omnipotence that remains with us throughout life. This omnipotence enables us to effectively deal with the inevitability of our own death, and it is this very defense against death anxiety that is most responsible for its presence.

The perception that one is part of a life cycle destined to end in death requires a conceptual leap; as children emerge from their omnipotent world of timelessness, they begin to discover that people dear to them can be lost. They learn the word "death" and the verb "to die." As the concept formation proceeds the child discovers that adults represent later stages in the life cycle to which he is irreversibly joined. He begins to recognize his own life cycle and perceives the future in terms of space-time. He opens himself to the essential human experience of seeing the finiteness of man.

As long as one is moving, growing, developing, and possessing a strong sense of self, the future is tolerable. The "ego chill"[3] associated with thoughts of death is not threatening. Thoughts of death may become prominent when identity and self are not in continuity, when the ego function is weakened or in isolation or without adaptive ability.

THE PROBLEM TO BE STUDIED

Cancer: Aberrant Cellular Growth

The problem of cancer is a problem of aberrant cellular growth, of disorder and anarchy in the usual patterns of cellular reproduction. Since the feedback control systems that normally stop cellular growth after a certain number of cells have developed are no longer obeyed, all systems of the body are due to be involved. Every resource of the individual with a malignant neoplasm is involved in the body's struggle for control of energy production. The autonomous cells of the neoplasm soon demand and utilize essentially all of the nutriment available.

Medical research is now focused on discovering the cause of the loss of control and discipline in malignant cellular behavior. Antineoplastic drugs and radiation have helped to combat and delay the spread, but there remains no universal cure.

The Threat of Death in a Child

Mark was five and one-half years of age, the oldest of three children in his middle-class family. His first admission to this metropolitan medical center occurred because of leg pain, limping, and palpable swelling of the distal left femur. Following an inguinal lymph node biopsy and x-rays, a diagnosis of osteogenic sarcoma, which is a primary malignant tumor arising in the bone and producing osteoids, was made. Cobalt therapy was prescribed and initiated, and Mark was discharged after nine days of hospitalization. He returned one month later because of recurrences of lymph node enlargement. The day after this second admission, another biopsy was done. The tumor had now vascularized, causing an erythematous left thigh. X-rays demonstrated metastasis to the sternum and lung fields.

Assessment of Mark's internal disorganization was indicative of the ego's struggle to maintain the integrity of the self. Energy deprivation leads to distortion, compensation, and contraction of the self, in this case the self of Mark. He could be considered a low-energy system and his therapeutic environment a high-energy system. The problem became one of supporting the child and his family through the continual struggle for self-affirmation; a problem of the several systems struggling toward equilibration.

No one who has not mastered or fulfilled his potential of existence wants to die, and so Mark asked that those other open systems in his life-space help him toward equilibration — toward the state of self-affirmation. He needed to feel whole, even though near death.

Waechter[4] found that children between the ages of six and ten, even though not directly informed as to the nature of their life-threatening illness, showed considerable preoccupation with death in fantasy, demonstrating feelings of loneliness and isolation and a sense of loss of control over the forces impinging upon them, along with a sense of incapacity to affect the inner and outer environment. They perceived threats through altered affect in the total environment and from the parents' anxiety communicated nonverablly.

THE CHILD'S NEED FOR SUPPORT THROUGH HIS STRUGGLE FOR SELF-AFFIRMATION

Fear of Being Alone

During the eight days of this hospitalization, Mark grieved over the loss of his parents, especially his mother. His ability to express verbally his feeling of loneliness was a positive way of dealing with his loss. Whatever the actual underlying cause, the feeling was very real to him, and an attempt to maintain that reality was provided by telling him that I would return each evening. Such a promise provides continuity during the transition the child must make after his loved ones leave.

Talking may spontaneously lessen the threat, eliciting the gratification needed to maintain self-control. When Mark seemed to be struggling to believe that he would return home again, I verbalized my perception of his feeling, as well as my understanding and acceptance of his having the feelings. He was then able to further express his loss. During periods of loneliness, when Mark exhibited sadness and despair, physical closeness was provided by stroking his hair, rubbing his toes, and letting him sit on my lap.

Long daily visits from Mark's parents provided him great comfort and self-preservation during the day. During the visits, they were encouraged to share in games and stories from home. Exchanges of small tokens of themselves, such as picture drawings, or leaves from the yard trees, also helped to preserve emotional ties and counteract the feelings of loss.

Midway through this hospitalization, Mark seemed to have difficulty evoking imagery of his sisters, pet, and home, tending to talk less of them. Thinking perhaps that he had little energy left, I asked Mrs. L. to bring Mark some snapshots of his "lost love objects." He happily showed them to me the evening they were brought to him, relating descriptions of their activities. Daily use of these pictures in the evening presented fear of permanent loss.

Sleep was used as a protective mechanism against the true loss he felt, as if it allowed him time to regain or conserve lost energy. The sound of any other child crying usually evoked a response such as:

M: "Why is that baby crying?"

N: "What do you think makes the baby cry?"

M: "When Kerry is wet or hungry, my mommy has to go to her. I know my mommy had to go home and put my sisters to sleep. My daddy will be here in the morning. Will you stay with me until I go to sleep again tonight?"

When he knew it was time for me to go, he would close his eyes and turn his head to the side. Sleep came quickly.

Fear of Intrusive Procedures

Daily cobalt had added much to Mark's pain and irritability, and I was beginning to surmise that his irritability was a transference of his anger at his own body. Encouraging Mark to talk about what he was feeling did not help. However, he was, with assistance, able to project his feelings in other ways.

In a hospital coloring book, there were several pictures demonstrating environmental scenes he was presently experiencing. When asked to tell me a story about what he thought was happening in the pictures, he did so in very general terms, almost with indifference to the details.

However, the operating room scene caused a concerned expression to come over his face. After a long pause, he pointed to his groin and said that there had been a "lump" there, and the picture showed where the doctor had taken him to take it out. His hand touched his erythematous thigh, and he verbally responded with: "It hurts. He did it. I hate him." Refusing all attempts to comfort him, he finally regained his self-control. When he was told that it was all right to get angry, he whimpered: "I know he didn't mean it. Let's read that story again about the boy who goes into the woods with his dog." Children often work out some of their problems by reading about others who may have similar problems, just as adults do.

Response to a child in such anger is difficult at times like this. Closeness, through physical and body expressions, and simple explanations are often enough to provide the emotional support needed to endure the trauma. In the "role playing" of parents and staff, the experience is too often characterized by a stoic kind of "make the best of it but let's not talk about it" atmosphere. The anxiety and embarrassment that occurs is found to be more detrimental than allowing the child opportunities to express his feelings in an accepting environment.

Active participation with independent behavior was encouraged in treatments as well as in self-care. It was of primary importance that Mark not be forced into the role of a passive recipient of the services we were to extend to him.

Fear of Death

The fact that someone in the family has died — in this case the paternal grandfather — just before the child becomes ill, is a factor normally conducive to curiosity and anxiety in the child. Mark's grandfather had died several months prior to the beginning of his own illness, following what was described as a debilitating process of cancer. Mark had seen him on several occasions, observing the suffering and wasting of his body and person.

Mr. L. related that following the death, Mark repeatedly asked him to stop smoking, so that he would not get sick like Grandpa, as he had heard that the death was caused by excess smoking. The L.'s had taken their children through the funeral services, supporting them with simple explanations of the burial process, and then prayer for the granting of heaven to their grandfather. Mark had been encouraged to express feelings of sadness, joy, love, and loneliness.

Mark was not felt to have experienced any heightened anxiety following the death, though he did remember his grandfather daily in his evening prayers. Discovering this, I wondered if Mark was not mirroring the observations of his grandfather now in his own altered body image and loss of body functioning. That evening Mark was asked if

159

there was any further preparation for bedtime he would like to make. "Will you help me say my prayers?" He ended a short recitation with, "God watch over Grandpa and make him happy in heaven." With a little encouragement through inquiring if he had remembered everyone that he wanted to, he added. . . . "God bless Mark and hurry and make him better faster, so that he can walk!" He smiled, and closed his eyes, saying "Stay with me until I fall sleep."

Mark took great care to protect himself from expressions relative to the inevitable "no return" thought that perhaps he had come to conceive of as death. The formation of an idea about death could have begun when he was actively initiated into projects of growing and becoming, such as with plants and animals, and an evaporation study.

Early in his hospitalization, Mark verbalized interest in becoming an astronaut. When he became "big," he would go to the moon by himself, returning to visit his parents; they could not go, as he never heard of mommies and daddies going to the moon. He watched the space science TV program with interest. Later, he used the TV manual control to turn the program off, no longer being interested in becoming an astronaut. With a puzzled, sad facial expression, he once asked: "Do astronauts always come back from the moon?" I said "Yes", pointing out that two had just recently returned, but encouraged him to tell me what he thought. "I think so, but I don't want to be an astronaut any more. Rub my toes. Gently!"

His test tube, an evaporation experiment begun at home, was taped by the window. Noticing that the water was nearly gone, Mark asked me one evening to give it to him. Sadly, he described what was happening to the water. The afternoon his mother brought the tube in, his description had been animated and directed with energy toward mastery of the understanding of the evaporation principle; now he seemed in conflict as to the results. He dropped the tube, angrily stating that it took too long for the water to evaporate, and he didn't see where it went in order for it to come back.

Children build their defenses to protect themselves from too much pain. It was not my goal to erect the defenses through my own silence or untruth, but to recognize them when the child uses them and to keep the bridge to reality open. Simply saying "Often when children are not feeling good, it is difficult for them to continue projects started when they were feeling good," gave him the hope for recovery, and he asked to return to working on a picture drawing to send home.

PARENTAL RESPONSES

Mark's parents were both involved in a grief process for they knew Mark's life expectancy was not long. They found it intolerable to think of their child's death as meaningless, and tried to resolve it by searching for an answer or clue as to a miracle cure for their son's cancer. Mr. L. invested much energy in attempting to understand the scientific whys and maybes in treating sarcoma. Hurt by their loss, they could only respond by showing their love and concern. Adults are often blinded to the child's anxiety because of their own fears and concerns and sense of helplessness.

Mrs. L. responded to her son as if in her own capacity to love was rooted the very affirmation of her own existence. She was constantly "on the go," in caring for the home situation and in long daily visits to Mark. Quiet moments and emotional interactions were avoided, as if she were attempting to control time. Her grief work was marked by guilt, by the feeling that she had nothing to offer Mark at this time except herself and the comfort this provided. Also she had been deeply involved with him in the phenomenon of all that lived and grew around them. "If I talk about how I feel, I'll cry and then I'll not be able to go in to him, and he needs me." The use of denial as a temporary defense is an adaptive means of control in an often unbearable life situation.

At first, she saw me as "Mark's friend," and openly expressed their appreciation for my staying with him after they left in the evening. If I returned during the day, my focus remained on Mark, as did Mrs. L.'s. One afternoon, she mentioned that Mr. L. would like me to visit while he was there in the morning.

It was Mr. L. who remained the instrumental force of that family throughout the three months of illness. He cognitively relived the phases of the illness with me during one of my visits. He talked of his shock in receiving the diagnosis, and the unempathetic manner in which the news was imparted to them; of needing to keep their own emotions under control from this terrible hurt, in order to be reassuring to Mark. From the orthopedic surgeon, they would only accept statements that there would be a hopeful turning point. Mr. L. said that deep down he knew it couldn't happen, but the hope kept them alive. The interactions with Mr. L., I believe, facilitated a working through process for him of what was going on in his family's world. He usually just talked, rarely asking questions.

As Mark had invited me to visit him at home, I agreed to the visit with the consent of the parents. It was eighty miles away, and I visited one week following his discharge. Mark had definitely retreated further into a withdrawal state, remaining in his bedroom except for infrequent trips out with his parents. Mrs. L. still remained close to her son, and so my visit was essentially with Mr. L. In one week, he had worked through many, many feelings, trying to grapple with the reality of maintaining the boy's, as well as his family's, self-integrity. As he related what actions he was taking, he asked for clarification of his feelings and those of his wife. He then asked me to share with him my own feelings of how best to help his son during this last stage of his life. He had come to some resolution of the finality of the process. Mark was their only son, and they wanted him home at any cost.

In the end, it was through what system theory would call his "distal systems" that I reached Mark: that is, it was his father who in effect helped his wife to comfort Mark. Mark died at home two weeks later.

THE NURSE'S INTERVENTION IN THE SYSTEM

Withdrawal was a protective device used in the later stages of Mark's illness. It was used when he was experiencing loss of self-control, especially in manipulating very simple body functions, and when he could no longer enter into an easy give and take with his environment. Withdrawal perhaps was inevitable, as energy was lost from his core body systems through the phenomenon of cancer disorganization. The hospitalized, dying child should come to know one nurse, who can be a consistent person in his environment, in order that mutual trust and energy replacement can be provided. The profession of nursing is left with a tremendous challenge: how to better understand and work with the loss of self-affirmation in children who are dying.

If the nurse is to be of assistance to the child and his parents who are dealing with a fatal illness, she must take a place in the environmental high-energy system. She must determine how she can best work with the many forces causing equilibration to prevent entropy from occurring. She continuously evaluates herself as a means of intervening in the feedback circuit, functioning to control variables and modify the reaction by inhibiting, constructing, or stimulating the whole system toward a goal of self-affirmation, even if it is limited.

"Every individual exists in a continually changing world or experience of which he is the owner". . .*Carl Rogers.*

ACKNOWLEDGEMENT

I am indebted to June C. Abbey for her use of general system theory as a focus of her lectures.

REFERENCES

1. Von Bertalanffy, Ludwig: General System Theory. New York, George Braziller, Inc., 1968.
2. Abbey, June C.: A General Systems Approach in Nursing. Unpublished paper, 1969.
3. Erikson, Erik H.: Young Man Luther. New York, W. W. Norton and Co., The Norton Library, 1962.
4. Waechter, Eugenia H.: Death Anxiety in Children with Fatal Illness. Unpublished Ph.D. dissertation, Stanford University, 1968.

Depressive and Psychotic States as Anniversaries to Sibling Death in Childhood

JOSEPHINE R. HILGARD

The concept of an anniversary derives from those cases who have annual symptoms, such as Easter and Christmas neuroses. However, the concept may be extended to other symptoms whose onset can be dated as a recurrence in some form of an event that happened at an earlier time. The recurrence need not be an absolute repetition, but there is something in common between the present and the past that is focal in precipitating the symptoms. Many types of anniversary reactions such as styes [11, 12], ulcerative colitis [1, 2], coronary occlusion [16], and depression [14] are reported in the literature.

Much of the earlier work in which the author and several co-workers collaborated concerned anniversaries that had as their background the loss of a parent by death in the patient's childhood [8].

In a four-year study of consecutive admissions at Agnews State Hospital in California a statistical test of the anniversary hypothesis was made with a sample of 82 women who had lost fathers and 65 who had lost mothers prior to the age of 16 [9]. These were patients, diagnosed psychotic or psychoneurotic, whose first entry to a hospital occurred after marriage and parenthood. The anniversary hypothesis was stated as follows: If a person had lost a parent by death in childhood, and that person, subsequently married, had children, and later became hospitalized for mental illness, the first hospitalization was likely to occur, beyond chance expectancy, when the oldest child of that person was within one year of the age the person was when the parent died. Here an anniversary connection is made through the patient's age at loss and the age of the patient's oldest child. If Mary's mother died when Mary was 8, the hypothesis would state that if she were hospitalized for mental illness after marriage and parenthood, there would be a likelihood that this hospitalization would occur at, or within one year of, her oldest child's eighth birthday. The anniversary hypothesis was not confirmed for women who lost fathers, the age-coincidences occurring only at a rate expectable by chance. For women who had lost mothers, however, there was a significantly greater occurrence of age-coincidences than would be expectable by chance, the appropriate test yielding a p-value of .032 (in a two-tailed test). Thus this aspect of the anniversary hypothesis was supported on a statistical basis.

Of course, we were interested in those many women who had lost a mother in childhood but had *not* become disturbed. These we located in a community sample survey. The kind of reconstructed home that overcame the trauma of parental death has been characterized, and this characterization has been published elsewhere [10]. In the present paper the emphasis is on sibling loss during childhood as it relates to anniversary types of mental illness much later in life. Naturally, sibling loss may have immediate consequences for the surviving child. We shall see later how these childhood cases are related to adult problems.

CASE NO. 1

Stekel [15], in an account of a case he saw many years ago, gives a vivid illustration of the way in which a child can be caught in the parental mourning consequent upon the death of a sibling.

On July 16, 1919, at 8 P.M., Stekel was asked to see a little boy who apparently had had a stroke. The previous afternoon, when the child, named Peperl, had returned home from picking berries, he was happy and merry, but half an hour afterward he lay down in the middle of the room and let his head fall and his extremities relax. His eyes had been closed most of the time, although now and again he rolled them. There were occasional convulsive movements. For 36 hours he had not eaten, had not talked, had not cried. On examination, Peperl appeared hardly alive. His eyes were closed except for brief moments when the lids opened, and the eyeballs rolled. There were occasional uncoordinated movements of the limbs. He did not react at all to talking. When his sister took him up and put him on his feet, he drew his legs in and fell down. Upon neurological examination the child did not utter a sound nor react to his head being pinched. His head wobbled helplessly on his shoulders.

Upon inquiry as to what could have happened in the half hour between Peperl's happy return from berry picking and the onset of symptoms, Dr. Stekel elicited the following:

The boy's mother had given birth to a baby a few hours before, and Peperl had been told of this event. Stekel learned that two years before, a baby had been born and an older child had died the same day. It had also happened that the preceding year the mother had given birth to a baby and on the same day a child of 2 became ill and died a few days afterward of meningitis. The family thought that this time the same thing would happen: when a baby was born, Peperl would become ill the same day and would probably die, too. They had all prayed for weeks over the boy, that he should remain healthy.

Dr. Stekel decided that only through energetic action could he succeed; otherwise any treatment might be useless. He asked the nine women who were already lamenting over the apathetic child to retire from the room.

"When left alone, I took him under his arms and shook him slightly, after which he opened his eyes. At this moment, I saw him drawing his mouth in a grimace for crying. I put him right on the floor and shouted at him: 'Stand up!' The child got up and hurried to his father with a cry, 'Daddy.' Half-an-hour's crying released the tension which had lasted 36 hours. One hour later the child asked for food—how successful was his treatment and how sudden was the change can be seen from the words of his father, 'Doctor, you have driven the devil out of Peperl.'" The night was spent by the child in quiet sleep. When the doctor visited the next day he found that the boy was cured.

Stekel summarized: "When the confinement was expected, the coming event was discussed long beforehand and Peperl, a child of three, was treated most carefully and prayed for. The latter listened to the chatter of the relatives. On the day of the birth he literally is taken ill, while his illness takes the form that he imagined his little brother had when he died, which he gathered from the talking of his parents."

This case illustrates the power of what I have termed the *family saga,* which can exert an unusual influence upon certain patients throughout their formative years. It can be particularly pervasive and assume malignant proportions where the patient's parent has suffered psychotic episodes and the patient throughout childhood has been openly and subtly likened to this disturbed and often disliked individual. Fisk and I have previously reported a series of such cases [7].

CASE NO. 2

Another anniversary of a depressive nature has been reported in a girl older than 3-year-old Peperl. Helena was 11. Dr. Albert Cain [3], to whom I am indebted for this case, said that she had been diagnosed at the pediatric neurology clinic of a midwestern university as suffering from a degenerative neurological disease.

When first seen in consultation, Helena was in a wheelchair, mute, not eating, not moving. It was quickly learned that she had been approaching and had now arrived at the anniversary of her sister's death; she was now 11½, the age at which the sister had died. Helena was treated primarily as an anniversary reaction, and, within a few weeks, she was eating voraciously, talking, walking, and running. Thus Helena, like Peperl, on the anniversary of a death of a sibling had reacted by reproducing death on a symbolic level.

CASE NO. 3

Now we turn to an adult case in which a suicide occurred on an anniversary date. The material presented here was gathered from sources close to the patient. In order to protect the anonymity of the individual and of his family, some coincidences in Matthew's life pattern which give further support to the anniversary nature of the suicide have been deleted. However, enough facts essential for our understanding of the case are presented intact.

Matthew, a distinguished lawyer whose publications showed elements of genius, died at age 43 after taking poison. The suicide occurred the day after his son, Matthew, Jr., reached the age of 12. The anniversary coincidence is with events in Matthew, Sr.'s childhood, when he was a boy of 12: the day after his twelfth birthday, his older brother had died suddenly, and unexpectedly, of encephalitis. Until his death, the two brothers had been separated by a wide gulf in temperament and achievement. While the older brother conformed, was brilliant, and excelled in school work, the younger, Matthew, was belligerent, frequently delinquent, and barely passed in school.

A few months after the older brother's death, the mother, to whom education was all-important, had Matthew tested and discovered to her delight that he was actually very bright. From then on he was cast in the role she had supported so successfully for the older son. Matthew became the anointed one, the older brother— and a brilliant career was launched.

As an adult, however, he told people he felt guilty because his success came only as a result of a death; he had been aware of his intense jealousy and death wishes against his successful sibling. Further, he said that he was convinced that if his older brother had lived, he would have continued as a delinquent and possibly ended a criminal: "I would have lived a life of crime." We see his turning to a career in criminal law as a probable defense.

Who was Matthew, Sr.? Who did he become? In his childhood, an older brother had died to make room for the younger one to succeed. As an adult he identified with his dead older brother and not with his relatively unsuccessful father. Matthew, Sr., as an adult in the role of his successful older brother, stepped aside through death, as his brother had done, to give Matthew, Jr., an opportunity to develop his potential. Matthew, Jr., would accomplish more if the "brother" who inhibited him were dead. In retrospect, this conviction was clear from an enigmatic statement that Matthew, Sr., had made to a friend, close to the time of his son's birth: "I probably have less than 15 years to live." Somehow he sensed that a tragedy was in the making. This strange reference to finite time means that in spite of his brilliant work during the intervening years, the underlying depression continued to his suicide on the day after Matthew, Jr.'s twelfth birthday.

As we find so frequently in this type of "fate neurosis" [6], no treatment had been sought. Knowledge of dynamics would have been important for the subsequent therapy if this first attempt at suicide had not been successful. Those dynamics would include not only the sibling rivalry but the family expectations or sagas which promoted that rivalry. Further discussion of this subject is presented in the section of this chapter on treatment.

CASE NO. 4

In this case, instead of suicide with actual death we have a psychosis with its symbolic death. Fortunately, this case proved treatable.

Evelyn, a 34-year-old housewife and mother of two sons, was hospitalized for three months. The diagnosis was paranoid schizophrenia. Treatment during this period consisted of chlorpromazine, group therapy, and weekly sessions of individual therapy. The husband also was interviewed. The onset of illness dated clearly to the time of the younger son's surgery in January, when the patient was described as depressed and very upset; her nervousness increased so that by February she thought she was hypnotized and she had ideas of reference. She had been hearing the voice of a person she loved, a man who told her about her past, and his voice was recorded on a record player. Further, he was somebody she had known as a child. The social worker who had taken the history and who sat in on the initial staffing with the patient recognized the name which the patient gave for the old friend as actually the name of a brother who had died when they were both children, i.e., Jimmy. When the social worker asked the patient if this was true, the patient immediately lost contact with the group and went into a complete psychotic withdrawal. It was a though a door had been slammed shut. Because of this exaggerated reaction the patient was referred to me.

I found the patient to be quiet, reserved, self-conscious, and clearly exercising extreme control. Most of the history at this point came from the husband and was corroborated later by the patient. After a fall from a bicycle, her brother Jimmy had died at age 10 of a ruptured appendix. Because the mother was on her way home from the hospital, the patient, who was then 8 years old, took the call from the hospital which announced Jimmy's unexpected death. The family had been going through a very deprived period, without adequate food, and the patient confessed to the therapist that her first thought, for which she felt very guilty, was, "Now I will have more to eat." She added that she had wished someone dead, she had had so little and wanted so much to have more. When this was first related, her face wore a bland, unfeeling expression; her only memory of her brother was of his death. She denied any recollection of his appearance, personality, or voice.

The patient's mother said that the patient had been inseparable from the brother; she had worshipped him and he was very tolerant of her. The patient's husband observed that on the first occasions when he met the family, years before, there were discussions of Jimmy's death.

Evelyn's two children, both boys, were 7 and 4 years old. While she felt that the children resembled her dead brother, the family said that the younger boy, Albert, showed a striking physical resemblance to him. Two years before, when the patient had sent her mother a picture of Albert, the mother had responded by sending the patient a picture of the dead Jimmy and it was clear that the two boys, separated by a generation, were incredibly similar in appearance. The operation on Albert that had triggered the patient's illness was a long one, but not serious. It was designed to correct a skeletal deformity.

The onset of the patient's illness definitely was related in time to the son's operation. The psychotic as well as the reality material indicated a close tie to her dead brother. It became apparent that the patient relived an anniversary which reflected a traumatic event from her childhood, i.e., the brother's hospitalization and death. Albert's suffering revived the feelings which Evelyn was unable to cope with successfully after the death of her brother. The strain was aggravated because at the time of her son's surgery, responsibility for the boys was solely hers. Her husband at the time was preoccupied with his work.

Evelyn loved her brother. He was a tolerant, interested, and protective person, almost a parent to her in a home where the parents were involved in their battles. As such, he must have supplied emotional support. She loved her brother but she also hated him, because, being a boy, he got more from their mother. In the light of her envy, the oral deprivation, and her death wishes, his death represented a magical accomplishment accompanied by guilt.

Because of the patient's initial strong reaction to mention of her brother, the therapist waited for several sessions to probe for possible acceptance of some elements of the anniversary hypothesis. Eventually, it was possible to present the anniversary in such a way that the patient could understand that as a child she had been caught in tragic circumstances beyond the capacity of any 8-year-old, and that a present threat had reinstated this old conflict and anxiety. While there were other features to her treatment, Evelyn, in common with other patients who have undergone major traumas on anniversaries, expressed relief that she could understand what had happened. She felt more in command of herself; the future looked less uncertain when the present emotional storm could be seen in perspective as belonging to a known sequence of events.

DISCUSSION AND INTERPRETATION

These four cases all involve sibling death, with the following different aspects:

The Influence of a Saga

A saga was pronounced in Case Nos. 1 and 2. The children's anniversaries belonged essentially to their parents. Sometimes it is the parent who expresses depression on an anniversary, and sometimes it is the child to whom the burden has been passed. The parent, through a series of complex interactions with the child, prominent among which is the saga, transmits the feeling or the action that the child then will enact. So it was with 3-year-old Peperl and with 11½-year-old Helena. Adults such as Matthew carry this saga as a built-in part of themselves.

The Replacement Aspect

Almost inseparable from the saga in a number of cases is the factor of replacement. We catch many glimpses of the replacement motif in the situations reported, the clearest being in Case No. 3.

The problems faced by a replacement child have been well studied and reported by Cain and Cain [4] and by Cain, Fast, and Erickson [5].

It is natural for parents who lose a child to wish to replace the dead child with another one. Where mourning is normal, the home is restructured in an adequate way. Where the mourning is abnormal, however (either excessive or almost completely denied), a burden can be placed on the replacement child. Vincent Van Gogh was a replacement child. Named for his predecessor who died before his birth, Vincent frequently passed the tombstone which read, "Vincent Van Gogh"—the family lived near the cemetery. We recall the extent to which Van Gogh was preoccupied in his painting and throughout his life with the subject of death.

The Development of Excessive Guilt

Up to this point the role of parents has been emphasized in the development of long-range anniversary reactions. In addition, the strength of the child's impulses also plays a major role. Children are in the process of coping with and developing an adequate resolution of their aggressive, competitive, and sexual feelings. The adult cases show the consequences of this.

Malamud and Linder [13] reported an interesting case of an Italian-Catholic woman whose infant child died of an infectious disease. In reaction to this she developed a depression, conceiving the idea that her child's death was punishment for her having been the cause of a younger brother's death. This incident had occurred when the patient was 16, after she had been left in charge of a 7-year-old brother. Their boat capsized, apparently through no fault of hers, and the boy had been drowned. It was clear that the precipitating cause of the illness, the loss of the infant child, was associated intimately with the earlier feeling of guilt over death of the brother. Needless to say, however, the death had occurred in a complex family and personal situation.

The case of Evelyn (Case No. 4) shows how the death wishes at the time of her brother's death produced guilt that doubtless increased her suffering when her son became ill.

Parental Suffering

A fourth aspect of these cases concerns the degree of parental suffering when children reach critical ages, critical events, or critical periods of development. In some adults the painfulness of the

171

relived experience (as indicated by the presence of depression, suicide, or psychosis) is out of all proportion to the suffering reported by the patient or seen by relatives at the time of the traumatic event in childhood. Basic to these reactions is an emotional immaturity in the adult accompanied by overidentification with a child.

Because of growth-inhibiting influences in the home, Evelyn (Case No. 4) had remained a child herself in terms of emotional development. She handled parenthood through close identification with her children in an effort to gain gratification for her own needs.

At the time of her son's operation, Evelyn found herself in conflicting roles; she found herself representing not one parent, but two. In her own role as parent, she wished to be the all-giving person, but she was faced now with the role of a mother who, like her mother, had experienced the death of a son. In other words, when Evelyn had to underwrite and support the painful operation for her son, her role as the all-good mother was gone. In its stead, she retained the role she most feared, that of the mother of a dying child.

Because of Evelyn's identifications, the child who went to the hospital was not only her son but to some extent her brother. She was afraid of repetition of the brother's death.

A "vicious cycle" had been set up. The image of "bad mother" and the fear of death exerted a force toward further regression. As she relived childhood experiences, either through her son's pain or through her guilt as a sister, the suffering became unbearable; the psychosis intervened as an expression of this suffering.

TREATMENT

As might be expected, there is no automatic magic in the anniversary idea as far as treatment is concerned. However, the arrival of a time or event with anniversary significance does constitute a precipitating factor in mental illness which, in the absence of a careful history, often is overlooked. Through careful investigation, with alertness to repetitions, anniversaries can be detected. Calling attention to them may prove helpful by assisting a patient to sort out and understand what was otherwise an incomprehensible and frightening experience.

Evelyn (Case No. 4) expressed it thus when she was interviewed at a checkup three months after her hospitalization: "My son had to have an operation and I became ill because of my brother's death when I was little." In her case the psychotic experience did not become isolated and encapsulated as did its prototype in childhood, largely because the childhood episode was understood and related to the present. The patient emerged from a major illness with greater knowledge about herself.

The therapeutic effort was directed toward the anniversary and, in addition, toward effecting some changes in the relationship of Evelyn and her husband. He realized that it was desirable to spend more time at home; she saw that being the all-giving and indulgent mother to husband and boys had to have limits, and they agreed that it was important to enjoy some activities together the way they had done early in marriage. While these general gains constituted valuable steps, they would not have hit the important target, the question, "Why an illness at this time?" Many elements are present in an illness, but the most significant is the precipitating one. That is where the anniversary hypothesis helped.

A word of caution belongs here. The possibility that the anniversary is present but not implicated always must be considered; in other words, the coincidence may prove to be a false positive. Thus a child may die in an accident at the same age his mother was when she suffered parental loss. The circumstances may not lead to any pathology associated with a traumatic anniversary. In our systematic survey of parent deaths, we met with some of these.

Assuming, however, that in a particular case the evidence for the anniversary is plausible, then the patient is apt to find greater strength in his ability to make sense out of what was a nightmarish disaster to his rational self.

The goal in treatment is to restore the equilibrium that was present prior to the anniversary, with enough insight to prevent or to minimize future occurrences of the same nature. The therapist may sense that broader goals in treatment are feasible, that the patient is capable of more change, and that longer-term therapy will prove useful. Psychotherapy then can continue along conventional lines. A word of warning is called for, however, in regard to the transference in many of these cases. If the patient has been very ill, understanding the transference requires unusual perception and skill on the part of the therapist. This factor should be taken into account before the decision for long-term treatment is made. The patient might be better off if he discontinued treatment but agreed to return if he felt the need for later help.

What of patients with anniversaries who do not recover—those who go on to become chronic invalids at home, in the community, or in mental institutions? This is the question of prognosis. While obviously we are dealing with a complex entity, it is possible to make a general statement: The more pervasive the negative self-image, the poorer the prognosis once the anniversary has precipitated a mental illness. It is possible to obtain a quick evaluation of this negative image by assessing the extent to which the patient reports negative experiences in her childhood. These may have revolved around intense rivalries with siblings, parents, or stepparents, or they may reflect the type of saga that surrounded the child. We know that, by and large, a negative saga provided parents with a convenient capsule for expressing disappointment in, or dislike for, the child; when such attitudes were incorporated as an integral part of the individual, the self-image became a predominantly negative one. Once a decompensation sets in, with its regressive features, including a reliving of childhood experiences, the positive ego with which the therapist must work is difficult to reach and difficult to maintain. For example, we studied cases in which a mother had been hospitalized permanently for psychosis during the patient's childhood. In some of these cases the patient had been watched for signs that she was like this disturbed absent person and, not infrequently, had been told that she was like her. In such cases the negative image was profound, and sometimes treatment problems proved insurmountable. Some of these patients persisted in reenacting the role of the isolated (hospitalized) and misunderstood mother.

In working with anniversary cases it is important to talk with other members of the family. One does not diagnose an anniversary entirely on the basis of what a disturbed patient says; other evidence is needed in order to evaluate a suspected presence or absence of anniversary material. If the anniversary is indeed operating, then there are unconscious elements that the patient is not prepared to talk about. However, a therapist who has clues to them can skirt the problem, coming in ever closer, often with reassurances that make it easier for the unconscious to become conscious. As has been mentioned, an evaluation of the self-image is important. By the time a patient is hospitalized, there is generally a distorted self-image; hence, this task is aided greatly by talking with outside sources.

What would we be inclined to say about treatment if Matthew, Sr. (Case No. 3) had lived? Sibling rivalry had to be understood in a family where parental expectations controlled the sibling roles. Before the brother's death, the saga spoke of pride in the achievements of the older child and of a continual disappointment in the level of achievement of the younger. We recognize that in certain families there exists a type of global competition, on an all-or-nothing basis, where one child is assigned the most successful role and another child is relegated to doing an outstanding job as the least successful. Needless to say, this is an unconscious mechanism; the parents express incredulity at their child's total failure.

Let us assume that after an abortive suicide attempt Matthew had agreed to begin therapy. While the anniversary constituted the trigger, it may well be that an anniversary explanation based primarily on sibling rivalry would not have made sense to Matthew. The problem was much broader than that and, since we must move fast in cases when the individual has come close to suicide, it is important to introduce the larger picture rather soon. The childhood rivalry would have had to be placed in the context of this particular family's expectations. If the therapist handled the rivalry without bringing in these valid extenuating circumstances, guilt would continue despite therapeutic interventions, because such interventions would not hit at the crux of the problem. It is essential that the patient understand the extent to which a global pattern of competition was underwritten by his parents when he was a child. He is then in a better position to see how much his present life reflects this same pattern, i.e., how much he feels that ability, as long as he is alive, always must dominate. A positive concept can be introduced, that of being unique in a number of areas but not in all. It is a relief to patients to realize that they do not have to excel in every area in order to be an excellent person.

Could these steps have permitted Matthew to live? Of course, we cannot know for sure. A negative self-image persisted through childhood to the age of 12; subsequent positive experiences were partially grafted upon, rather than integrated into, the basic personality structure. Since in therapy we need to work with the positive self, the question arises as to how much of that part we could have counted on.

One step would be to correct the negative image up to the age of 12 that had persisted, perhaps unconsciously. There must have been some strength in these early years for him to have been able to shift to the positive role so quickly after his brother's death. Perhaps it could have been pointed out how natural it was, for one in a position of competitive disadvantage, to cease to compete for approved goals and to turn instead to disapproved ones. If this had worked, then the later life might have had enough positive aspects so that a firm picture of himself as a person of strength might have emerged to displace the tendency toward self-destruction.

REFERENCES

1. Berliner, B. The psychogenesis of a fatal organic disease. *Psychoanal. Quart.* 7:368, 1938.
2. Bressler, B. Ulcerative colitis as an anniversary symptom. *Psychoanal. Rev.* 43:381, 1956.
3. Cain, A. C. Personal communication.

4. Cain, A. C., and Cain, B. S. On replacing a child. *J. Amer. Acad. Child Psychiat.* 3:443, 1964.
5. Cain, A. C., Fast, I., and Erickson, M. E. Children's disturbed reactions to the death of a sibling. *Amer. J. Orthopsychiat.* 34: 741, 1964.
6. Chapman, A. H. The concept of nemesis in psychoneurosis. *J. Nerv. Ment. Dis.* 129:29, 1959.
7. Hilgard, J. R., and Fisk, F. Disruption of adult ego identity as related to childhood loss of a mother through hospitalization for psychosis. *J. Nerv. Ment. Dis.* 131:47, 1960.
8. Hilgard, J. R., and Newman, M. F. Anniversaries in mental illness. *Psychiatry* 22:113, 1959.
9. Hilgard, J. R., and Newman, M. F. Evidence for functional genesis in mental illness: Schizophrenic, depressive psychoses, and psychoneuroses. *J. Nerv. Ment. Dis.* 132:3, 1961.
10. Hilgard, J. R., Newman, M. F., and Fisk, F. Strength of adult ego identity following childhood bereavement. *Amer. J. Orthopsychiat.* 30:788, 1960.
11. Inman, W. S. Clinical observations on morbid periodicity. *Brit. J. Med. Psychol.* 21:254, 1948.
12. Inman, W. S. Periodicity. Guy Fawkes Day. *Brit. J. Med. Psychol.* 23:220, 1950.
13. Malamud, W., and Linder, F. E. Dreams and their relationship to recent impressions. *Arch. Neurol. Psychiat.* 25:1081, 1931.
14. Scott, W. C. M. A Psychoanalytic Concept of the Origin of Depression. In M. Klein, P. Heiman, and R. Money-Kyrle (Eds.), *New Directions in Psychoanalysis.* New York: Basic Books, 1955.
15. Stekel, W. Anxiety Neurosis in Children. In W. Stekel, *Conditions of Nervous Anxiety and Their Treatment.* London: Paul, Trench, Trubner, 1923. Quoted courtesy Routledge & Kegan Paul, Ltd.
16. Weiss, E., Dlin, B., Robbin, H. R., Fischer, H. K., and Bepler, C. R. Emotional factors in coronary occlusion. *A.M.A. Arch. Intern. Med.* 99:628, 1957.

PSYCHIATRIC ASPECTS OF SPONTANEOUS ABORTION—II. THE IMPORTANCE OF BEREAVEMENT, ATTACHMENT AND NEUROSIS IN EARLY LIFE

L. Kaij, A. Malmquist and Å. Nilsson

Assumptions of a psychological influence on the course of pregnancy are common in many myths, but generally dismissed by modern scientists. Spontaneous abortions following mental trauma are usually explained as purely coincidental which is probably true in many cases. There is, however, a growing interest in the possibility of a relationship between abortion and various psychological factors of both temporary and more long-lasting nature in contemporary psychosomatic literature. The most current theory in this field, originally proposed by Deutsch, is that abortion may be an expression of a woman's unconscious conflict about her femininity. This conflict is supposed to originate from the early relationship with the parents, especially the mother. The theory is hard to prove and the evidence is indirect, sometimes based upon very small material derived from psychoanalysis of a few women.

In the present paper we wish to report some observations on bereavement, early personal relationships, and neurosis as they were remembered in adult life in an unselected sample of women with a history of spontaneous abortion.

MATERIAL AND METHOD

The sample was derived from a series of 861 women collected for a psychiatric study of the post partum year (Jacobson et al. [1], Kaij et al. [2], Nilsson et al. [3], Nilsson et al. [4], Jacobson et al. [5]). This study provided evidence of poorer post partum mental health in women with a history of spontaneous abortion. The aborters were subjected to a closer matched pair study with controls chosen from those women in the original sample who had no history of abortion (Malmquist et al. [6]). Probands (aborters) and controls were matched for seven variables, namely, age, parity, marital state, length of marriage, occupation, domicile, and the time between the last delivery and the original interview. This matching was almost perfect. Information was derived from the maternity hospital records and two mailed questionnaires. The second questionnaire was sent only to women in the matched sample. This comprised questions on childhood and adolescent neurotic symptoms, whether the parents were alive, with which of them the women had the best relationship during childhood, and a record of her pregnancies and their outcome. After unavoidable losses 84 complete pairs remained for study. As has been repeatedly stressed in previous communications the sample is completely unselected except for the defining criteria.

RESULTS

The results will be presented in terms of intrapair differences, which means that pairs who are concordant for a feature or combination of features are disregarded. The differences are statistically tested by the binomial test under the null hypothesis that it is equally probable that the control and the proband exhibit the feature. As all probability values refer to the binomial curve they can be directly compared as expressions of the strength of the associations.

In 21 pairs the father of the proband was dead and that of the control alive, the reverse being true in 9 pairs ($p = 0.022$), while the corresponding figures for death of the mothers were 13:9 ($p = 0.2611$).

TABLE 1. ASSOCIATIONS BETWEEN BEREAVEMENT, ATTACHMENT AND CHILDHOOD AND ADOLESCENT NERVOUS SYMPTOMS EXPRESSED AS χ^2 VALUES IN THE TOTAL SAMPLE

	Md	F+	M+	N+
Father dead (Fd)	0·302	0·475	0·010	0·035
Mother dead (Md)	—	0·000	0·834	1·430
Best relation to father (F+)		—	—*	1·328
Best relation to mother (M+)			—	0·033
Early neurotic symptoms (N+)				—

* Mutually exclusive variables.

TABLE 2. DISTRIBUTION OF THE PAIRS IN RESPECT OF DIFFERENT COMBINATIONS OF BEREAVEMENT OF FATHER AND EARLY NEUROSIS

		Aborters				
		Father living		Father dead		Total
Controls		No early neurosis N−	Early neurosis N+	No early neurosis N−	Early neurosis N+	
Fl	N−	27	7	10*	8†	52
	N+	11	2	1	2	16
Fd	N−	4*	5	5	1	15
	N+	0†	0	1	0	1‡
	Total	42	14	17	11‡	84

* $p = 0·180$
† $p = 0·008$
‡ $p = 0·006$

TABLE 3. DISTRIBUTION OF THE PAIRS IN RESPECT OF DIFFERENT COMBINATIONS OF BEREAVEMENT OF MOTHER AND EARLY NEUROSIS

		Aborters				
		Mother living		Mother dead		Total
Controls		No early neurosis N−	Early neurosis N+	No early neurosis N−	Early neurosis N+	
Ml	N−	33	12	6	6*	57
	N+	11	3	0	1	15
Md	N−	6	2	1	1	10
	N+	1*	0	1	0	2
	Total	51	17	8	8	84

* $p = 0·124$

In 13 pairs the proband and in 5 pairs the control reported that the best relationship was with the father. The probability that 13/18 is a chance distribution is 0·048. The corresponding figure for best relationship with the mother was 20/42.

Neurotic symptoms during childhood and adolescence were discordantly reported by probands in 21 pairs and by controls in 13 pairs ($p = 0·1151$).

Possible interactions between bereavement and attachment on the one hand and early neurosis on the other were also sought. No intercorrelation between these variables in the total sample was found (Table 1).

Tables 2 and 3 show the distributions of the pairs in respect of the 16 possible combinations

179

TABLE 4. SUMMARY OF THE MOST RELEVANT FINDINGS FROM TABLE 2

Intrapair difference of combinations to be tested		Distribution Aborters/controls	p
Father dead	/ father alive	21 / 9	0·022*
Early neurosis	/ no early neurosis	21 / 13	0·062*
Father dead + early neurosis	/ any other combinations	11 / 1	0·006
Father dead + early neurosis	/ father alive + no neurosis	8 / 0	0·008
Father dead + no neurosis	/ father alive + no neurosis	10 / 4	0·180

* One-tailed test.

TABLE 5. SUMMARY OF THE MOST RELEVANT FINDINGS FROM TABLE 3

Intrapair difference of combinations to be tested		Distribution Aborters/controls	p
Mother dead	/ mother alive	13 / 9	0·130*
Early neurosis	/ no early neurosis	21 / 13	0·062*
Mother dead + early neurosis	/ any other combinations	8 / 2	0·110
Mother dead + early neurosis	/ mother alive + no neurosis	6 / 1	0·124
Mother dead + no neurosis	/ mother alive + no neurosis	6 / 6	—

* One-tailed test.

when both early neurosis and the death of the father and mother respectively are considered in terms of intrapair differences. The interpretation of contingency Tables of this kind is quite complicated as no satisfactory statistical method exists to treat the whole distribution. Therefore the cells, rows and columns must be considered separately. Summaries of the relevant features are given in Tables 4 and 5 respectively. As we had no *a priori* hypotheses for this part of our study two-tailed tests of significance are used in the following.

The most striking features in Table 2 are the marginal values of the 4th row and the 4th column. Among 12 pairs where one member had a dead father and a history of early neurotic symptoms and the other member any other combination, the proband reported the first-mentioned combination in 11 pairs and the control in only one. This distribution is unlikely to be due to chance ($p = 0.006$). The main part of this difference can be attributed to the two opposite cells, the upper right vs. the lower left, i.e. pairs where one member had a dead father and early neurosis, the other a living father and no neurosis. The distribution 8:0 pairs is also highly significant ($p = 0.008$). The combination dead father + no neurosis vs. living father + no neurosis is still to the disadvantage of the aborters (10:4), but this distribution is not significant ($p = 0.1800$). Thus our results indicate that aborters more often than non-aborters have a dead father and that the difference is emphasized if early neurotic symptoms are combined with the bereavement. Bereavement of the father in the absence of early neurosis is less disadvantageous.

The corresponding analysis of the influence of the bereavement of the mother shows a similar trend but none of the differences reaches a significant value (Tables 3 and 5).

Table 6 shows the distribution of the 36 possible intrapair combinations of childhood relationship and early neurosis. This very unwieldly Table is condensed in Tables 7 and 8. The relevant data are summarized in Tables 9 and 10. In Table 7 the relationship with the father is contrasted to "not-best" relationship with the father, i.e. best relationship with the mother or equally good relationship with both parents. In Table 8 the relationship with the mother is analogously "purified". The orders of the rows and columns are slightly modified for easier reading.

In Table 7 the most striking feature is that best relationship with the father in the absence of early neurosis (4th row and column) was more common in aborters than in controls (10:1, $p = 0.012$). In 8 pairs the probands had best relationship with the father and denied early neurosis, the controls had "not-best" relationship with the father and no neurosis, while the reverse was true in one pair (right upper and left lower cells respectively). The probability that this distribution is due to chance

180

TABLE 6. DISTRIBUTION OF THE PAIRS IN RESPECT OF DIFFERENT COMBINATIONS OF ATTACHMENT TO PARENTS AND EARLY NEUROSIS

Controls		Aborters						Total
		Best relation to mother M+		Equally good relations to both parents FM		Best relation to father F+		
		No early neurosis N−	Early neurosis N+	No early neurosis N−	Early neurosis N+	No early neurosis N−	Early neurosis N+	
M+	N−	7	6	11	3	3	1	31
	N+	0	0	2	0	1	1	4
FM	N−	10	5	9	5	5	1	35
	N+	2	0	4	2	1	0	9
F+	N−	0	0	1	0	0	0	1
	N+	2	1	1	0	0	0	4
	Total	21	12	28	10	10	3	84

TABLE 7. DISTRIBUTION OF THE PAIRS IN RESPECT OF DIFFERENT COMBINATIONS OF ATTACHMENT TO FATHER AND EARLY NEUROSIS. CONDENSED DATA FROM TABLE 6

Controls		Aborters				Total
		F−		F+		
		N−	N+	N−	N+	
F−	N−	37	19†	8*	2	66
	N+	8†	2	2	1	13
F+	N−	1*	0	0	0	1
	N+	3	1	0	0	4
	Total	49	22	10	3	84

* $p = 0.040$.
† $p = 0.054$.

TABLE 8. DISTRIBUTION OF THE PAIRS IN RESPECT OF DIFFERENT COMBINATIONS OF ATTACHMENT TO MOTHER AND EARLY NEUROSIS. CONDENSED DATA FROM TABLE 6

Controls		Aborters				Total
		M−		M+		
		N−	N+	N−	N+	
M−	N−	15	6	10	5	36
	N+	6	2	4	1	13
M+	N−	14	4	7	6*	31
	N+	3	1	0*	0	4
	Total	38	13	21	12	84

* $p = 0.032$.

TABLE 9. SUMMARY OF THE MOST RELEVANT FINDINGS FROM TABLE 7

Intrapair difference of combinations to be tested		Distribution Aborters / controls	p
Best relation to father	/ equal or best relation to mother	13 / 5	0·048*
Best relation to father + no early neurosis	/ any other combinations	10 / 1	0·012
Best relation to father + no early neurosis	equal or best relation / to mother + no early neurosis	8 / 1	0·040
Best relation to father + early neurosis	equal or best relation / to mother + no early neurosis	2 / 3	—
Equal or best relation to mother + early neurosis	equal or best relation / to mother + no early neurosis	19 / 8	0·108

* One-tailed test.

TABLE 10. SUMMARY OF THE MOST RELEVANT FINDINGS FROM TABLE 8

Intrapair difference of combinations to be tested		Distribution Aborters / controls	p
Best relation to mother	/ equal or best relation to father	20 / 22	0·323*
Best relation to mother + no early neurosis	/ any other combinations	14 / 24	0·144
Best relation to mother + no early neurosis	equal or best relation / to father + early neurosis	0 / 6	0·032
Best relation to mother + no early neurosis	best relation to / mother + early neurosis	4 / 4	—
Best relation to mother + early neurosis	/ any other combinations	12 / 4	0·012

* One-tailed test.

is 0·040. Thus best relationship with the father was more strongly correlated with abortion in the absence of neurosis.

In the case of best relationship with the mother the interesting difference is found among pairs where both members had such a relationship but differed in respect of early neurosis (Tables 8 and 10). In all 6 pairs the neurotic was the aborter ($p = 0·032$). Pairs in which one member had best relationship with the mother and was neurotic and the other had any other combination were distributed as 12:4 to the disadvantage of the aborters ($p = 0·012$).

DISCUSSION

Hypotheses concerning a psychological influence in spontaneous abortion are based on psychoanalytical theories of the importance of identification as expressed, i.e. in Freud's theory of the Oedipal complex. Some authors (Mann [7], Javert [8], Tupper [9], Grimm [10], Cappon [11]) have found an unsuccessful identification with the mother to be common in habitual aborters and assumed a causal relationship. The mothers are described as possessive, dominating, punitive and intolerant, while the fathers are absent, dead or detached. As a result the relation to the mother is either submission to her domination or rejection.

182

In the latter case we believe that the woman may attempt to identify with the real or, when he is not available, an idealized father. Any of these solutions may result in a failure to achieve a normal psychosexual development into mature femininity of which a successful motherhood is considered the final proof.

It is very difficult to test these theories in a scientific way. The results are often based upon small samples derived from psychoanalysis of a few women. The studies have further been almost exclusively concerned with women with habitual abortion to which no organic cause could be traced.

Our sample differs from those of earlier studies in that it is not based upon aborters but upon parturient women with at least one abortion in their history. Thus we have not selected habitual aborters nor tried to exclude women with organogenic abortions. Hence it can be safely concluded that the sample represents the most "benign" group of aborters. There were 25 women with a history of more than one abortion, but this group is too small to permit separate statistical treatment.

Possible bias factors as well as our method have been extensively discussed in previous communications. The method is admittedly superficial but has the advantage that the women are not aware of the aim of the investigation, nor of the selection criteria.

The results supply some indirect evidence of the above-mentioned theories.

Thus bereavement and especially loss of the father seem to have a detrimental effect in some women. This effect is more pronounced in those who have had childhood or adolescent neurotic symptoms than those without.

A closer attachment to the father on the other hand was stronger related to abortions in the absence of early neurosis. Early nervous symptoms were more strongly associated with abortions in combination with better relationship with the mother and contrariwise closer attachment to the mother was most favourable in the absence of early neurosis.

It is clear from the correlation matrix (Table 1) that bereavement, attachment and early neurosis are not correlated in the total sample. The question is whether the different associations in the aborters are due to different mechanisms or whether they can be tracked back to some common denominator.

This question can naturally not be answered but it seems feasible to make an attempt to construct a model, bearing the hypothesis of an unsuccessful female identification in mind.

The importance of the absence of the father or a better relationship with a living father might be that in fact the mother was "bad", i.e. inacceptable as an identification object. In the case of the bereavement this might imply that the daughter was at the mother's mercy and the conflict laid bare, thus resulting in neurotic symptoms. A living father on the other hand might be accepted as an identification object and "protect" his daughter from symptom neurosis. In the first case the result might be a personality pattern as one of the two described by Tupper which also corresponds to the type of aborters in the samples of Mann, Grimm and Javert, i.e. dependent immature women; while the women who were more attached to their fathers might belong to Tupper's second type, i.e. the "independent women who seek their rewards in the men's world".

Whatever the mechanism or mechanisms may be, the hypothesis of the importance of female identification in abortion is supported by the fact that best relationship with the mother in the absence of early neurosis is associated with a negative history of abortion.

A quite independent observation may further support the theory. In a sample of identical twins discordant for motherhood examined by two of us (Kaij and Malmquist [12]), there were 8 pairs in which one member was more favoured by the mother, the other by the father. In 7 of these pairs the twin favoured by the mother was herself a mother, a distribution significantly different from chance.

Alternative explanations to our findings are hard to find. A reverse causality, e.g. that an abortion should distort the memory of relationship or nervous symptoms in childhood, is hardly conceivable particularly considering hard data such as bereavement.

The importance of our findings may be hard to parcel out among all possible explanations of spontaneous abortion. However, it seems necessary to at least consider psychodynamic aspects when dealing with this problem.

SUMMARY

Eighty-four women who had had spontaneous abortions and a control sample matched for seven relevant variables were chosen from an unselected series of parturient women. The women were interviewed with the aid of a mailed questionnaire in respect of parental attachment, bereavement and childhood neurotic symptoms.

Bereavement, especially the loss of the father was more common amongst aborters than controls, and the difference was more pronounced when bereavement was combined with childhood neurotic symptoms. Compared to their controls the aborters were more often closer attached to their fathers during childhood. This was especially true in the absence of early neurosis.

The implications of the findings are discussed.

REFERENCES

1. JACOBSON L., KAIJ L. and NILSSON Å. Post-partum mental disorders in an unselected sample. Frequency of symptoms and predisposing factors. *Br. Med. J.* 1, 1640 (1965).
2. KAIJ L., JACOBSON L. and NILSSON Å. Post-partum mental disorder in an unselected sample. The influence of parity. *J. Psychosom. Res.* 10, 317 (1967).
3. NILSSON Å., KAIJ L. and JACOBSON L. Post-partum mental disorder in an unselected sample. The psychiatric history. *J. Psychosom. Res.* 10, 327 (1967a).
4. NILSSON Å., KAIJ L. and JACOBSON L. Post-partum mental disorder in an unselected sample. The importance of the unplanned pregnancy. *J. Psychosom. Res.* 10, 341 (1967b).
5. JACOBSON L., KAIJ L. and NILSSON Å. The course and outcome of the post-partum period from a gynaecological and general somatic standpoint. *Acta Obst. Gynec. Scandinav.* 46, 183 (1967).
6. MALMQUIST A., KAIJ L. and NILSSON Å. Psychiatric aspects of spontaneous abortion. A matched control study of women with living children. *J. Psychosom. Res.* 13, 45 (1969).
7. MANN E. C. Habitual abortion. *Am. J. Obst. Gynec.* 77, 706 (1959).
8. JAVERT C. T. *Spontaneous and Habitual Abortion.* McGraw-Hill, New York (1957).
9. TUPPER C., MOYA F., STEWART L. C., WEIL R. J. and GRAY J. D. The problem of spontaneous abortion. I. A combined approach. *Am. J. Obst. Gynec.* 73, 313 (1957).
10. GRIMM E. R. Psychological investigation of habitual abortion. *Psychosom. Med.* 24, 369 (1962).
11. CAPPON D. Some psychodynamic aspects of pregnancy. *Can. Med. Ass. J.* 70, 147 (1954).
12. KAIJ L. and MALMQUIST Å., *to be published.*

Object Loss and Grief

The Linking Objects
of Pathological Mourners

Vamik D. Volkan, MD

S TUDIES conducted since 1966 in the psychiatric department of the University of Virginia have
disclosed the adoption and use of inanimate objects by
pathological mourners. These studies defined the phenomenology of pathological grief in adults, recorded the impact of "known" loss and the attempted restitution that
followed it, and assessed the effectiveness of a brief psychotherapy of "re-grief work" for pathological mourners.[1-5]

The Recognition and Description of Linking Objects

The data for this report come from a study of 55 patients whose diverse symptoms had appeared on the clinical level at the time of the loss of a loved/hated person,
immediately following the loss, or on the anniversary of
its occurrence. Sixteen of the 55 patients were treated in
re-grief therapy of four or five weekly sessions for three
or four months, with follow-up according to the patients'
availability. Seven of the 55 went into psychoanalytic psychotherapy on the basis of two or three visits a week, and
one went into a successful psychoanalysis after his re-

A preliminary version of this paper was read before the fall meeting of
the American Psychoanalytic Association, New York, December 1970.

griefing. The long-term observation possible in the case of these eight patients permitted extended assessment of their reactions to death and the part grief played in their psychiatric difficulties. The rest of the group of 55 were, with few exceptions, inpatients averaging between 30 and 40 days of hospitalization during which they were treated by psychiatric residents under the supervision of the investigators. The age range of the patients, who were of both sexes, was from 17 to 45.

Reactions to loss can be seen as distributed along a spectrum. Engel[6] suggested that uncomplicated grief appearing at one end of the scale might be classified as an illness since it has a discrete syndrome with relatively predictable symptomatology. Bowlby[7] described three phases of mourning. Parkes[8] amplified the scale to include four phases—numbness, yearning (to recover the lost object), despairing disorganization, and, finally, behavioral reorganization.

On the other end of the scale from uncomplicated grief appears that reaction to loss which has turned into a depression or other identifiable neurotic, psychosomatic, or psychotic clinical entity so that the clinical diagnosis of pathological grief reaction is inappropriate. I have attempted[3,4] to show that between these two extremes lies the clinical entity of pathological grief, with predictable symptomatology, a psychodynamic constellation, and characteristic findings. Among these findings was the typical use of certain objects by pathological mourners, most of whom were aware that they had invested the objects with symbolism but unaware of just what was being symbolized.

These objects can be placed in four categories, with some overlapping in classification: (1) objects which had been worn by the deceased, like a dress, a watch, a ring, or eyeglasses; (2) objects which had not been worn (in the usual sense) by the dead but which could be viewed in the psychoanalytic sense as an extension of their bodies, like a camera—an extension of visual intake; (3) objects with realistic or symbolic resemblance to the deceased, often a photograph; and (4) objects at hand when the news of the death came, or present at the funeral—things that could be considered "last minute objects" related to the last moment in which the deceased was seen as alive.

The objects to which the pathological mourners clung had no common physical characteristics such as softness, color, or odor. They were not put to use in the way for which they had been designed. A watch previously belonging to a dead person, for example, was never worn, but kept in a drawer. One patient did shave at times with his dead father's electric shaver, which had become a linking object, but he did so only with great anxiety. He did not regard it as a serviceable tool, and was unable to clean it after use, fantasizing the merging of hairs from his face with those from his father's.[5]

Linking objects are jealously protected. One patient kept his murdered sister's identification bracelet hanging from the sun visor of his car, and when the car was demolished in an accident this was the only thing he saved, going to great lengths to retrieve it from the wreck. The linking object must be available to be looked at or to be touched whenever the unconscious need arises, but physical distancing from it is always possible. In some cases it must be avoided, although the patient requires reassurance of its availability. The man who kept the watch in a drawer, for example, had arranged for it to be out of sight but within reach. One patient used his father's broken cameras as linking objects. They hung for 14 years after the death in a clothes closet where the patient could glimpse them each morning as he dressed. The linking object characteristically exerts an eerie fascination for the mourner. One of our patients demonstrated this by locking himself in a room and gazing at his dead father's picture until he sensed his reincarnation.

In these ways linking objects are clearly differentiated from *inherited items* simply put to appropriate use. One who has completed his mourning successfully may, for example, wear a ring previously worn by the deceased, and be able to do so without anxiety, feeling no undue compulsion to protect it, and no conflict between a desire to see it and a wish to keep it out of sight. In this case, the ring would not be a linking object but a keepsake, the difference lying in that indefinite area between the pathological and the normal. The more ambivalent the relationship with the one who died had been, the more likely it is for something inherited to become a linking object.

Theoretical Considerations

An extensive review of the literature on the psychodynamics of mourning is not required here, nor is it necessary to point out the similarities and dissimilarities of mourning and depression, which have been studied as twin subjects since the publication of Freud's *Mourning and Melancholia*.[9] Siggins'[10] critical survey of the literature on mourning, and Gaylin's[11] collection of relevant papers show changing theoretical formulations. To understand linking objects, however, it is important to recognize that the state of the ego in true pathological mourn-

188

ing is different from that in depression. In the latter there is a state of helplessness,[12] but in pathological grief there is a chronic hope and a continuing effort to regain the lost one.[3,4] Bowlby[7] defined a "persistent seeking of reunion." This process of searching for the deceased is unconsciously intensified, and it is habitual and specific enough to be called a mechanism of defense—defense mainly against the tension of ambivalence and the eruption of derivatives of those aggressive and libidinal drives originally directed toward the deceased.

The introject of the deceased is kept as his representation like a foreign body within the mourner, who continues to have a conflictual relationship with it. Three of our patients actually referred to a foreign body in the chest; during re-griefing they exhorted it to leave them, shouting, "Get out! Get out!" A detailed account of this appears elsewhere.[5] If the boundaries of this foreign body disappear, and it melts into the rest of the patient's personality, we speak of identification with the deceased. Some identification may be adaptive, some may be symptomatic. Total identification does not occur in the typical pathological mourner, as Pollock[13] also demonstrated. As Abraham[11] said long ago, the purpose of identification is "to preserve the person's relation to the lost object." The patient may be so convinced of the persistence of the dead person within himself that he engages in continual inner conversations with him. One patient, whose brother had drowned, not only reviewed conflictual issues in these inner conversations, but even sought from the introject (his brother's) advice about his daily affairs.

Temporary identification with the deceased also occurs in pathological grief through *merging*, as Schafer[15] described it. His view showed merging with another to be essentially a phenomenon of the primary process which, like other primary process phenomena, may be represented consciously in spite of its being more customarily an unconscious experience.

Approaches to complete merging of subjective self and object are evidenced by a high degree of fluidity or ambiguity in localizing attributes and experiences in the subjective self or the object, as if self and object freely substitute for each other, as if interest in individuation has been pretty much suspended, and as if, ultimately, it is undifferentiated unity that is experienced or sought rather than the relation of one person to another.

The clinical difference between relating to an introject and actually merging with the deceased is clear. The introject is regarded as if it had existence of its own. In merging, however, the mourner loses awareness of his differentiation from the one he mourns, in a total but tempo-

189

rary identification with him. This transient experience is usually abrupt, and many patients have spontaneously used the word "merging" in speaking of it. An example can be seen in the patient who, throughout a therapy hour, feels that the tone of his voice and the gestures of his hands are not only his but those of the one he mourns. It is usual for such an experience to be "shaken off," only to reappear suddenly on occasion.

In pathological grief the psychodynamic process of the work of mourning is frozen. Indeed, the pathological mourner frequently uses the word "frozen" in describing his "typical" dream[2-4] in which the struggle of keeping the dead person alive appears. The lost one is both killed and not killed, is both buried within the mourner, and not buried within the mourner. Excessive use of the splitting mechanism, as Freud showed,[16,17] creates a fence-sitting man who is ready to jump to either side—to acceptance of the reality of the loss or to the other possibility of keeping the deceased alive.

The meaning of the linking object as a tie with the deceased is clarified by this understanding of the psychodynamics of the pathological mourner. The linking object belongs both to the deceased and to the patient himself, as if the representations of the two meet and merge in an externalized way. The ambivalence which had characterized the relationship with the dead one is invested in the process of distancing the object in a representation of psychic distancing, but at the same time keeping it available. The mechanism used here resembles the one used by the so-called satellite patients Corney and I described,[18] in whom ego development arrested at the separation-individuation phase of childhood found a malignant compromise in the adoption of the role of satellite to the mother—or, in later life, to her substitutes.

The satellite is suspended, as it were, between engulfment by regression to symbiosis with the mother and annihilation through separation from the mother. For the satellite to move in either direction (regression or progression) would precipitate a clinical psychotic state.

In these individuals the experience of physical separation from the mother usually becomes symbolized, representing the experience of psychic separation. Like the satellite doomed to orbit around the mother but able to control the distance from her, the pathological mourner, doomed to keep his linking object, can control its distance.

All of the psychoanalytic literature on identity formation is relevant to the problem of object loss and the mechanisms of introjection, identification, projection, and projective identification. However, in earlier times introjection and identification were emphasized. I have already referred to the pathological mourner's attempts at reunion with the lost one by means of introjection. The presence of the linking object indicates a special emphasis in pathological mourning on projection and externalization, in the broadest sense of these terms.[19] The linking object itself is evidence of the externalization of what is painful—the work of mourning and the persistence of external object relationship. Jaffe[20] has reemphasized the dualistic and conflictual nature of the mechanism of projection which

involves the psychic apparatus in a continuously ambivalent mode of dealing with object relationship. On one end of the continuum, the annihilation of the object is predominant; while on the other, the identification with and preservation of the object is paramount.

The dual role of the linking object, which evokes both the impulse to destroy it and the impulse to preserve it, can be understood in this light. The two opposing impulses can be maintained externally in a dynamic conflict which is not a dominant feature of depression and which thus further differentiates it from pathological grief.

In the cases illustrating these theoretical considerations, only material relevant to the genesis of pathological grief and to the significance of linking objects will be reported.

Case Abstracts

CASE 1.—A 23-year-old married man, whose course through regriefing and subsequent psychoanalysis has been reported elsewhere[5] was the oldest son of a surgeon and a manic-depressive mother whose hospitalization on several occasions during his childhood left her son sensitized to separation. Her instability led him to depend on his own resources. He developed into a child who masked his basic dependence by an air of great self-reliance and a fiercely protective interest in his rights.

He was frightened during his childhood and puberty by the seductive behavior his mother exhibited toward him during her manic phases. In a dream reported during his later analysis, the Gulf of Mexico represented the mother who could engulf him. He felt that she had engulfed his father during the act of intercourse. The father seemed bewildered by his wife's behavior, and was dominated by an older brother and his own father, a veritable clan leader. At the death of the clan leader the patient's father asserted himself, gained prestige in his profession, and followed his successful brother to the fashionable part of town. He took an interest in his son, prepared him for medical school, and was the only one to favor his projected marriage.

The son responded with constructive attempts to identify with him. The father had made a point of checking the boy's testicles during his puberty to assess his sexual potency, and this interest had given the child misgivings, leaving him with the feeling that his only proof of being a man would be to impregnate a woman. When his father died suddenly in his sleep at a vacation resort, the patient was 22 years old, and unable to go through an uncomplicated course of mourning. In an obvious effort to prove his manhood, he made his fiancee pregnant. On the first anniversary of his father's death, the patient was hospitalized with a severe case of anniversary reaction, showing symptoms of pathological grief.

One of his linking objects was a photograph of his father which his mother had sent him after the death. Except for an occasional glimpse he was unable to open the folder enclosing the picture. His father's corpse was flown back from the resort where he had died, and the son experienced conflict about looking at it, deciding finally not to do so. The covered photograph can be seen as a representation of the father in his coffin. The patient tried to resolve the work of grief in an externalized way by placing the photograph where it was dampened by slowly leaking water in a representation of (1) his tears over the dead father, and (2) an attempt to repeat the death scene, which had followed a day of snorkeling during which, his son felt, the father had probably taken enough sea water into his lungs to account for his subsequent heart congestion. During his treatment the patient gave clinical evidence that he was afraid of weeping lest he be drowned in his tears. Identification of the linking object that appeared during his re-griefing was validated by the fact that in the re-griefing process it lost its magic. The patient then voluntarily framed it and made a place for it on his study desk. No other linking object replaced it during his three years of psychoanalysis.

CASE 2.—A 27-year-old Jewish patient went through re-griefing and is now in the second year of three-times-a-week psychotherapy. He was born in Nazi-occupied Belgium, and his first 17 months were spent in hiding. He had internalized the anxiety and helplessness felt by his parents during his childhood, and his capacity to express emotion had necessarily been stifled. At the age of 7 he accompanied his parents to the United States, and in later life somatized some of his affective expressions as his father had done. The father had hoped for success in the new world, but developed a survivor's syndrome[21] and died in an iron lung after a year of suffering from multiple sclerosis. His son was 13 when the death took place.

The patient had taken care of his father, and at his death could not discharge the anger which would have been an indication of the separation. He identified his aggression with the Nazis; it did not surface at all except when it overflowed in an occasional temper tantrum. For 14 years he exhibited symptoms of pathological grief and attempted reunion with his father. His collection of linking objects included his father's two cameras, a pair of sunglasses, and a watch. All were broken, representing the father broken with multiple sclerosis. At times the son thought of having them repaired, but did not do so. This response was consistent with his unconscious fantasy of his father's being both alive and dead.

One of the cameras, which hung like a skeleton in his closet, had a syringe-like "time-delayer." This represented the delayed work of mourning as well as the syringe which the patient had used in giving injections to his sick father. The injections evoked ambivalence. They were given as a life-saving measure, but after completing them the son had to carry the shrunken body to a toilet, and there he fantasized flushing it away. The syringe-like object also represented a snake with which the patient had tried to resolve his work of mourning in an externalized and symbolic way. He caught the snake six months after his father's death, put it in a bottle of acid, and watched it decompse like the dead man's body in its grave. Through the mechanism of internalization he simultaneously developed boils—his own skin started to "rot."

His other linking object was the watch with his father's initials, S.M., engraved on it in the reverse of M.S. (multiple sclerosis). The broken watch represented the broken father, and the patient felt compelled to keep it in a drawer as a link with him. When we discussed this in therapy he volunteered that he could see why it had been so hard for him to win his M.S. degree. Because of the tension generated by ambivalence, a distancing from the father with his M.S. (multiple sclerosis) was a necessity. This patient is in his second year of psychoanalytic psychotherapy on a three-times-a-week basis after his initial re-griefing. His linking objects have lost most of their magic, but he still clings to them and from time to time asks his therapist about disposing of them. The therapist has refrained from giving advice or suggestions about them.

CASE 3.—A 38-year-old man had a successful hiatus hernia operation a year before the death of his 79-year-old father. Soon after the death, the patient's surgical scar began to give him pain, and he became impotent. It was necessary to hospitalize him on the first anniversary of his father's death because of these symptoms.

The patient was obsessed with fear that physical activity would reopen the scar on his chest. It became evident that, appearing as it did on a hairy skin surface, it represented a vagina to him. He was regressed to dependency, and needed care from his wife and mother, toward both of whom he felt unexpressed rage. As a child he had noticed his mother's preference for his younger brother, and had reached up to his father in an effort to pair with him. However, pre-oedipal sibling rivalry and a sense of being rejected by his mother interfered with the development of normal oedipal conflicts, renunciations, and identifications. Accordingly, motivated by an unconscious attempt to avoid the unpleasant aspects of the pregenital phase by reaching up the ladder of psychosexual development, he became preoccupied with being in his father's company and being an athlete. Similar psychodynamics in another case are described elsewhere.[22]

This attempt did not lead to a real solution of the oedipal conflict nor to the establishment of an adaptively useful identification with the father. The original oedipal father of the external world survived in the acutal father during the post-oedipal phase of the son's conflict. Although in the course of time he married and engaged in his own profession, the patient remained geographically close to his father. The hiatus hernia operation was a symbolic castration and also an obstruction to the satisfaction of

193

his oral needs, since it involved his stomach. The operation was performed a year before the death of the father, who still predominantly represented the original external oedipal father. It was then that the patient reported that "Father Time caught up with" him. It was clear that Father Time was his father who, like the symbolic representation of Time, had a beard, lived a long time, and died at one minute after midnight. In the mind of this patient, Father Time, his own father, and the surgeon who had put a "vagina" in his chest were all condensed.

Besides these symptoms, the patient exhibited the typical characteristics of pathological mourning. He could not allow his father to die, and kept attempting reunion with him. Among his symptoms of pathological grief was his use of his father's old car as a linking object. Although he was poor he spent as much as $1,000 yearly to keep the car and its motor in good condition in spite of the fact that he never took it out on the road. The fate of his linking object subsequent to his discharge from the psychiatric service is unknown, as we had no further communication with him after he left the hospital.

CASE 4.—An unmarried black woman in her early 30s exhibited a pathological grief reaction after the death of her mother. While she realized intellectually that her mother had died, her behavior denied this. She spent her days fantasizing her mother as being still able to observe her actions and, perhaps, being able to "come back."

The patient was the youngest of six children. The mother-child unit had been disturbed because the mother had been severely burned when the child was six months old. Bedfast for a year, she had been unable to function adequately as mother or wife. The continued symbiotic relatedness turned into a sadomasochistic relationship between mother and daughter, the closeness of which was reflected in the patient's need to keep her mother alive after death. Although the other siblings moved away, the patient had remained at home with her mother, who became a widow and, during the last ten years of her life, an amputee because of diabetes. To care for her mother the patient had given up college scholarships, opportunities for a good marriage, and any independent social life. Although she sometimes wished her mother would die, she was in the habit of telephoning her on a regular schedule three times a day "to see if she was OK." She slept at night at the foot of her mother's bed and awakened periodically "to make sure she was still alive."

After her death the mother often appeared in her daughter's fantasies and dreams, wearing the red robe in which she had died. The patient had purchased this luxurious robe for herself during one of her infrequent holidays, but had ended up by presenting it to her mother, who asked for it. It became a linking object, belonging to both women, and an ambivalence-strained link which had to be externalized and put aside. The daughter became actually afraid of it, but kept it carefully. When asked to show it to us she instructed her sister to bring it to the hospital in a paper bag. When the bag was in the room, she fantasized that the dead woman would come out of it, and gave a lively display of appro-

194

priate fearful affect. After going through enough re-griefing therapy she spontaneously burned the robe, the genetic aspect of this act referring to her mother's burns suffered so many years earlier. Follow-up two years after the completion of her re-griefing indicated no return of symptoms of pathological grief.

CASE 5.—A patient in his mid-30s was diagnosed as a paranoid schizophrenic when he had a delusion that his wife was trying to poison him. He was convinced that a yellow spot at the bottom of his coffee cup was poison. Because his symptoms had started nine months before at the time when his 19-year-old half-brother drowned, he was accepted by the study group because of the possibility that he was suffering from pathological grief. This proved to be the case, and his psychotic symptoms cleared in therapy when he was helped to grieve effectively.

His mother had died of melanoma, and he and his sister had both had operations for the same disease. The half-brother who drowned was the child of the patient's father's second marriage. The delusion about the spot of poison could be understood against the background of a horror of death from melanoma and death by drowning in muddy waters. Therapy disclosed that the spot represented melanoma, and the coffee represented muddy waters.

This patient's linking object is an example of the fourth category—an object recalling the last moment during which the dead person was thought of as being alive. Word of his brother's accident had reached the patient as he was putting records on the record player. The first word was that the boy had not surfaced after a dive and the search was still in progress. Another call a few hours later reported the discovery of the body. The records on the record-player became highly symbolized for the patient, who insisted that they remain where they were, as if the act of playing them had been frozen. Unable to listen to them, he was equally unable to remove them and put them away. At last he played the records and went into an abreaction. Even after they were put away, the records contained a heavy investment of his unfinished work of mourning, and were not used until the patient was well into his treatment. An exercise of his re-griefing was the playing of the records and weeping over his dead brother while listening to them. A two-year follow-up of this patient indicated that no pathological grief symptoms persisted, nor were the records any longer symbolized.

The Linking Object, Fetishes, and the Transitional Object

When the term *fetish* is seen in its etymological reference it may seem a suitable term to apply to the linking object. However, since the linking object is unique and specific in its institution, its usefulness in maintaining psychophysical balance in the face of a loss, and in the related psychodynamics, a special descriptive term to distinguish it from the fetish in the psychoanalytical sense and from the transitional object as well, seems warranted.

It is outside the scope of this report to review the literature on the fetish or the transitional object, but it will be profitable to refer to articles by Greenacre[23, 24] in which the clinical forms and functions of each are compared. In these papers Greenacre uses the term *fetish* in the limited sense of adult fetishistic perversion. After summarizing her information about the fetish and the transitional object I will compare them to the linking object. I will also refer to fetishism in children as Sperling[25] describes it, and the "instant mothers" used by the psychotic children studied by Speers and Lansing,[26] who applied the insights of Mahler.[27] All these kinds of uniquely significant objects overlap in function and description, but they are recognizably different from one another.

Transitional Object.—The "transitional object" was described by Winnicott[28] as "an object that becomes vitally important to the child . . . more important than the mother, an almost inseparable part of the child." He considered this a universal phenomenon in normal emotional development. Agreeing, Greenacre emphasized that the transitional object is a temporary construction to help the infant toward a sense of reality and the establishment of his own identity. Usually chosen, from whatever is available to the infant in the first year of his life, on the basis of texture, odor, visibility, and movability, it is a consolation for the separation of going to sleep. It may be an old blanket, for example; or the mother herself can be treated as a transitional object. It absorbs neglect and even abuse, as well as the most loving closeness. If it is lost, the baby usually finds as a replacement a new object like it. It represents symbolically the first not-me, but it is never totally not-me. It links not-me with mother-me. It fades away ultimately, and its memory is not subjected to active repression.

Childhood Fetish.—Differing from Winnicott, Sperling suggests that the transitional objects he describes are pathological manifestations of a specific disturbance in object relationship. Before the age of 2 the child becomes attached to an inanimate object, something concrete and real; when it is a part of the child's own body it is a replaceable feature like fingernails. The child does not accept weaning, but replaces the mother's breast with the fetish, the symbolic function of which concerns separation anxiety (1) during weaning; (2) at the height of the anal phase (in reference to clinging to or letting go of feces—the mother equivalent); and (3) during the oedipal phase, when the mother is renounced as the sexually gratifying object. In summary, the childhood fetish represents a pathological defense against separation from the mother

196

on the pre-oedipal levels, and may or may not lead to adult fetishism.

The observation of psychotic children brought to the attention of Speers and Lansing[26] a similar phenomenon resembling Sperling's childhood fetishism in its dynamic meaning. These children created "instant mothers" through the use of movable inanimate objects. Mahler[27] gave clinical examples of the "psychotic preoccupations" of children with an inanimate object (the "psychotic fetish") such as a fan, a record player, a jar—even a thread to wind around the finger. These she described as a form of transitional object.

The Fetish.—In the classical sense, the fetish represents the illusory penis of the mother, and it may represent the last moment in which the woman could be regarded as phallic;[16] thus it is a special solution of the castration threat. The roles of pregenital sexual experience, of aggression, and of other aspects of fetishism have been studied extensively since Freud. Bak,[29] summarizing points in the development of fetishism, included: weakness of ego structure; fixation in pregenital phases; the representation by the fetish of breasts, skin, buttocks, feces, nipples, and the female phallus, separately or in combination. He emphasized the importance of identification with the penisless mother, in which the wish to give up the penis creates marked intrastructural conflict.

The classical fetish used by the adult pervert, usually a male, can be described according to Greenacre's summary. It is an inanimate object the presence of which is necessary if the pervert is to sustain potency for the completion of sexual intercourse. It is often an article of clothing, such as a shoe. The color black (representing pubic hair) is important, as are odor and visibility. It symbolically combines male and female attributes; the fetishist's mother-me combination is concerned with genitals. In adult perversion the fetish is a link between the denial of sexual differences and their affirmation, and must be indestructible. There is no spontaneous recovery from fetishism.

The Linking Object.—Like the others, the linking object appears in relation to loss understood in the broadest sense to include psychical separation. The transitional object, a normal and transitory manifestation (in spite of Sperling's suggestion to the contrary), provides restitution for the loss of total oceanic symbiosis and identity formation. In the adoption of the childhood fetish the separation anxiety due to the loss of the pre-oedipally satisfying mother is more important than castration anxiety. "The childhood fetish represents a pathological defense against separations from the mother on the pre-oedipal (oral and anal) levels."[25]

I cite Bak's paper[29] from the extensive literature on fetishism in adults to illuminate the separation aspect of this phenomenon. Bak saw the fetish as a compromise between separation and castration, reflecting (1) the wish to give up the penis in order to identify with the penisless mother and avoid the danger of separation from her, and (2) the alternative danger of castration. As indicated in one of his reported cases, the anxiety of being abandoned may mobilize fetishistic ceremonies. In this instance the response to the threat of loss can be clearly seen.

Like fetishes in the classical sense, linking objects are seen in adult men and women. In our study, the physical loss through death occasioned the adoption of a linking object. The loss involved in the use of a fetish is usually symbolic and diffuse. To adult males, the classical fetish represents the mother's penis, and this remains its highest significance in spite of the interweaving of pregenital aspects with the genital. The chief function of the linking object for the adult, however, is the response to an obvious loss (with its condensed aspects from different levels of psychosexual development). Paraphrasing Freud, I[1] have suggested that the linking object is a "token of triumph" over loss. Although the loss involved in the establishment of childhood fetishism concerns the pre-oedipally gratifying mother, the loss by death may represent to the pathological mourner separation from representations of a greater diversity of important objects from every level of psychosexual development. For example, I noted in one of my case histories that the dead father—or Father Time—represented the original oedipal father needed for the resolution of the oedipal conflict and the completion of the superego. In this instance the patient wanted to avoid separation at the oedipal level. The inherited car parked in the front yard with its motor in working order probably represented both his father's penis and his own, and the patient defended himself against both separation and castration anxiety by using his linking object. In such a case it is difficult to distinguish between a true linking object and a fetish, but since the symbolization of the car definitely corresponded in time with the death I considered it to be the former.

Other inanimate objects not descriptively identical with either the classical fetish or the linking object are used to handle separation anxiety. Elsewhere[22] we have reviewed accounts of man's psychological connection with his machines and reported the case of a 16-year-old boy who, dur-

198

ing treatment, employed a series of machines, some of which he made himself. In considering the many possible meanings of his inanimate objects (machines), we were struck by his attempt to reconstruct the equilibrium of object relationships at the time of a critical separation. Further generalizations arise from the work of Searles,[30] who completed an extensive study of man's kinship with his nonhuman environment. He wrote,

". . . the nonhuman surroundings possess psychological significances for us which are not confined to their serving as such a shock-absorbing background; . . . *to the degree that* some differentiation between ego and surrounding nonhuman environment has been achieved, various specific elements of the nonhuman realm (such as machines) can be reacted to by the developing ego which is engaged in a defensive struggle, as symbols of the warded-off drives and affects."

Productions in the psychic field like delusions and hallucinations used to link the mourner with the dead should have consideration. The Schreber case clarifies this point. Niederland,[31-33] whose investigations have done so much to shed light on Schreber's childhood, demonstrates how some of the patient's childhood experience emerged in the form of "miracled-up" delusions during the psychotic process. These are projected in the *Memoirs* "as if the pages of the manuscript which Schreber filled with his delusional descriptions had served him as a welcome screen for the externalization and concretization of his fantasies."[33] Niederland called my attention to Schreber's hallucination of "divine miracles" as constituting *linking* references to manipulations which Schreber's father had practiced on his son's body and which the sick son later "miracled-up" in order to revive the infantile tie between himself and his father. I suggest that this may be called a *linking phenomenon* in an extension of the concept of the *linking object*.

In adult life, linking objects mark a blurring of psychic boundaries between the patient and the one he mourns, as if representations of the two persons, or parts of them, merge externally through their use. Winnicott[28] believed that the transitional object is held in memory without repression, gradually becoming decathected, and that it may reappear in later life when deprivation threatens. It would be enlightening to know whether pathological adult mourners using linking objects had used a transitional object excessively in childhood or had the type of childhood fetish described by Sperling. Among the patients in our study and seen in treatment over the years we failed to establish the earlier use of a childhood fetish. The relationship must remain speculative for the present. However, problems of psychic separation from the mother seem evident in three cases cited—that of the first patient who was later analyzed, that of the man born in hiding, and that of the woman whose mother had been burned. Further research into the genetic aspect of the linking object is required. It is hoped that the recognition of the phenomenon of the linking object will direct the attention of other analysts and psychotherapists to its appearance during the treatment of suitable patients.

The distancing used with linking objects also distinguishes them from the fetish and the transitional object. The child holds, sees, and smells the transitional object. The adult pervert needs at least the sight of the fetish in order to feel sexually potent. With the linking object in pathological mourning, knowledge of its whereabouts is highly important, but it is as usual for the patient to distance himself from it as to embrace it. In the example of the red robe, it was avoided in spite of the fact that its existence was important. In another case, the dead father's picture was placed under a leaking pipe, where it served to resolve externally some of the patient's conflicts without directly involving his sensory perceptions. One might even consider the linking object a higher-level symbol, since it does not have characteristics easily associated with body parts, but takes its importance instead from the individual's ideation.

As Greenacre[23] indicated, the fetish contains congealed anger, born of castration panic. The linking object also contains anger, and is similarly an instrument for the control of expressions of anger arising from separation panic. I suggest further that the linking object is more significantly invested with the aggressive drive than is the fetish; this characteristic accounts for the phenomenon of distancing and avoidance.

The linking object may represent the "last moment" in which the dead individual was felt to be alive; the fetish is the object of the "last moment" in which the mother can be considered to have a penis.

The linking object provides a means whereby object relationships with the deceased can be maintained externally. The ambivalence of the wish to annihilate the deceased and the wish to keep him alive is condensed in it, so that the painful work of mourning has an external reference and thus is not resolved. Recognition of linking objects and formulations regarding them may provide technical suggestions for dealing with pathological mourners as we deal with the phobic patient who, after sufficient analysis of its symbolic meaning, needs to confront the dreaded object. The pathological mourner needs to stop using the linking object to bring it with all its implications fully into the field of therapeutic working through.

References

1. Volkan VD: Normal and pathological grief reactions: A guide for the family physician. *Virginia Med Monthly* **93**:651-656, 1966.
2. Volkan VD, Showalter CR: Known object loss, disturbance in reality testing, and "re-grief" work as a method of brief psychotherapy. *Psychiat Quart* **42**:358-374, 1968.
3. Volkan VD: The University of Virginia study in pathological mourning. *Tip Dünyasi* **42**:544-551, 1969.
4. Volkan VD: Typical findings in pathological grief. *Psychiat Quart* **44**:231-250, 1970.
5. Volkan VD: A study of a patient's "re-grief" work through dreams, psychological tests and psychoanalysis. *Psychiat Quart* **45**:255-273, 1971.
6. Engel GL: Is grief a disease? A challenge for medical research. *Psychosom Med* **23**:18-22, 1961.
7. Bowlby J: Process of mourning. *Int J Psychoanal* **42**:317-340, 1961.
8. Parkes CM: "Seeking" and "finding" a lost object: Evidence from recent studies of the reaction to bereavement. *Soc Sci Med* **4**:187-201, 1970.
9. Freud S: Mourning and melancholia, in *Collected Papers.* London, Hogarth Press Ltd, and the Institute of Psychoanalysis, 1956, vol 4.
10. Siggins LD: Mourning: A critical survey of the literature. *Int J Psychoanal* **47**:14-25, 1966.
11. Gaylin W: *The Meaning of Despair.* New York, Science House, 1968.
12. Bibring E: The mechanism of depression, in Greenacre P (ed): *Affective Disorders.* New York, International Universities Press, 1953.
13. Pollock GH: Mourning and adaptation. *Int J Psychoanal* **42**:341-361, 1961.
14. Abraham K: A short study of the development of the libido in the light of mental disorders, In *Selected Papers.* London, Hogarth Press Ltd, 1949.
15. Schafer R: *Aspects of Internalization.* New York, International Universities Press, 1968.
16. Freud S: Fetishism, in *Collected Papers.* London, Hogarth Press Ltd and the Institute of Psychoanalysis, 1956, vol 5.

201

17. Freud S: Splitting of the ego in the defensive process, in *Collected Papers*. London, Hogarth Press Ltd and the Institute of Psychoanalysis, 1956, vol 5.

18. Volkan VD, Corney RT: Some considerations of satellite states and satellite dreams. *Brit J Med Psychol* **41**:283-290, 1968.

19. Rapaport D: Projective techniques and the theory of thinking. *J Projective Tech* **16**:269-275, 1952.

20. Jaffe DS: The mechanism of projection: Its dual role in object relations. *Int J Psychoanal* **49**:662-677, 1968.

21. Niederland W: Psychiatric disorders among persecution victims. *J Nerv Ment Dis* **139**:458-474, 1964.

22. Volkan VD, Luttrell A: Aspects of the object relationships and developing skills of a "mechanical boy." *Brit J Med Psychol* **44**:101-116, 1971.

23. Greenacre P: The fetish and the transitional object. *Psychoanal Study Child* **24**:144-164, 1969.

24. Greenacre P: The transitional object and the fetish with special reference to the role of illusion. *Int J Psychoanal* **51**:447-456, 1970.

25. Sperling M: Fetishism in children. *Psychoanal Quart* **32**:374-392, 1963.

26. Speers RW, Lansing C: *Group Therapy in Childhood Psychosis*. Chapel Hill, NC, University of North Carolina Press, 1965.

27. Mahler MS: *On Human Symbiosis and the Vicissitudes of Individuation*. New York, International Universities Press, 1968, vol 1.

28. Winnicott DW: Transitional object and transitional phenomena. *Int J Psychoanal* **34**:89-97, 1953.

29. Bak RC: Fetishism. *J Amer Psychoanal Assoc* **1**:285-298, 1953.

30. Searles HF: *The Nonhuman Environment*. New York, International Universities Press, 1960.

31. Niederland W: Schreber: Father and son. *Psychoanal Quart* **28**:151-169, 1959.

32. Niederland W: The "miracled-up" world of Schreber's childhood. *Psychoanal Study Child* **14**:383-413, 1959.

33. Niederland W: Further data and memorabilia pertaining to the Schreber case. *Int J Psychoanal* **44**:201-207, 1963.

THE IMPACT OF OBJECT LOSS ON A SIX-YEAR-OLD

Morton Chethik, M.S.W.

Introduction

In recent years there has been much interest in tracing the young child's reaction to object loss and sharp controversy about his capacity to deal with it. Can he accept the finality of death? Can he experience grief? What developmental milestones must be reached before he is capable of managing the painful decathexis from the lost object —the complex psychic process of mourning? Some authors (Furman, 1964a; Barnes, 1964) citing clinical examples note that children who have solidly reached the phallic level of object relations (those who have mastered the ambivalence of the anal-sadistic stage and are beyond magical thinking) can deal with major losses and death in a way similar to that of the healthy adult. Many others, however, strongly disagree and feel that the capacity to mourn can be achieved only much later in development. Some (Wolfenstein, 1966; Nagera, 1969) state that the phase of "object removal" which naturally transpires in adolescence, is a necessary precondition and precursor for the ability to mourn in adult life. It is in this context of conflicting positions and points of view that I present the case of Mark. Mark was six years old when it was discovered that his mother had cancer. In fact, his birthday coincided with her first hospitalization. During

The author would like to express his appreciation to Dr. Jane Kessler who supervised the treatment, and to the Child Therapy Program (Cleveland, Ohio) for their helpful discussion of this case.

his sixth year, his mother deteriorated under the impact of this disease, and she died two months before Mark became seven. I here trace the events of these ten months dealing primarily with the content of Mark's analysis.

I chose to describe this material because it brought to my mind sharply the *enormity* of the task facing the child during this kind of crisis, and it clearly exposed, I felt, the additional psychic burdens a child must often struggle with when he attempts to master tragedy early in life. I shall also comment on the problems involved in mourning that this child presented and discuss their implications for death and young children in general.

HISTORY AND THE INITIAL TREATMENT PERIOD

Mark was a little over five years old when I began to work with him. He was a rather short but extremely well-built, well-proportioned child who looked "ready for action." He had a pleasant appearance, with strikingly dark features and coloring, just like his mother's. His crewcut, turtleneck polo shirt, heavy corduroy trousers, and tennis shoes further accentuated a picture of premature manliness. One often found Mark climbing, twisting, hurdling, and maneuvering with unique agility rather than walking from place to place.

Mark had been in analytic treatment (five times a week) for seven months before the cancer discovery. We found, in that early period of treatment, that he was already in a severe developmental struggle. Mark was enuretic, soiled, and sucked his thumb, but the most pressing problem which motivated the parents to seek help was his uncontrolled behavior. It appeared to be a diffuse aggressiveness, a striking out, which often seemed unprovoked. In the analysis, accompanying fantasies quickly showed us that Mark often feared sadistic attack. His aggression was a counter-reaction and warding-off of an imagined danger. In addition, there seemed to be another important motive for his attacks: he often wanted to be controlled and physically stopped so that he could gratify passive anal aims of being subdued or beaten.

It was clear from the history that an intense fighting relationship existed between mother and son. The difficulties with Mark seemed to have started during his second year, when mother (Mrs. L.) became pregnant. (There were three boys in the family; Brad, two years older than Mark, and Michael, two years younger.) It had been a particularly hot and humid summer, the mother explained, and she had found "carrying" her child difficult and tiring. Mark was a very active and curious toddler, and she grew increasingly impatient and exasperated with him. She had told Mark about her impending delivery, and she recalled that the night before Michael was born, Mark began to climb out of the crib.

When mother returned with the new baby, the difficulties were compounded. One evening she found Mark straddling the baby, and she began the practice of locking Mark in his room at night. Now Mark was perpetually climbing out of his crib. Mrs. L. and her husband, in an effort to keep him in bed, built larger and higher barriers to his crib; with superhuman determination, Mark scaled all obstacles.

The same difficulties carried into Mark's toilet training which mother began six months later. Mark was forced to sit on the potty, but soiled right after he got off, at which mother lost her temper. Mark's toileting problems continued until he began treatment. Mrs. L. also described a pattern of provocative soiling, when Mark simply pulled down his pants and defecated on a neighbor's lawn.

As his horizon broadened, so did Mark's misbehavior. He became somewhat of a "terror" in the community. He was often very aggressive with street friends, suddenly hitting and punching without provocation. He led little forages into neighbors' yards, turning on hoses to let the water flow into kitchens and basements. As mother remembered, they had become "real popular" on their street.

From my early contacts with Mrs. L, it was clear that she had formed a special identification with Mark. Despite the misery his aggressive behavior caused, she felt an underlying pleasure in the "manliness" he conveyed. Mrs. L. herself was a strong, controlling, charismatic person (in contrast to her indecisive, faltering husband), and in many subtle ways she reinforced the dare-devil, exciting, and heroic qualities in her son.

What was our concept of Mark's illness? While he was bright, verbal, and well endowed, his explosiveness and uncontrollable behavior were at times quite extraordinary. There seemed to be a definite weakness in the balance between drives and ego, and the ego function which seemed most damaged was his reality testing. Fantasies overwhelmed him. One must think of Mark in terms of trauma. Some of the recent Hampstead research has been helpful in fixing the possible trauma point. Mark's mother, as noted above, reported a significant withdrawal from him during her pregnancy, which occurred when he was little more than a year old. Some of the studies of the prehistory of uncontrolled and delinquent London children found that changes in the mother-child relationship at that time of life, namely, the beginning of the anal phase, have far-reaching and important consequences for the child. This is a crucial time during which the dependent need and the love stemming from it keep sadism, aggression, and drive expression under control. A change for the worse in the relationship (a mother's absence, illness, birth of next baby, etc.) can severely disturb the fusion with libido of the normal aggression and sadism of that period, and appears to be a factor in the development of many unmanageable children. This was a major conception in our attempt to understand Mark, and one for which we found increasing evidence throughout the entire analytic period.

During those first seven months of treatment, before we learned of the mother's cancer, we made some definite gains with Mark. He had established a good deal more self-control; this growth was partly the result of much better and consistent parental handling and partly the result of his growing ability to separate inner and outer fears, to distinguish his "mind thoughts," as we came to term them, from what was really happening.

THE CRITICAL EVENTS

It was in September, 1965 that the crisis began. Several days before Mark's birthday, Mrs. L. called me to tell me the news. During the physical examination, the doctor confirmed her own discovery of suspicious lumps on her right breast and arm and suggested immediate exploratory surgery. Later the same day, Mrs. L. met with me to focus on preparing the children for the event; she did an excellent job in discussing the "lumps" realistically with the boys, and the need to find out if they were dangerous. Her only comment to me about this discussion, was that she was not sure she had "reached" Mark.

Several days later, the malignancy was uncovered. A radical mastectomy was performed, and several lymph nodes were removed from under the arm. The following week, Mrs. L.'s ovaries were removed as a preventative measure against further metastasis. She stayed in the hospital three weeks, and during that period a widowed aunt cared for the children. With much trepidation Mark's father conveyed to the children what was occurring. "Mother's bosom had to be taken off, several lumps were taken from her arm . . . they were dangerous to mommie if they were allowed to remain in her." In answer to their questions, he assured them that the doctors had removed all of the lumps, and that the *doctor said* she would be all right. The father commented to me however, that while he felt the older brother understood, he wasn't sure if Mark "heard."

For the first week or so, while his mother was hospitalized, Mark was overtly sad during his sessions. He was quiet, said almost nothing, and gave no verbal recognition or acknowledgement to my comments about missing mommie, or of things changing at home. He sat near me for comfort, quietly touching familiar objects we had used over the months. He asked me to read, from a "Little Bear" book, stories about how a mommie bear kept her little bear warm during the winter, and in another story, how she made a surprise cake for his birthday. No, Mark told me, he himself did not miss his mommie for his birthday, only for his Jewish consecration (his word for confirmation). "Would you come instead?" He made Jewish presents to send to his mother—flags and stars—and I was given the job of mailman.

Then one day there was bedlam. Mark couldn't stand his lunch: he threw his sandwich across the room, scattered potato chips, and jabbed his apple with a pencil. Chairs were overturned and materials flew. When I physically restrained him, he screamed in terror that I was hurting him, and he ended the hour with a bowel movement in his pants. At home, eating immediately became a problem. He refused food, messed with it, and meal-times were utterly impossible.

The chaos continued during his sessions, and many themes seemed all fused together. His food was filled with germs and potential danger. These germs were spread from person to person; he became a giant and a strong man to ward off injury. All was acted out, and led to further excitement, aggression, and guilt. Slowly, however, a predominant theme seemed to emerge. Mark constantly sought out all openings in the office and proceeded to fill them to the brim; his thermos bottle, the pillow cover, etc. Then as the apertures became tightly packed, a giant explosion took place, and Mark scattered the contents about the room. On the basis of my previous experience with him, I recognized this as his exciting fantasy of birth. Food was eaten, the contents gathered in the stomach, and babies came out after the bursting. He confirmed this interpretation by telling me to watch my step in the room: I might unwittingly walk on and crush one of the scattered babies. I then told Mark he was making a very big mistake! He thought his mommie was in the hospital to have a baby! This was absolutely untrue! Her being there had nothing whatsoever to do with babies! I then repeated what he had already been told many times. Mark was absolutely incredulous at first. He said, "This is really something serious," and he would have to go home to tell his brothers about it.

The unusual and unexpected aspect in this situation was that Mark did not retain any conscious knowledge of what was happening in the hospital. The event seemed to be denied completely and unavailable for reality appraisal. It appeared that, as with younger children, Mark used the mechanism of denial in fantasy. He substituted an exciting, pleasurable fantasy for an external painful event. When confronted directly with this fantasy, and when I described his denial, there were then reality inroads. Mark began asking some appropriate questions about his mother.

Shortly afterwards, Mrs. L. returned from the hospital, still showing many of the effects of her surgery. Mark's soiling reappeared, and he again became a severe management problem, reversing our apparent analytic gains. In the hour, I noted that he was secretly straining, as if to force out a BM surreptitiously. When I commented to him that I was aware that the BM problem was coming back, he expressed it more directly. "Fart, burp, and blow" entered his vocabulary, and he practiced making anal noises at me with his mouth. In a provocative way, Mark would find imaginary pieces of "doodie" all over the office, which, in mock play, he threw at me.

The character of Tarzan of the Ape Men appeared at this time, and a most sadistic character he was. He fought viciously in the jungles and killed the enemy tribesmen with a great deal of violence and gore. Heads came off; feet came off; stomachs were cut out. He fought snakes, panthers, lions, and they were not only killed, but dismembered. One day, in his travels, Tarzan came across a little boy who was being spanked very, very hard by his mother. With no hesitation (and to my complete surprise) he plunged a knife into the mother and took the boy with him. For a period of time, he comforted and cared for the little boy. He took him into bed with him, rocked him, and let him "make in his pants" if he wanted to. But then Tarzan himself turned on the boy and punished him cruelly. Guilt attached to the mother-murder then appeared, and Mark acted out with me, in an attempt to get me to be angry with him. We saw this as a regression. The striking element was the open sadism, for Tarzan attacked the mother with absolutely no signs of ambivalence. The present separation experience and hospital procedure seemed to reawaken a primitive earlier anger that came through with little ego modification.

Because Mark's anger was also being expressed at home, we were anxious to find some means of controlling it. And because it affected the mother, we were concerned abut later additional guilt. Our emphasis at this point was to attempt to separate realistically the two periods in Mark's mind. I told Mark these were *old* angry feelings that he had had when he was a little boy, and had imagined that thoughts and wishes could really hurt people. We could talk about those ideas. Now (appealing to whatever sense of reality I hoped was there), I told him he was much older and he could really understand that his mommie had to go to the hospital because she had a sickness. Her illness had nothing to do with people's thoughts.

As Mrs. L. recovered, and again became an available object, there was a period of ego growth. In early December, Mark decided to make a "Heart Book" to give his mother for Christmas. While this book expressed many of his positive feelings toward his mother, we could also call it a "Reality Book", for it dealt with the wholesome desire to understand and integrate all the recent events.

The book itself had a very "grown up" quality. It must have many pages, for the thicker it was, the more adult it was. It must use pen and ink, rather than babyish pencil. Everything must be written in "script", because the early grades used printing, and cursive writing was for the older boys.

Before we began, Mark subjected me to interesting little tests, as if to measure the soundness of my reality judgments. He might say this month of September was a real good month, and he waited for me to point out that it was December. He told me he would visit his aunt for Christmas and swim in the nearby lake. I thought it might be too cold, and wondered if the lake weren't frozen over with ice. After I apparently met his requirements, we proceeded.

The first page of his book began with a prayer: "Mommie, Mommie, I don't want you to be sick. I don't want to get angry with you and have a fight." Then he proceeded to ask many questions, in great detail, about death. "What makes people die? How are they buried? How far down are they put in the ground? Do they have boxes for children—are they smaller ones? Would it hurt to touch a dead person? Where was his grandpa buried? What would he look like?" I answered these questions as factually and directly as I could, for there seemed to be a desire for real knowledge. I also injected that the questions must be coming from worries about Mommie.

Mark then recalled frightening early events, and we entered them into the book. He remembered how his older brother, Brad, went to the hospital after swallowing a coin. He told of the time the family received the news that the grandfather had died. This was by telephone, and he recalled that they couldn't finish eating their supper. Finally, he mentioned his mother. When his mommie was in the hospital, he was afraid she was going to die. He described how much she had changed; she stays in bed more, seems so tired, and never puts on any of her dresses. He listened and accepted my explanation of the slow path of recovery from severe surgery.

He had many questions about God. "Where was God? Was he invisible? Was he up there in the sky, or was he in the room? Was his grandpa with God?" Inasmuch as his parents were not strong believers, I confirmed that his grandfather was only in the box in the ground.

During these talks he at times playfully became the little boy. He suddenly lapsed into baby talk, walked on his knees, and on a couple of occasions, became so "dumb" that he walked into the wrong room "forgetting" that we worked in room number-six. In contrast, at other times, he wore his grown-up equipment which consisted of a watch, and a ring. He carefully set the time so that it coincided exactly with mine, identifying directly with the grown-up qualities he endowed me with. There was a tremendous change at home; he was under perfect control, he was helpful and understanding, fair in play with his brothers, and doing well in school.

The most difficult part of the book Mark was making related to mommie's missing breast. For a period of time, he endowed it with life. He wanted to know where it was now, and how it was doing. After that, he wondered if it would grow back. He would ask, "Is it still off today?" and when I emphasized that it couldn't return, he seemed quite sad. He demanded that *I* not forget that *I* write down that the bosom would never return. Mark became realistically interested in the operative procedure. "How did they take it off? How did they sew her up? What kind of scar would she have? Did it hurt her there?" He was puzzled at times, because his mother looked as if she had two breasts, and we explained that she wore a false one made of rubber.

Dealing with the breast was difficult because it related so directly to castration. It was a genital organ that had been amputated in reality. From time to time I injected that I thought this idea made Mark have worries about his own body too.

While he was preparing the "Heart Book," Mark was very much intact. For instance, on one occasion there was a pending visit to the pediatrician to receive a shot. With only a little effort on my part, he talked freely about his worries. He wanted to know the different kinds of shots and how they helped. He recalled his measles shot—how it hurt, and how his arm swelled. The visits to the doctor went well. This quality of integration made me think much more of a child on an oedipal level of functioning. He used many ego processes that seemed more age appropriate at this point.

This adjustment temporarily evaporated when the parents took a vacation to Florida, and some of the old Mark immediately returned. A second "Reality Book" contained a map of Florida and Cleveland. Calendars which counted the days the parents were away seemed to help Mark acquire perspective on time and distance of the separation.

During the early months of 1966, we continued to experience a reality "lull" wherein no new major events occurred. Though Mrs. L. had some pain and fatigue, she again ran the household and there was no breakdown of routine. When she was tired, she directed household procedures through her husband or hired help. She was determined not to give up the reins and to keep functioning. She also continued her involvement in her son's analysis. She kept all her office appointments with me and called fairly frequently. Mrs. L. spoke intellectually of helping her family cope wtih her illness, but understandably she needed to avoid many feeling areas. The material of our sessions began to shift, more and more, to practical arrangements. We planned how Mark was to be brought to his sessions, which neighbors were best to use, how much Mark should visit others, whether he should attend camp in the summer. Implicitly, Mrs. L. wanted help so she would not break down and express her despair with the children. When she became uneasy over her ability to control herself when Mark seemed to be more provocative or aggressive, her phone calls increased. I must add that she maintained herself remarkably well. Mark's overall picture of his mother was that she was functioning at home, though she was often tired. He was aware of a natural withdrawal. Mrs. L.'s interest beyond herself was only maintained by strong effort.

During this "lull", when we had no immediate crises to cope with, Mark continued to show conflicts that were more typical of the oedipal period. He became concerned about castration. For the first time, he was much more openly fearful, and every injury was a major concern. Scratches, a little rash, a cold became evidence for Mark that something was really wrong. This behavior was in contrast to the earlier Mark who never reacted to injury overtly, even severe ones. Fritzie, a neighborhood dog with whom he played, became much more ominous.

Mark began to have more frightening dreams and nightmares in which he was chased by lions and tigers who bit off arms and legs. The most prominent and frightening animal of this period was the gorilla, who, in the dream, ate Mark and spit out his head. In other dreams, his own aggression was expressed. The gorilla attacked his father or mother and bit or ate them. Mark shuddered at the prospect of sleep, and he gathered all his stuffed animals and special protecting necklace in bed with him before he would face the night.

His fears spread beyond the nighttime. He became frightened when he saw his younger brother wearing a heavy jacket or pajamas, because the furry quality of the material he wore made him look like an animal. His work in school began to deteriorate. He seemed suddenly to lose his ability to read and distinguish letters. In his sessions, his play was an attempt to master the dreams.

He climbed to the windowsills or stood on the table to keep out of the reach of the snapping jaws of the animals. He asked demanding and repeated questions. "Can the lions get out of their cages? Can they escape from the circus? Did I ever see a lion on the street?" He wanted immediate direct reassurance. He wanted to make sure that all doors were locked in the office so the animals wouldn't get in. He promised me he would never go to the circus or zoo, and he would avoid looking at any books which had gorillas or animals in them. Magic was prominent. A drawing he made of a gorilla became lifelike, endowed with aggression and had to be ripped into little pieces.

All my attempts to show him what he was doing, were simply not heard. In his terror, he would get out of control during the hour. At times he was very remorseful, telling me he wanted to be good, but he just couldn't help it. He brought me cookies as presents, in his desire to make up for bad days. Intermittently I attempted to return to writing and making our books, but Mark was unable to continue. He managed sometimes, under my direct suggestions, to simply use a color book, and he promised himself that he would try to stay within the lines.

In time, I became the feared object. Mark began to say he hated me. I was the one who made him dream. He didn't know if I was a gorilla or not. I could change. I should take off my clothes to prove I wasn't. He wouldn't be so scared if he didn't have to come to see me, since, he pointed out, he was absolutely fine on Saturdays and Sundays. Mark's resistance became more active, and for a period of three weeks he stayed out of his sessions totally. We handled this development as we would other phobias. While he wasn't forced to enter my office, he was brought every day by his mother who "expected" him to attend and who waited the full time. It was to his mother that Mark verbalized how absolutely terrified he was of me.

After the verbalization he himself felt its unreality and was able to return.

These few months were a period of striking anxiety for Mark. We saw an enormous increase in castration anxiety, partly because Mark had been watching his mother *literally* being cut to pieces. One could see in this material characteristics of how Mark handled conflicts that were evident throughout the treatment. The intensity of his anxiety, the inability to control the flooding, seemed to be typical of Mark whether he was dealing with phallic problems or problems of other phases. Being overwhelmed made all work difficult, no matter what the level. In this period, in some ways, despite the age-appropriate quality of his struggle, there were many regressive features or perhaps aspects that indicated arrest. Magic and animism appeared and seemed to affect his reality testing. His brothers and therapist could turn into animals, and Mark fleetingly lost his ability to distinguish objects clearly. The ego function of perception became involved. He was unable to distinguish letters and to read, a facility he had recently acquired. Aggression involved the sadism and primitiveness on a two-year-old level.

During these months it was extremely difficult to work with Mark. There was little observing ego, little free ego that could be used in alliance with the therapist. For instance, at one point I attempted slowly to lay the groundwork to show Mark that he was dealing with an inner rather than an outer anxiety. I'd comment about how strange it was that every day he'd worry about a new and different animal—a lion, tiger, shark, or gorilla. But Mark couldn't hear me. He did not have the capacity to listen to the idea; he simply heard the word "gorilla," and this was enough to make him frightened again. At points I managed to stop Mark's expanding anxiety temporarily by loudly saying things like," You are making another big mistake. Mr. Chethik is not a gorilla. I haven't changed yesterday or today, and I won't change tomorrow. It is your 'mind idea' again." But I, and Mark's faltering ego, could not control the onrush of anxiety during many sessions.

In April two important events occurred. By some unbelievable and horrible coincidence, Mark's grandmother became acutely ill. In surgery it was discovered that she too had cancer. She deteriorated swiftly. In contrast to Mark's mother, she experienced marked outer

214

physical changes: rapid loss of weight, and bloating of the body; these things Mark saw. About ten days after this discovery, Mrs. L. herself had a reoccurrence of the malignancy—growths were discovered in her neck and hip. She underwent cobalt X-ray treatments which caused many secondary effects such as severe nausea and extreme fatigue. These events dramatically and directly affected Mark. He was brought to his session by a friend of the family. The best way I can describe interviews during this period is to call them fragmented. They were fragmented in several senses. The interviews were filled with scattered themes: Mark's thoughts and ideas seemed to move from one area to another without any apparent connection. It seemed as if the new thought or anxiety suddenly intruded itself upon Mark and simply displaced an earlier idea. Mark appeared almost helpless in the process of these changing ideas. Contact with me was fragmented. At times I was there talking and relating to him; the next moment I no longer existed for him. This process was also evident in school, according to descriptions from the teacher. Mark would begin an arithmetic paper, answer the first two questions correctly and thereafter seem to wander into drawings or scribblings.

There were a few occasions in the hour when Mark took fleeting glimpses at the changing realities with me. "Why is Mommie so tired? Why does she take strong medicine (referring to the cobalt treatment) if it hurts her? What's wrong with Mommie's leg? Will Mommie die soon?" For a short period I could respond to these questions and be heard, and then Mark seemed to drift away. It was clear that he often moved to some thoughts which involved an identification with his mother's illness. For instance, he might become preoccupied, feeling his forehead, and I could deduce that he worried that he had some fever. (His mother was running a high temperature at that time.) My words could not reach him at this point, but I could follow his thoughts through his behavior. Mark would use his food to care for himself in his illness. He might divide up his lunch and hide sections of it in corners of the room, as if to use it carefully when needed. Then he might change his mind and gorge himself, as if looking for strength. Momentarily, a Hercules or Tarzan would appear, but Mark seemed to have little strength for sustaining these characters. I was impressed with my total inability to reach him, and I could only describe his behavior as some form of temporary withdrawal. Certainly it was a major regression from the quality of the relationship we had before.

Throughout this fragmented period I realized that I was dreading my interviews with Mark. I felt a great sense of helplessness. I was concerned that in some ways I was overidentifying with Mark; that perhaps he and I were helpless together against this enormous disaster that was occurring. If I could define my role, I could represent some reality, some support that Mark could fall back on and use from time to time. Mark was going through a crisis that terribly weakened his reality controls and day-to-day functioning.

Mrs. L. was rehospitalized at the beginning of June for the last time. She died on the 30th of that month. The final cause of her death was hepatitis (cancer had invaded the liver), but for the entire period of the last hospitalization her mind was affected. Though she was conscious, only intermittently did she understand where she was, and for the most part she reacted to her own delusions and hallucinations. Therefore the children were unable to visit or speak with her. At the beginning of June, when mother was hospitalized, Mark used his relationship with me to attempt to ward off loss. He reported all his accomplishments to me, instead of to his missing mother; how he flew his kite, built his airplane, how he felt about his new camp uniform, and the new high diving he did in the pool. He began to take care of the office. He helped me open the door, straighten the chairs. This growing mother-child relationship between us took on oedipal overtones. We were to get married, and he came in singing "Here comes the Bride." He made a beautiful poster of two babies who were made by Mr. Chethik and Mark and he wanted it hung prominently. The gay, happy, united couple he attempted to make of us during the hour contrasted with the rest of his reality day. To some degree I gingerly pointed out the disparity. He also used the transference to help him cope with many feelings he had about his mother. Some days he only whispered, and we came to understand how he felt when he could not hear a direct word from his mother. He wandered out of the office some days, and he wanted me to look for the lost Mark as he himself looked for his lost mother. When I interpreted the passive into active mechanisms, Mark showed some moments of sadness.

About a week before Mrs. L.'s death, Mark's father could no longer reassure his children. No letters or messages were sent from home by the children because Mommie had become too sick to see or understand them. In the hour, Mark reacted to this reality with total regression. His only form of communicating with me was to ask how much time was left in the session, which meant how much time did mother have left to live. He became like a child who had suffered great narcissistic injury. He lay on the pillow, comforting himself, slowly touching himself and going over each and every area of his body. He opened his shirt to touch his skin. Much of the time he fell asleep, but he slept very uncomfortably and fitfully, awakening with starts. He sucked his thumb and periodically stroked his penis. He wet his pants and sometimes seemed to have momentary frightening dreams.

When his mother's death came at last, Mark attended the funeral. He missed several sessions because he wanted to stay at home. He was able to show some sadness and cry in company with the other members of the family. This seemed to be more of a sympathetic reaction with others, than a real expression of his own sorrow. His comment to his father after returning from the funeral, a prelude to later denial, was that he could not see the "box" (coffin).

Mark continued the autoerotic activity I described earlier (to some degree this was evidenced at home too). Thumbsucking, touching, fitful sleeping was evident, and he added a rhythmic counting. This lasted for several weeks. He complained of monster dreams coming every night, and screamed at me that I couldn't talk of Mommie. That's what made him dream. I tried to help him with some verbalizing, but he couldn't discuss his sadness or anxieties, and I had to be content with making remarks such as "Maybe you can't feel your sad feelings, but you show them to me all the time."

On the few occasions when verbalization was possible, he described his idea of his mother's death. She was reading a book in the hospital and grew tired. As she was putting out the light she slipped out of bed and hit her head. That was how she died. The illness aspect was denied, and her death was conceived in simple terms. It was described in terms of an experience that could happen to him and as something he could imagine. In addition, finality of death was denied, since Mark was sure that his mommie had taken at least $100 with her to use. He also told me that Michael, the younger brother, wasn't sad because he didn't really believe that Mommie died.

Mark did express more feelings about my coming vacation, displacing some of his primary reactions from his mother. He began wetting himself and also tearing at his scratches or scabs until they bled. I spoke of how awful he felt that there seemed to be no one to take care of him now. To this remark, he could cry some. He brought string to the hour and spent several sessions tying us or our chairs together. On one occasion, as I spoke of the anger he must be feeling because I was going on vacation, he began to spit, and he spat and spat at me until there was no saliva left. When he was totally spent, his tears came. Slowly then he seemed to rally. He related to the calendar that showed the time I would be away, talked realistically of his impending activities, and said he planned to write to me. He spoke directly of his fear that I also was going away forever, but he reassured himself that he had too many problems remaining for that to happen.

In the following months several themes appeared related to his mother's death. I became much more of a direct replacement for his mother. Mark attempted to have something from me each hour, and this had become increasingly important to him. A story we worked on together, a paper I folded, a paper clip or rubber band from my desk, all had special meaning for him. In return, he brought more of his daily realities to his sessions. He described his neighborhood, making maps of all the houses on his street, showing me who lived where so I could follow his activities. Similarly with school, he drew a diagram of the class, indicating where each child sat, and these charts of his daily life were hung in the office. He seemed to be attempting to bring the full day and the activities of his whole life to his therapist-mother.

The terminal quality of the death remained denied. We created a new, extensive book which had the form of the "torah," the Jewish holy scroll. In it, he had prayers to his mother; through it, he communicated directly with her. "Dear Mommie: You have passed away and we are missing you. I miss you because I love you, and I won't be bad for you. You died." In the body of the book were illustrations and stories. One prominent drawing was of Jack and the Beanstalk.

Jack could climb the beanstalk into heaven where the castle was. In heaven lived the beautiful lady whom Jack could reach. The mother, therefore, was attainable. The stories Mark dictated had a similar form. Bozo the clown came home to find his mother gone. He and his brothers searched for her, but she couldn't be found anywhere. Maybe she had been in a car accident. Bozo came home tired after the search, and sat down to take a nap. Suddenly he heard a click at the door and he turned around to find Mommie taking a nap in a chair beside him. I allowed these fantasies and only attempted to make small inroads into the reality situation. When Mark had his seventh birthday, he reminisced about how his old parties used to be. When I wondered why he only had three children at the party this year, he screamed out, "Because my mommie is dead, stupid." Despite a few inroads, the denial in fantasy remained a vital necessity.

Mark continued in treatment for a year and a half after his mother's death. Treatment took the form of a modified analysis with the work centered on helping Mark with affects and defenses, rather than direct work on impulses. A central issue continued to be the theme of difficulties with reality testing, to help Mark distinguish between inner and outer perceptions. Rather than helping Mark mourn (which did not seem possible) we devoted ourselves to "after death work." We came to understand together many difficult affects aroused by the death. For example, Mark became enormously jealous of his siblings and school peers whom he felt, always "had something" or attained something he longed for. We could connect these missing feelings to his Mommie-missing feelings. Stories or fantasies, however, where sudden reunions with the beautiful lady occurred, continued throughout the treatment.

Mark had many difficulties with mother substitutes. He reacted strongly to several housekeepers and the "new mother" when father remarried a year later. He came to understand his feelings of disloyalty when he began to like the new person. We could also work through his enormous anxiety lest he drive away the new mother, as he felt he had driven away the old mother.

At the point of discharge, Mark was functioning in public school and was generally a socially acceptable youngster. However a major symptom remained. He continued to wet his bed several times weekly.

Clearly, Mark was not able to accept the death. He denied the finality of the loss. In his situation, to what degree was denial absolutely essential? Did Mark face more than the usual tasks involved in accepting death? It appears to me that to accept the loss of his mother, Mark faced, in addition, a severe developmental crisis. He faced the enormous danger of further massive regression. If he accepted the fact that his mother was gone, then, to him, all her influences were also gone. Her prohibitions and reality-defining qualities, which seemed so essential for his development, were gone as well. Did Mark need to ward off the mother's death because of the danger of personality disintegration? Did keeping her alive keep her influence available?

In our theory of object relations we are very much aware of the crucial role of the object tie in development. At first, the child has no ego or superego organization to control instinctual expression. The object serves as the first control, and much of what the child does is to satisfy the wishes of the parents. He begins to develop controls because he fears that the object will withdraw or remove his love. There is a long process before these controls become internalized. There is a long period during which the parents must serve as the auxiliary ego and superego.

In our early months of treatment with Mark, we attempted to capitalize on this important developmental influence. We used the mother to help Mark with reality reinforcement. There were innumerable instances when Mark wanted support for his magic at home, and his mother (through her growing understanding of his problems) undercut this process, but this was a very small part of what she did naturally and intuitively to establish reality. Every routine and daily request made by the mother, having to do with eating, sleeping, or washing, interrupted Mark's active fantasy life. The omnipotent Tarzan, Hercules, and giant fantasies were constantly tempered when the mother demanded that her child behave like a little boy. When this reality support is removed during the developmental process, we can expect a threat of ego regression.

In a similar way, we can look at superego formation. Full development of an internalized superego often comes later in childhood, after resolution of the oedipal struggle. With Mark, it appeared that much superego development was still tied to the parents. Again, during the early part of the analysis, I worked with the mother to have her forcefully and consistently prohibit many of Mark's impulsive acts. Prohibition in this instance was tied directly to the mother. Only slowly could we expect that some internal sanctions (independent of the parents) would evolve. Can we not say, then, that some of the instinctual regression we saw in Mark during the 10-month period of mother's deterioration appeared because mother in her illness was less effective?

It seems to me that the mother's dangerous illness and death had a very important double meaning for Mark. He not only faced the loss of an object, but even more directly, *he faced the loss of a part of himself.* The attack on the life of his mother appeared to be a direct attack on the development of the ego and superego processes within him. It challenged the very integration of his personality.

Was Mark's burden in facing the death unique to him or is this a general difficulty with young children? As I noted earlier, there is controversy as to whether children have the capacity to mourn. Some authors (Furman, 1964 and Barnes, 1964) show that grief and the mourning process in young children seem possible. Other authors stress the child's inability to mourn. Rochlin (1953) describes fixations, regression, and heightened narcissism among children as reactions to object loss. Shambaugh (1961) describes a child in treatment whose ego could not cope with the task of grief, because it had to deal with the burden of regression. I was interested to note that those authors who felt children could not mourn found that severe ego disintegration or the threat of disintegration played a prominent role.

It appears to me, using Mark as an example, that mourning is much more difficult to attain when a significant degree of internalization of the object has not already occurred. We would need to know how far the development of identifications had proceeded before the death, in order to assess whether acceptance of the death is at all possible. In Rochlin (1959) and Shambaugh's (1961) case material, as with Mark it appears that loss is much more significant because the child still depends on the presence or proximity of the object. When massive regressions are a danger, when there is a threat to the integrity of the ego, there is a greater need to ward off and deny the loss, and mourning could not possibly follow. In this context, to assess mourning potential one would have to follow closely the course of development. Two six-year-olds could react differently to similar tragedies depending on the degree to which each child had developed in object relations and the process of identification.

While I have stressed the threat of disintegration of the self as an impediment to accepting the death, I am aware that there were other important factors that made it difficult for Mark to achieve this. His problem with his aggression was an important factor. The primitive quality of his aggression (the fantasied knife-killing of the mother, for instance) aroused enormous guilt and responsibility for her death. His anger also had a magical quality, as though death thoughts could become real. We can say that Mark needed to deny the death because it would stimulate great guilt, as well as fear of retribution on another level. Did Mark ward off facing death because of increased castration threat? Could he allow acknowledgment of the death when it involved the amputation and annihilation he feared to himself and his own body? All of these seemed to be additional factors in deterring mourning.

REFERENCES

BARNES, M. J. (1964), Reaction to the death of mother. *The Psychoanalytic Study of the Child*, 19:334-358. New York: International Universities Press.

FURMAN, R. (1964), Death and the young child: some preliminary considerations. *The Psychoanalytic Study of the Child*, 19:321-334. New York: International Universities Press.

—— (1964a), Death of a six-year-old's mother during his analysis. *The Psychoanalytic Study of the Child*, 19:379-398. New York: International Universities Press.

NAGERA, H. (1969), Children's reactions to the death of important objects: a developmental approach. Unpublished monograph.

ROCHLIN, G. (1953), Loss and restitution. *The Psychoanalytic Study of the Child*, 8:288-309. New York: International Universities Press.

—— (1959), The loss complex. *J. Amer. Psychoanal. Assn.* 7:299-317.

SHAMBAUGH, B. (1961), A study of loss reactions in a seven-year-old boy. *The Psychoanalytic Study of the Child*, 16:510-522. New York: International Universities Press.

WOLFENSTEIN, M. (1966), How is mourning possible? *The Psychoanalytic Study of the Child*, 21:93-127. New York: International Universities Press.

"SEEKING" AND "FINDING" A LOST OBJECT:
EVIDENCE FROM RECENT STUDIES OF THE REACTION TO BEREAVEMENT*

C. Murray Parkes

Abstract—Evidence is presented from several studies of bereaved adults which supports Bowlby's claim that "the urge to recover the lost object" is a principal component of grief. This is revealed in abortive "searching" behaviour.

At other times bereaved people tend to feel and act as if the dead person were still present even though they know that this is not so. Thus "seeking" and "finding" are juxtaposed.

The implications of these findings for traditional theories of ego defence are discussed and the place of "searching" is considered in wider context as a consequence of the frustration of goal-corrected behaviour.

GRIEF is the reaction to loss of an object of love. It is a complex process which, as Bowlby [1] has pointed out, passes through a succession of phases before it is resolved.

This article is concerned with one aspect, the most obvious and, to many, the pathognomonic feature of grief, restless pining for the lost object. It is our contention that this represents a frustrated search common to all social animals who maintain attachments to other objects in the life space.

"The urge to recover the lost object" has been described by Bowlby as a principal component of the reaction to loss. The evidence which he cites is largely derived from studies of animals and young children, and although much of it is anecdotal in form, its consistency and clarity carry weight. The behaviour patterns which Bowlby finds in accounts of the separation behaviour of several different species and from which he deduces a common urge to recover a lost object are crying, searching and angry protesting, all of which are directed towards the object. These behaviour patterns have evolved and have obvious value in ensuring the survival of the individual and/or the love object. Thus crying and searching help the separated parties to find each other, and protesting, according to Bowlby, punishes all concerned with the loss and makes it less likely that it will occur again.

It is not intended to repeat here the evidence upon which Bowlby bases his theory nor to cite evidence for the occurrence of this behavior in children and animals. There is a need for systematic studies in this area and current work such as that of Hinde [2] on the behavi-

* The first 7 pages of this article formed the basis of a paper read at the "Symposium on Anxiety" held by the World Psychiatric Association in London in November 1967. The proceedings have been published as a Royal Medico–Psychological Association Special Monograph under the title "Studies of Anxiety".

our of infant rhesus monkeys separated from their mothers can be expected to throw further light on the situation.

In this paper evidence will be drawn from a series of studies of bereaved human adults which have been carried out by the writer in recent years. These studies show that when an adult human being learns of the death of a person to whom he is attached he tends to call and search for that person; at the same time his awareness that such a search is useless, reinforced by lifelong restrictions on the expression of "irrational" behaviour and the knowledge that fruitless searching is painful, cause him to avoid, deny and, in many ways, restrict the expression of the search. The result is a compromise, a partial expression of the search which varies in degree from person to person and even, within a single person, over time.

In focussing on searching rather than on crying and protesting as Bowlby does, it is not intended to belittle the importance of these other features. But both crying and protesting are relatively non-specific phenomena. A bereaved person has many reasons for tears and many causes for anger. It is only when the anger and tears are clearly related to the lost person that they can be regarded as a specific part of grief. Searching, by its very nature, implies the loss or absence of an object; it is thought to be an essential component of grief and important to an understanding of the process.

The data drawn upon comes from three sources:—

1. *Unselected widows*

22 unselected widows under the age of 65 who were interviewed systematically at intervals during their first year of bereavement. These were referred by their General Practitioners and whilst there were a few who declined to volunteer for the project those who did agree to be seen seemed to constitute a representative sample of London widows. Case examples from this series are prefixed by the letter U. Further details of the study are given in the Appendix.

Most of the information on which the conclusions of this paper are based comes from this study which was concerned with the typical grief of typical London widows. But there is much to be learned about the normal from studying the abnormal and it has been found helpful to include two further studies in which information was obtained from psychiatrically disturbed bereaved patients. To avoid confusion with data obtained from the unselected widows case examples taken from the two psychiatric studies will be prefixed by the initials I and C and enclosed in brackets.

All numerical data and statistics refer to the sample of unselected widows.

2. *Psychiatric interviews*

21 psychiatric patients whose illness had come on within six months of the death of a spouse, parent, child or sibling. These were interviewed at the Bethlem Royal and Maudsley Hospitals. Additional information was abstracted from their case notes. Other details of this and the series which follows are described elsewhere [3]. Case examples are prefixed by the letter I.

3. *Psychiatric case notes*

Other examples are taken from the case notes of 95 psychiatric patients who had suffered a bereavement during the six months preceding their illness. This group were not accessible for interview. Case examples from this series are prefixed by the letter C.

224

Although we tend to think of searching in terms of the motor act of restless movements towards possible locations of the lost object, it also has perceptual and ideational components. Thus in the normal course of events the motor activity of searching is likely to bring the lost object within the perceptual field. The perceptual apparatus must be prepared to recognize and pay attention to any sign of the object. Signs of the object can only be identified by reference to memories of the object as it was. Searching the external world for signs of the object therefore includes the establishment of an internal perceptual "set" derived from previous experience of the object.

A woman is searching for her missing son. She moves restlessly about the likely parts of the house scanning with her eyes and thinking of the boy; she hears a creak and immediately associates it with the sound of her son's footfall on the stair; she calls out, "John is that you?" The components of this behaviour sequence are:—

(1) Restless movement about and scanning of the environment.
(2) Preoccupation with thoughts of the lost person.
(3) Developing a perceptual "set" for the person, namely a disposition to perceive and to pay attention to stimuli which suggest the presence of the person and to ignore those that are not relevant to this aim.
(4) Directing attention towards those parts of the environment in which the person is likely to be.
(5) Calling for the lost person.

Each of these components is to be found in bereaved men and women, in addition some grievers are consciously aware of an urge to search.

Evidence for each component as it appeared in the three studies under discussion will be presented:—

1. *Motor hyperactivity*

All save two of the unselected widows studied said they felt restless and fidgety during the first month of bereavement and none of them felt retarded or anergic. Observations by the interviewer confirmed this report and assessments of restlessness at interview averaged over the whole year were found to correlate highly with estimates of general muscle tension ($r=0.83$, $p<0.001$). These findings confirm Cobb and Lindemann's quantitative study of bereaved subjects using the Interaction Chronograph technique [4]. Lindemann's [5] account of this feature cannot be bettered, "The activity throughout the day of the severely bereaved person shows remarkable changes. There is no retardation of action and speech; quite to the contrary, there is a rush of speech, especially when talking about the deceased. There is restlessness, inability to sit still, moving about in aimless fashion, *continually searching* for something to do. There is, however, at the same time, a painful lack of capacity to initiate and maintain normal patterns of activitity." (My italics).

It is contended that in fact the searching behaviour of the bereaved person is not "aimless" at all. It has the specific aim of finding the one who is gone. The bereaved person, however, seldom admits to having so irrational an aim and his behaviour is therefore regarded by others and perhaps even by himself as "aimless". His search for "something to do" is bound to fail because the things which he can do are not, in fact, what he wants at all. What he wants is to find the lost person.

Taken alone restlessness cannot be regarded as convincing evidence of search. There are other factors such as anger which are also likely to give rise to restlessness.

TABLE 1.

CORRELATION COEFFICIENTS OF MEAN YEAR SCORES OF
FEATURES DESCRIBED IN TEXT

	Preoccupation with thoughts of deceased	Clear visual memory of deceased	Sense of presence of deceased	Tearfulness	Irritability and anger
Restlessness	0·18	0·04	0·08	0·32	0·65†
Preoccupation with thoughts of deceased		0·73†	0·58†	0·54†	−0·05
Clear visual memory of deceased			0·56†	0·38	−0·18
Sense of presence of deceased				0·42*	0·02
Tearfulness					0·41

* $p < 0.05$ † $p < 0.01$

Table 1 shows cross correlations of six components described in this paper. Quantitative assessments were made at each of five interviews during the course of the first year of bereavement and the mean figures obtained in each case were cross correlated. Further details of the component features are given below.

It will be seen that whilst "Preoccupation with thoughts of the deceased", "clear visual memory", "sense of presence" and "tearfulness" correlate quite well together, "restlessness" and "anger" correlate only with each other.

Despite this there was one widow whose motor activity did seem clearly related to the urge to look for her husband, she (Case U 1) showed a tendency to keep glancing over her right shoulder. She did this, she said, "Because he was always on my right".

2. Preoccupation with memories of the lost person

Whilst we have no sure means of knowing the thought content of young children and animals during the period of searching, it seems reasonable to suppose that their thoughts are focussed on the lost object and maybe on the events and places associated with the loss. This is certainly the case with adult humans for whom preoccupation with thoughts of the lost person and the events leading up to the loss is the rule.

During the first month of bereavement 19 of the 22 unselected widows interviewed were preoccupied with thoughts of their dead husband ("I never stop missing him," case U 4); and 12 of them still spent much of their time thinking of him a year later.

Throughout the year a clear visual picture of the dead person remained in the minds of most of the widows and they reported no blurring as preoccupation grew less. This visual image was sometimes so clear that it was spoken of as if it were a perception.

U 22 said, "I can picture him in any given circumstances . . . I can almost feel his skin and touch his hands," U 1, "I keep seeing his very fair hair and the colour of his eyes," U 5, "I can always see him," U 11, "I can see him whenever I want to". U 16 , "I still see him, quite vividly, coming in the door". U 24, "I can see him sitting in the chair".

The amount of preoccupation with thoughts of the dead person assessed at interview and the widow's report of a clear visual picture of her husband were highly correlated ($r = 0.73$, $p < 0.001$) Although there were a few times when widows complained that they were unable to recall the appearance of their spouse such episodes were transient blocks in recall rather than lasting states of mind.

It is postulated that maintaining a clear visual memory of the lost person facilitates the search by making it more likely that the missing person will be located if, in fact, he is to be found somewhere within the field of search.

3. Perceptual "set" for the lost person

Clear visual memories are associated with a change in the perceptual "set" such that incoming sensory data is scanned for evidence of the lost object. From time to time ambiguous sensory data will fit the image of the lost object. When this occurs attention is focussed on the data and further evidence sought to confirm the initial impression. Occasionally, an ambiguous sensation is misidentified as deriving from the lost person. 9/22 widows described actual illusions of the lost person at some time during the first month of bereavement. These usually involved the misidentification of existing environmental stimuli. Case U 3 thought she heard her husband at the door; U 4 repeatedly heard him cough at night; U 7 heard him moving about the house; U 10 said, "I think I catch sight of him in his van, but it is the van from down the road". U 11 woke to hear her husband calling her in the night; U 14 repeatedly misidentified men in the street who seemed to resemble her husband; A Nigerian girl, U 15 said, "Everywhere I looked I saw his picture. Ordinary things would have his face." U 20 thought she heard the door opening and her husband coming in.

4. Focussing of attention on those parts of the environment which are associated with the person

Half the widows said that they felt drawn towards places or objects which they associated with their dead husband. For example, Case U 1 kept visiting old haunts and planned to go to spiritualist meetings in the hope of making contact with her husband. (Spiritualist Meetings were also attended by six psychiatric cases C 34, C 39, C 46, C 95, I 99 and I 111.) U 3, U 4 and I 119 were unable to leave home without experiencing a strong impulse to return there. U 11 and U 21 felt drawn towards the hospital where their husbands had died and the latter actually walked into the hospital before realizing that such behaviour was pointless. U 3, U 21, U 24, C 7 and I 97, felt drawn to the cemetery and 6 of the unselected widows returned compulsively to places which they had visited with their husband. As U 18 said, "I walk around all where we used to go". 19 widows treasured possessions which they associated with their husband and 4 returned repeatedly to these, for instance, U 2 kept searching and gazing at her husband's clothes.

Even when conscious efforts were made to avoid painful reminders of the dead person there was a sense of conflict as if the bereaved person was pulled two ways. U 14 for instance tried sleeping in the back bedroom to get away from her memories but found she missed her husband so much that she had to go back to the front bedroom to be near him.

Several turned over in their minds the idea of killing themselves in order to join the dead person in an after life. One girl, aged 12 (Case I 101) was admitted to hospital because of serious weight loss after the death of her mother. She had refused to eat and her father said, "You'll become like mother," whereupon she replied, "That's just what I want to do, I want to die and be with Mummy". Suicidal ideas were also expressed by I 106 who had seen the face of her husband after death, "He looked so happy in death," she said, "it made me think he was with her (his first wife)".

5. Calling for the lost person

"Dwight, where are you? I need you so much," wrote Frances Beck in her "Diary of a Widow" [6]. Crying is, of course, a frequent feature of grief and one which occurred in 16 out of 22 widows when discussing their husbands a month after bereavement. The fact that they cried does not, of course, mean that they were necessarily crying for their husbands. Had they been asked it is doubtful if many would have acknowledged that a cry needs to have an object at all. On occasion, however, the object towards whom the cry was directed was quite clearly the husband. For instance, faced with the fact that she would never have her husband back again, one widow (U 4) shouted out, "Oh Fred, I do need you," and then burst into tears. (Case C 94 cried out for her dead baby during the night. Similarly Case I 111 called to her dead sister at night, she went to several spiritualist meetings and dreamed repeatedly that she was searching for her sister but couldn't find her.)

Tearfulness significantly correlated with preoccupation with the memory of the dead person ($r=0.54$, $p<0.001$), sense of the presence of the dead person ($r=0.42$, $p<0.05$) overall negative affect ($r=0.73$, $p<0.001$) and tension ($r=0.43$, $p<0.05$). All of these features are associated with severe grief and with the focussing of ideation and perception described above. The association seems to suggest that, whatever other factors contributed to cause these widows to cry, an important one was the memory of the lost husband.

6. Conscious recognition of the urge to search for the lost person

The adult human being is well aware of the fact that searching for a dead person is irrational and will therefore resist the suggestion that this is what he wants to do following a bereavement. Exceptions occur among those who recognize the irrational components of their own behaviour, in psychotic patients and in children who are less bound by reality than adults.

The following statements were made by four of the 22 unselected widows interviewed:

Case U 1. "I walk around searching for him." "I felt that if I could have come somewhere I could have found him." She was tempted to go to a spiritualist séance but decided against it.

Case U 3. "I go to the grave . . . but he's not there."

Case U 9. "I'm just searching for nothing."

Case U 21. "It's as if I was drawn towards him."

Searching for the lost person was also apparent in several bereaved psychiatric patients:

Case C 78. An Australian woman lost her adoptive son and her true son in the war. Their deaths were announced within a few weeks of each other. When told of her son's death she refused to believe him dead and eventually persuaded her husband to bring her from Australia to England in search of him. On arrival in Britain she thought she saw her son coming towards her on the stair, she became very depressed and cried for the first time since her bereavement.

Case C 79. Received a report that her son had been killed in action in Belgium. She reacted severely and four years later, when the war was over, persuaded her husband to take her to visit her son's grave to make sure that he was dead. Returning home, she said, "I knew I was leaving him behind for ever."

Case I 116. After the death of her baby this patient kept going to the bedroom in search of her dead baby.

Case I 117 admitted that she went to the street door to look for her husband. She found this kind of behaviour so painful that she consciously resisted it, "I think, there's no good going into the kitchen, he'll never come back".

Children who persisted in a search for lost parents extending into adult life have been described by Stengel [7–9] who believes that some wandering fugues can be accounted for in this way. A young man seen at a case conference in Professor Romano's Department in Rochester had been an adoptive child and had spent large sums of money in hiring private investigators to locate his true mother. A singular change occurred when he succeeded in finding his mother. She came to stay with the patient and he was disappointed that she did not live up to his idealized picture of her. Their relationship, however, did become quite good and the patient's restless anxiety diminished considerably.

To sum up, each of the components which go to make up searching behaviour has been shown to play a part in the reaction to bereavement. Motor restlessness, preoccupation with a clear visual memory of the lost person, development of a perceptual "set" for the lost person, direction of attention towards those parts of the environment in which the person is most likely to be found, and calling to him have been found in some or all of the bereaved people studied. In addition, despite the irrationality of such behaviour a number of bereaved persons were consciously aware of the impulse to search.

The studies from which this evidence is derived were not designed to test the "search" hypothesis. If they had been there are a number of other questions which could have been asked and which might have thrown further light on the problem. For instance in none of these studies were the respondents asked whether or not they were aware of the need to search. There is a danger, however, that if such an intention had been in the mind of the investigator he could have phrased his questions in such a way that he would have exerted undue influence on the respondent to give replies which would confirm his expectations.

Additional evidence could be cited from dreams and from interpretation of behaviour which seems to represent displaced searching, but the chain of inference in such cases grows long and it has been thought preferable to confine attention to the evidence presented.

Searching is only one aspect of the reaction to bereavement. Other components such as anger, guilt, identification phenomena and loss of appetite for food and other forms of gratification are not relevant to this paper. Neither is it intended to describe in detail the forms of secondary elaboration which modify the components of the search. It is, however, necessary to describe another major aspect of bereavement which is, at first sight, the antithesis of searching, disregard of the fact of loss.

DISREGARD OF THE FACT OF LOSS

When searching the bereaved person feels and acts as if the lost person were recoverable although he knows intellectually that this is not so. Similarly, bereaved people may feel and act as if the dead person were still present even though they know that this is not so.

Commonly the two forms of disregard [10] alternate with periods of each occurring many times in the course of a day. Disregard of the fact of loss, however, is most prominent in the earliest stage of bereavement whereas searching does not reach its peak until a week or so later.

Disregard of the fact of loss is seen most clearly during the final illness and immediately after the loss. This involves disbelief [10] in the fact that the loss has or is about to occur, but this is seldom complete. (For instance, one bereaved patient (Case I 99) said, "I just didn't want them to talk about it because the more they talked the more they'd make me believe he was dead.")

Of 22 widows 19 had been warned of the seriousness of their husband's illness before his demise. They were later asked how they had reacted to this information. 12 said that they did not believe what they were told; either they disbelieved the correctness of the diagnosis or they accepted the diagnosis but questioned the correctness of the prognosis. 7 said that they believed what they were told but at least 3 of these described how they had subsequently distorted the information or "pushed it to the back of their minds".

The significance of death itself is also likely to be disregarded. Half (11/22) the widows described feelings of "numbness" or "blunting" during the first few days following bereavement. The feeling was variable in its intensity and was well described by one widow (Case U 3) whose husband died during an attack of asthma. She had found the body hanging over the bannisters and her first thought was to get her children out of the house. As the door closed behind them she recalls that she heard herself wailing: "I suddenly burst. I was aware of a horrible wailing and knew it was me. I was saying I loved him and all that. I knew he'd gone but I kept on talking to him". Shortly afterwards she began to feel "numbed solid"—"It's a blessing . . . everything goes hard inside you—like a heavy weight". It enabled her to carry on without crying.

Even after the numbness had passed most widows still had difficulty in accepting the reality of what had happened and realizing its implications. In 12 cases this was still present from time to time a year later, although in only one case was it a pronounced feature. Four widows said they felt they were waiting for their dead husband to come back and most of them consciously attempted to avoid situations and thoughts which would remind them of their loss and bring about painful pangs of longing.

A comforting sense of the presence of the lost person was experienced by 15/22 widows. This was often associated with a temporary reduction in restlessness and pining which seems to indicate that this phenomenon is accompanied by mitigation of searching.

Case U 4 said, "I still have the feeling he's near and there's something I ought to be doing for him or telling him . . . He's with me all the time. I hear him and see him—although I know it's only imagination." U 12 said, "I still feel that he's around". U 14, "Spiritually he's near". U 21, "When I'm washing my hair it's the feeling he's there to protect me in case someone comes in through the door." The sense of his presence was particularly strong in the cemetery—"It's terrible if it's raining. It's as if I want to pick him up and bring him home." Later the feeling became more general, "He's not anywhere in particular, just around the place. It's a good feeling."

Whilst the above examples are probably illusions, there were other cases in which hypnagogic hallucinations occurred. These were clearly unrelated to pre-existing sensory stimuli. Thus U 13 saw her husband coming through the garden gate, C 39 saw her dead father standing by her bed at night, and C 62 saw her dead husband gardening with only his trousers on whilst she was relaxing in a chair on a Sunday afternoon.

Some bereaved subjects actually spoke to or did things for the absent person whilst others were aware of resisting the impulse. "If I didn't take a strong hold on myself I'd get talking to him," said U 14. U 4 often became tearful in bed at night, "I talk to him and I quite expect him to answer me."

It almost seems that for these people the search has been successful.

That "seeking" and "finding" occur close together is hardly surprising. Measures of "sense of presence" correlated with "clear visual memories of the deceased" ($r = 0.56$,

$p < 0.01$) and "preoccupation with thoughts of the deceased" ($r=0.58$, $p < 0.01$). It will readily be recognized that these phenomena, which have already been referred to as components of searching, can equally well be components of finding. In fact, it seems that whilst searching and finding cannot, logically, occur simultaneously, they may be so closely juxtaposed as to be inseparable. Thus a widow may be preoccupied with a clear visual memory of her husband. At one moment she is anxiously pining for him, and a moment later she experiences a comforting sense of his presence near her. As time passes and the intensity of the affects diminish pain and pleasure are experienced as the "bitter-sweet" mixture of emotions which characterize nostalgia.

"Memorials" are built to "keep alive" the memory of a dead person. To many of the bereaved they seem to bring the same sense of comfort of having "found" the lost one, as that which is obtained from the sense of presence.

Perhaps the most striking illustration of the way in which the search for a lost person can be associated with a sense of the presence of that person was found in case I 99.

This was a woman of 30 who had been very attached to her dominating mother. When her mother died her search was consciously directed towards making contact with the departed spirit. At her sister's home she improvised a planchette and "received" messages which she believed came from her mother. At the same time she noticed a Toby jug which resembled her mother. She became convinced that her mother's spirit had entered into this jug and persuaded her sister to give it to her. During the next few weeks she kept the jug in a prominent position at home but became increasingly frightened by it. Against her will her husband eventually smashed the jug and she noticed that even the pieces "felt hot", presumably a sign of life. Not long afterwards she was offered a little dog. Her mother had said that if she returned it would be in the form of a dog.

When interviewed by the writer three years after her bereavement she said of the dog, "She's not like any other animal, she does anything. She'll only go for walks with me and my husband. She seems to eat all the things that mother used to eat. She doesn't like men."

Another type of ideation which seems to imply a partial disregard for the fact of loss is the repeated reviewing of memories of events leading up to the death. Unhappy reminiscences of such events were reported by over half the widows studied—"I go through that last week in the hospital again and again . . . It seems photographed on my mind" (Case U 14). "I think if only I'd woken up early, perhaps I could have saved him," (Case U 3).

This is associated with a great deal of anxiety and cannot be regarded as a comforting defence. Such reminiscences obtrude upon the mind much as anticipatory worrying preoccupies people who fear a possible misfortune. Such anticipation has been called "Worry Work" [11] and when it occurs before a misfortune it has the effect of focussing attention on possible dangers and providing an opportunity for appropriate planning. Once the misfortune has occurred, however, this is no longer possible and the most that can be hoped for is that the affected person will learn something from the "post mortem" which might prevent a similar occurrence in the future. In practice, the painful reminiscences which follow bereavement are particularly fruitless. Not only is there nothing which can now be done to bring back the dead person but there is rarely anything which can be learned from such reminiscence which will prevent future disasters. Anxious reminiscence thus resembles the searching behaviour of bereaved people in being a behavioural sequence which, in the normal course of events, is a valuable activity but which, in the special case of permanent loss, has little positive value.

Disregard of either the fact of loss or its permanence has, in the past, been regarded as a consequence of ego defence and the principal mechanism postulated has been denial. More recently, Maslow and Mittelmann [12] have preferred the term "coping mechanisms" when speaking of crisis reactions in order to stress the positive value of such processes in helping the individual to cope with an otherwise intolerable situation.

But there are difficulties arising from such terms which limit their usefulness in the special case of grief. In the first place ego defence mechanisms are usually presumed to reduce anxiety. Disregard of the fact of loss certainly does this but searching and the type of reminiscing described above can hardly be said to reduce anxiety. Furthermore bereaved persons often go to great lengths to avoid such painful thoughts—in terms of ego defence they are defending themselves against a defence or using one coping mechanism to cope with another.

Similar difficulties arise when we try to understand the "function" of grief. Freud asserts that the function of "mourning" is "to detach the survivor's memories and hopes from the dead" [13], yet in "searching" behaviour we have an important component of mourning which seems to have the opposite function, the restoration of the object.

We know, however, that even in animals unrewarded searching does not persist for ever. With repeated failure to achieve reunion the intensity and duration of searching diminish, habituation takes place, the "grief work" is done. It seems that the human adult must also go through the painful business of pining and searching if he is to "unlearn" his attachment to a lost person.

A REVISED CLASSIFICATION OF THE PHASES OF GRIEF

John Bowlby, in his classification of the phases of mourning [1], regards "the urge to recover the lost object" as the first phase of grief and "giving up" as characteristic of the second phase, which he calls the phase of Despair or Disorganization. He follows this with a third phase, the phase of Reorganization in which the grieving person again takes an interest in the external world and finds fresh objects to replace the lost one. Bowlby emphasizes that distinctions between these three phases are not clearcut and that elements of each phase persist into and alternate with elements of the other phases.

The findings described above indicate that an additional phase should precede Bowlby's first phase, a phase of numbness or blunting during which the fact of death is disregarded. This corresponds to the "Impact" phase described by Tyhurst [14] in his account of the reaction to community disasters. After discussion with the writer Bowlby agrees to renumber his original three phases so that they now become phases 2, 3 and 4. The following classification is therefore recommended:

First phase—Phase of Numbness—during which the fact of loss is partially disregarded.

Second phase—Phase of Yearning—during which the urge to recover the lost object predominates and searching takes place. In this phase it is the permanence rather than the fact of loss which is disregarded.

Third phase—Phase of Disorganization and Despair—during which both the permanence and the fact of loss are accepted and attempts to recover the lost object are given up.

Fourth phase—Phase of Reorganization of Behaviour.

In the widows who were interviewed by the writer the third phase, the phase of despair, was less obvious than the first and second because its features were less dramatic. As the pangs of grief diminished and pining subsided depression, apathy and aimlessness were more noticeable. One year after bereavement 15/22 widows declared that they still preferred not to think about the future and five more regarded their future as distinctly unpleasant. Few of them had begun to expand their circle of acquaintances and in 11 cases social relationships were clearly fewer than they had been before bereavement. Nevertheless there were a few widows who, by the end of their first year of bereavement, had begun to resume object relationships and to plan their lives afresh. These and other details of the reaction to bereavement will be described elsewhere.

"SEARCHING" AND "FINDING" IN CONTEMPORARY PSYCHOLOGY AND ETHOLOGY

It is necessary to relate the search for a lost object to a more general conceptual framework. Traditional theories of psychology have paid little attention to this category of behaviour and it is only recently that the significance of searching has been recognized.

In analysing animal behaviour ethologists have assumed most behaviour to be "chain-organized". That is to say it is made up of behaviour sequences which commonly lead to a biologically useful end result. The appetitive and consummatory (terminating) activities which make up these sequences do not presuppose awareness of the end result in the animal itself.

Miller, Gallanter and Pribam [15] point out that most human behaviour (and some animal behaviour also) is not "chain-organized" but is planned so as to achieve a pre-set goal: successive behaviours are repeatedly modified as their consequences relative to the overall goal become apparent, and cease only when the goal is reached. Thus the organization of the behaviours resemble that of a homing missile. To distinguish behaviour organized on these lines Bowlby [16] has proposed the term "goal-corrected".

It is clear that searching behaviour is normally "goal-corrected" and is consequently likely to be more adaptable and versatile than it would be if it were "chain-organized". But what happens if none of the usual paths look like leading to the goal? At this point the behaviour can be said to be "frustrated". The term "frustration" can be used to indicate both the situation of a person or animal whose goal-corrected behaviour is baulked and the subjective discomfort to which this characteristically gives rise.

C. S. Lewis [17] has described the sense of frustration of the mourner, "I think I am beginning to understand why grief feels like suspense. It comes from the frustration of so many impulses that had become habitual. Thought after thought, feeling after feeling, action after action had H. (his wife) for their object. Now their target is gone. I keep on through habit fitting an arrow to the string; then I remember and I have to lay the bow down. So many roads lead through to H. I set out on one of them. But now there's an impassable frontier-post across it. So many roads once; now so many *culs de sac*".

In all goal-corrected behaviour there is an element of searching, of finding the right "fit" between action and perception. In the behaviour which mediates attachment to a human being the search element is more explicit. We speak of love as a "tie". The strength of a tie is its resistance to severance. The behaviour patterns mediating attachment are patterns of interaction; clinging, smiling, following, searching, calling, and so on. Some of them, such as smiling and clinging, require the presence of the object for their evocation, Others, such as calling and searching occur only in the absence of the object.

The situation to which these behaviour patterns normally lead is an optimal proximity to the loved person, and when this is achieved the behaviour ceases. When the loved person is lost, however, the behaviour persists and with it the subjective discomfort which accompanies unterminated striving. This is experienced as "frustration".

However, the behaviour patterns mediating attachment are not the only behaviour patterns to be evoked following bereavement. There are many activities which require or have benefited from the collaboration of the lost person but which are not themselves examples of attachment behaviour. Some of these are habits established over the years, in which both parties shared; getting the children off to school on time, planning leisure activities, washing up. When circumstances cause these patterns to be initiated the sense of frustration and restlessness occur but alternative means of doing without the lost person are likely to be readily available and the bereaved person soon learns to cope. When, however, attachment behaviour is evoked (e.g. a woman reaches for her husband in bed or interprets a noise as the gate slamming at a time when he is due home from work) no substitute is acceptable. It is this that accounts for the persistence of the impulse to search for the lost person long after habits such as laying the table for two have been unlearned. C. S. Lewis was right in regarding the persistence of habit as a cause of frustration but it is not the only cause. The suspense which he describes would seem to indicate the expectation that something important is about to happen. To the griever the happening which seems most important is the finding of the one who is lost. And in social animals from their earliest years the behaviour pattern which is evoked by loss is searching.

Less clear is the occurrence of consummatory behaviour following the frustration of searching. There are many examples of this phenomenon in the form of the "Vacuum Activities" described in the ethological literature. For instance, the behaviour of the male stickleback, deprived of a mate, carrying out its "courtship dance" in an empty tank [18] is reminiscent of the widow (U 4) who regularly talked to her husband in bed at night and the mother (C 94) who got up at night to rock the cradle of her dead baby. It seems reasonable to postulate that in such cases there is a sensori-motor "set" which predisposes the individual to seek for and to find something, however tenuous, towards which consummatory behaviour can be directed.

APPENDIX

Methodology of the study of unselected widows

This study will be described in full detail elsewhere.

General Practitioners in the London area were asked to invite any woman under 65 registered with them who lost a husband in the course of the study to take part. 26 widows were referred, four of whom were excluded from the analysis of the data because they did not remain available for a full year after bereavement. Those widows who were not referred were thought by their G.P.'s to be no less emotionally disturbed than those who were referred.

Each widow was visited 1, 3, 6, 9 and $12\frac{1}{2}$ months after bereavement and at other times if need be. Systematic assessments were made at each visit of the presence and intensity of each of a number of psychological and physical symptoms. These were recorded on rating scales and treated as scores for purposes of statistical analysis. Figures given in the text of the article are based on inter-correlation of mean year scores (i.e. the mean of all five scores for each feature).

The features referred to in the text include six which were rated at each interview on a five point scale; tearfulness, tension, hyperactivity, preoccupation with thoughts of the deceased, sense of the presence of the dead person near at hand, and irritability or anger. The points of the scale were defined as:

1. Absent—no evidence of the feature.
2. Mild—not evident at interview—said to be present but inconspicuous at other times.
3. Moderate—*Either* not evident at interview but conspicuous at other times,
   Or inconspicuous at interview and moderate at other times.
4. Marked—conspicuous but only occasionally during interview.
5. Very marked—conspicuous throughout interview.

Clear Visual Memory of the dead person implied a tendency to recall the deceased person in clear visual form. It was rated as absent (1), probable (2), definite (3) or marked (4).

Overall negative affect was rated for each month of the year by consensus of widow and interviewer. The scale used was scored:

1. None—No more emotional disturbance than usual.
2. Mild—Only occasionally more disturbed than usual.
3. Moderate—Disturbed less than half the time.
4. Severe—Gross disturbance most of the time.
5. Very Severe—Gross disturbance most of the time with clear suicidal ideas.

Scores were punched on I.B.M. cards and the data analysed at the Harvard Computing Center. Product–moment correlations were calculated from the mean-year scores and the significance of these measured by the "*t*" test.

Acknowledgements—Thanks are due to Dr. John Bowlby and Dr. Robert Hinde for their constructive criticism of the drafts, and to Dr. Kenneth Jones for statistical help. Most of the research was undertaken with the support of a senior fellowship from the Mental Health Research Fund.

REFERENCES

1. BOWLBY, J. Processes of mourning. *Int. J. Psychoanalysis*, **62**, 317, 1961.
2. HINDE, R. A. Some recent trends in ethology, in KOCH, S. (ed.) *Psychology: A Study of a Science*. Study 1, Vol. 2, 561–610, McGraw-Hill, New York, 1959.
3. PARKES, C. M. Bereavement and Mental Illness. Part I. A clinical study of the grief of bereaved psychiatric patients. Part II. A classification of bereavement reactions. *Br. J. Med. Psychol.*, **38**, 1–26, 1965.
4. COBB, S. and LINDEMANN, E. Neuro-psychiatric observations of the Coconut Grove Fire. *Ann. Surg.*, **117**, 814, 1943.
5. LINDEMANN, E. The symptomatology and management of acute grief. *Am. J. Psychiat.*, **101**, 141, 1944.
6. BECK, F. *The Diary of a Widow*. Beacon Press, Boston, 1965.
7. STENGEL, E. Studies on the psychopathology of compulsive wandering. *Br. J. Med. Psychol.*, **18**, 250, 1939.
8. STENGEL, E. On the aetiology of the fugue states. *J. Ment. Sci.*, **87**, 572, 1941.
9. STENGEL, E. Further studies on pathological wandering. *J. Ment. Sci.*, **89**, 224, 1943.
10. "Disregard" and "disbelief" are used in preference to the more traditional term "denial" to avoid ambiguity. Loss is seldom explicitly "denied".
11. JANIS, I. *Psychological Stress*. John Wiley, New York, 1958.
12. MASLOW, A. H. and MITTELMANN, B. *Principles of Abnormal Psychology: The Dynamics of Psychic Illness*. Harper, London, 1941.
13. FREUD, S. Totem and taboo. *Complete Psychological Works*, Vol. 13, Hogarth, London, 1913.
14. TYHURST, S. S. Individual reactions to community disaster. The natural history of psychiatric phenomena. *Am. J. Psychiat.*, **107**, 764, 1951.
15. MILLER, G. A., GALLANTER, E. and PRIBAM, K. H. *Plans and the Structure of Behaviour*. Henry Holt, New York, 1960.
16. BOWLBY, J. *Attachment and Loss*. Vol. 1. Attachment. Hogarth, London, 1969.

17. Lewis, C. S. *A Grief Observed.* (First published under pseudonym N. W. Clerk in 1961). Faber, London, 1964.
18. Tinbergen, N. *The Study of Instinct.* Oxford University Press, 1951.

AUTHOR INDEX

Beckwith, J. Bruce, 141
Bergman, Abraham B., 141

Chethik, Morton, 203

Ellard, John, 11

Gramlich, Edwin P., 65

Hilgard, Josephine R., 163

Kaij, L., 178
Kennell, John H., 128
Klaus, Marshall H., 128

Maddison, David, 72, 78, 89
Malmquist, A., 178

Nilsson, Å., 178

Pacyna, Dorothy A., 154
Parkes, C. Murray, 223
Paul, Norman L., 36
Pomeroy, Margaret A., 141

Silverman, Phyllis Rolfe, 112
Slyter, Howard, 128

Townes, Brenda D., 53

Volkan, Vamik, 22, 186

Walker, Wendy L., 89
Wallace, Elspeth, 53

KEY-WORD TITLE INDEX